REDUCE MY PRISON SENTENCE

Stephen C. Sharp

Sunbelt Publishing Co.
Port Orange, Florida – 2013
www.ReduceMyPrisonSentence.com
www.SunbeltPublishing.net

© Copyright 2013 by Stephen C. Sharp

All rights reserved. No part of this book may be reproduced or utilized in any form or by any means, electronic or mechanical, including photocopying, recording or by any information storage and retrieval system, without permission in writing from the Publisher. Inquiries should be addressed to Sunbelt Publishing Co., 2134 Springwater Lane, Port Orange, FL 32128.

Printed in the United States of America
First Edition   10 9 8 7 6

ISBN – 978-0-9838592-4-6
Library of Congress Control Number – 2011913140

This publication is designed to provide information in regard to the subject matter covered. It is sold with the understanding that the publisher and author are not engaged in rendering legal, accounting, or other professional services. If legal advice or other expert assistance is required, the services of a competent professional person should be sought.
--- From a Declaration of Principles jointly adopted by a Committee of the American Bar Association and a Committee of Publishers.

Acknowledgements:

This book is dedicated to my family who I thank dearly for their love and support during the tough times which we all endured. To my mom and dad, I say thank you and I love you. To Lee and Savannah, I say thank you for being my best friends; I love you. Special thanks also to Robert G., Joe S., Chris S., Steve G., Doc P., Dusty M., Al S., Mike C., George M., Deb M., Scott M., Jake M., Creedon M., Jack B., Lise B., and Marc L. You all made my time pass easier.

DISCLAIMER

Because of possible unanticipated changes in governing statutes and case law relating to the application of any information contained in this book, the author, publisher, and any and all persons or entities involved in any way in the preparation, publication, sale or distribution of this book disclaim all responsibilities for the legal effects or consequences of any document prepared or action taken in reliance upon information contained in this book. No representatives, either express or implied, are made or given regarding the legal consequences of the use of any information contained in this book. Purchases and persons intending to use this book for the preparation of any legal documents are advised to check specifically on the current applicable laws in any jurisdiction in which they intend the documents to be effective.

Please note that throughout this book the word "he" has been substituted for all genders. Using the repeated term "he and/or she" would be awkward for the reader therefore we have chosen to use the simple pronoun "he".

Chapter 1 – Fed Up   8
    Two Ways
    The Investigation
    Statute of Limitations
    The Indictment
    Finding the Right Attorney
    To Plea or not to Plea
    The Pre-Sentence Report
    Criminal History
    Plea Bargaining
    The Sentencing Hearing
    The Road to Prison

Chapter 2 – Reduce my Sentence
    Single Mother Factor
    Separation from Children
    Irreplaceable Caretaker
    Financial/Caretaking
    Single Parent
    Abusive Spouse

Chapter 3 – Medical Factors

Chapter 4 – Other Mitigating Factors
    Age
    Charitable Works
    Victim's Conduct
    Diminished Capacity
    Rehabilitative Efforts
    Aberrant Behavior
    Coercion and Duress
    Lesser Harms
    Risk of Abuse in Prison
    Acceptance of Responsibility
    Mitigating Role

Chapter 5 – The 5K1 Motion

Chapter 6 – Getting Around Mandatory Minimums

Chapter 7 – Take a Year Off

Chapter 8 – Post Sentencing Reductions
    Compassionate Release
    Commutation of a Sentence
    RDAP
    Halfway House Placement
    Rule 35
    The Appeal

Chapter 9 – Year and a Day

Chapter 10 – Putting it all Together

Chapter 11 – Prison Blues

Chapter 12 – Prison Diary

Chapter 13 – Prison Directory

Appendix
    Inmate Resources

Index

Introduction

Are you or someone you know staring a federal prison sentence in the face? Have you or someone you love already endured the heartache of a federal judge's order to report to federal prison? Are you in a federal prison right now and in need of some easy to understand solutions and remedies that may be able to help you? If you answered yes to any of the above questions then fear not, there are better days and help ahead! Just like the proficient pilot dealing with an engine failure in a single engine aircraft in the middle of the night, the most important thing to do when dealing with a crisis (e.g., threat of possible prison time) is to stay calm and focused. As hard as this may sound, trust me when I say, *"You will get through it!"* Using rationale and common sense during these difficult times will help in the end.

One thing is for sure, federal prison is no joke. Sometimes though, the prison sentence that accompanies the offense is something to laugh at; in a facetious way of course. The disparity between sentences from one defendant to another for similar offenses is clearly an ongoing problem here in the U.S., and the average individual can be in for big trouble if he does not educate himself about some federal sentencing basics, regardless of having a qualified attorney on his side or not. After reading and studying the contents of this book, you should have a bigger and hopefully brighter picture about how the federal sentencing system works and the many ways to make it work in your favor.

After having the unfortunate opportunity to a ring side seat in a federal prison camp in what seemed to be the epitome of injustice commingled nicely with a dose of political corruption, I decided that enough was enough. I woke up after my second week in a South Carolina federal prison camp and made the commitment to dedicate every minute of my remaining time to deeply and intensely research the federal justice system and to ultimately determine, bottom line, the secrets, if any, arguments, tactics, and techniques that really work in the federal justice system to help reduce one's sentence.

After hearing dozens of stories from other inmates about ineffective counsel, errors on their PSIR, and little, if any, mitigating arguments made by their attorneys on and before sentencing hearings, I promised to write a book to help others who suddenly find themselves being a defendant in a federal court. My relentless research and analysis successfully uncovered several federal cases that involved years and years of long recommended prison sentences, most which inevitably resulted in terms of home and community confinement or probation – prison free results! How did this happen?

I continued my research and discovered the most successful arguments and proven techniques that can help shorten a sentence before and after one is incarcerated. I then dissected the pure essentials that all inmates and defendants, not only their attorneys, should have knowledge about when dealing with sentencing reducing provisions such as the *"Rule 35," "5K1," "Safety Valve,"* etc.

After dozens of interviews with inmates and prison employees I also discovered what it takes to get more time in a federal halfway house than the next guy. After hundreds of hours spent in the law library and only after reading through the archives of not less than six hundred federal cases, was I able to isolate the real tips, tricks, secrets, and techniques that have enabled so many defendants and inmates to wipe months and years off of their otherwise lengthy prison sentences.

I continued on with my studies and successfully outlined a set of mitigating factors that statistically work best when attempting to secure departures below the recommended sentencing guidelines for specific federal offenses. The pages that follow will deliver critical information vital to anyone dealing with a federal prison term and provide a clearer understanding about the many remedies that are available to those sentenced in federal court. Please read this book with an open mind to get the wheels turning in the event that your future involves a visit to federal court or even worse; prison.

1
Fed Up

Are you or someone you know the target of a federal investigation? Have you been charged with a federal crime or maybe facing future charges? Have you or someone you know been indicted on, or convicted of, a federal offense? Is federal prison lurking around the corner? If so, then take a deep breath and continue reading on.

My name is Stephen Sharp, and back in 2008 I was the target of a federal investigation named "Operation True Test." This was a follow up to "Operation Pipedream," a similar investigation which landed Tommy Chong from *"Cheech and Chong"* in federal prison for nine months for selling bongs, not drugs, only smoking pipes, over the internet. Mr. Chong was the only defendant without a criminal history that received prison time in the raid that involved dozens of companies. Ironically, I was the only person in Operation True Test without a criminal history that received prison time also.

Operation True Test was orchestrated by the same Pennsylvania District Attorney, Mary Beth Buchanan, who spearheaded Operation Pipedream. She has been toted as one of the worst District Attorneys to ever hold the position, and she spent millions of dollars in taxpayer's money in worthless prosecutions such as U.S.A. vs. Wecht, in which Mr. Cyril Wecht, a Pittsburgh coroner, was prosecuted for using the business fax machine for personal use, or U.S.A. vs. Fletcher, in which Buchanan ensnared Ms. Fletcher for writing online stories that portrayed her childhood memories of being molested and sexually abused, and of course who can forget the poor comedian Mr. Tommy Chong who had to go to prison for selling smoking pipes over the internet.

Back in 1999 I invented a product called "You're In The Clear" which was sold as a detoxification supplement to help cleanse one's body of drug toxins. This product was originally created to be sold with the many bodybuilding supplements that my nutrition store carried, many which contained all natural ingredients such as tribulus terrestris and deer antler; these and other herbal ingredients were known to have the potential to cause false positives on a urine drug test. Since many of my customers were calling me asking about the chance of a failed drug test, I determined it was in my best interest to offer some type of dietary cleansing supplement that they could use with my natural bodybuilding products. It would put their mind at ease and help me keep my customers coming back for more of our fitness supplements. I then researched and created this all natural detoxification product and added it to my store in 1999. It consisted of natural ingredients, mainly psyllium husk and other vitamins and minerals; a natural cleansing formula. Little did I know that this one little product would give me the ride of my life a few years later. My web site talked a great deal about unfair drug testing and this likely raised some red flags, but since there were no laws preventing the sale of such products I exercised my right to sell it and did so successfully from 1999 and onward until 2008 when I voluntarily removed it from my store after our house was raided by DEA and FBI agents.

In December 2000 I received my private pilot's license and by 2005 I was employed as a first officer for a regional airline. You can probably now see where the door was open for problems. While it may have been a lot easier to simply stop selling that one product when I got hired by the airline, I honestly never thought twice about it. I was sure that there was no law prohibiting its sale and called several other companies that sold drug testing kits and cleansers to further confirm the legality of these products. Furthermore, my nutrition store also had a slew of drug testing kits for sale. Did I ever think about the legality of these too; of course not. How can these items be illegal? They are sold in stores like Walmart. Well I was in for the shock of my life.

To make a long story short, the feds, as directed again by District Attorney Mary Beth Buchanan, raided our house in addition to five other non-related online businesses on May 7, 2008. An intense investigation was conducted for nearly two years, obviously due to the premature belief that I was some kind of drug dealing airline pilot. Of course this was not the case though, but with all the money spent investigating me, the government wanted a conviction on something.

money, and if this attorney is not getting any more money, it is likely that there is not any time for additional litigation.

A private attorney is almost always paid in full before he starts defending his client. The amount he is paid by the defendant can be thought of as the base defense package. This is purely my opinion but it has been backed up by case after case that I heard of and read about. It is like driving your car through the car wash. On the top is the basic wash for $5. That gets your car through the wash with the basics, but if you want the works it will be $10. Since attorneys can't really ask you if you want the standard service or the works it is safe to assume that most of us end up with the standard package. If a public defender is being used by the defendant, then he is not receiving any compensation from the defendant. In this situation, it is quite possible that the defendant is receiving only a small portion of the attorney's capacity and professional capability. Why should a public defender work his fingers to the bone and fight with his last bit of might for you? Because it is his job you say? Well that may be true for a very small percentage of legal eagles but the fact of the matter is that a public defender is not too much concerned if your sentence will be ten months in prison or twenty months. But to you this can mean a whole lot and that is why you must learn some of the guidelines regarding sentencing procedures and motions. These are perfect examples of why any defendant should do his homework in a federal case. You need brilliant results in this fight of your life.

One of the biggest flaws in the system is the procedure in which a private attorney is paid to defend someone. When a defendant decides to retain the services of an attorney, that attorney is usually paid up front via a retainer. The retainer is commonly drawn up as a non-refundable payment and contains language that places that attorney as legal counsel for the defendant for the alleged charges. The caveat to this is obvious though. Everyone knows that when an individual pays for a particular service up front and in its entirety, the performance of that service will likely be adversely affected at some point and especially during the final phase(s).

Here is a typical scenario that I heard too many times while interviewing other inmates: A defendant hires an attorney. This attorney gets all of the money owed to him up front and initially defends the case with a head of steam in the early stages. As this criminal case lingers along, the fire begins to die down and performance slacks. By now several months have gone by and the attorney has two fresh new cases to defend with fresh deposits being made. Communication with this original defendant is gradually degraded and then all of a sudden the defendant's important case, a matter of life and death, is stuck in second gear and situated neatly on the back burner. This complacent performance almost always leads to a less than favorable sentence in the end. This happens all too often; trust me.

In any criminal case one should think of themselves as a log and the attorney as the fire. When the attorney is first hired, his fireplace is full of logs and a fierce blaze is roaring. As time goes by, the fire fades and flickers here and there. It will be at this precise time in one's case that the defendant should have an arm full of fresh logs to dump on the fire and keep it roaring. This book will outline the methods available to keep that fireplace full of burning logs and discuss the various procedures to help reduce one's overall offense level and resulting sentence. Keeping an attorney's mind full of fresh ideas and arguments will prevent the entire case from being *"back burnered."* Constant contact and communication is imperative to keep the ball moving forward and the case fresh in the attorney's mind. Mere occasional contact by an attorney's client can convey the feeling that this particular case is not as urgent as other cases on his desk.

I remember in my particular case nothing would happen unless I would initiate the call to my attorney and shed some light on new ideas, theories and arguments regarding the facts surrounding my case. If I was not persistent with my phone calls and emails, and if I did not keep pushing and pushing for results, then I am confident that the outcome would have been much different. What started with a possible maximum sentence of twenty-eight years in federal prison and three felony charges, concluded in September of 2010 with a plea of guilty to one single count of interfering with a government function and a nine month sentence in a minimum security federal prison camp. After applying some real life arguments to substantiate extra time in a halfway house, I was able to walk out of the Estill, SC federal camp after only seven months, that's almost twenty-five percent of my total sentence substituted for community confinement.

The bottom line; going to prison is not fun for anyone, but as I stated before anyone can get through it. Being the sole provider of my beloved family and a dedicated, hard working husband and father, and then having my entire world crumble right in front of me was clearly devastating. But when dramatic events like this take place in one's life there is some type of inner strength and spiritual power that helps guide us through to the other side.

For several weeks prior to surrendering to federal prison I would wake up in the morning only after a few hours of poor sleep and then pace around the house all day. Looking at and thinking about my family definitely helped me through the tough times. I took all these horrible things that were transpiring in my life and then weighed it all against the health and safety of my family. I knew that they would be healthy and safe no matter where I was and promised from that day on to move forward with a positive attitude and dedicate my time towards helping others faced with the threat of federal prison.

With regard to prison, it really is all what you make of it. Staying busy while in any prison is the key to success. My salvation while incarcerated consisted of getting in great shape and learning how to take my writing skills to the next level. This book is an example of what anyone can do while serving time and how to use the system to one's advantage. Sure, the system will do its best to strip you of your dignity and self-pride but don't let it. I remember my first and second day in federal prison being the worst of all and then it went all uphill form there. My second day was when I got to exchange my temporary white jumpsuit for the stylish green inmate uniform. I was called into the laundry room early in the morning around 6am. Inside, the inmates who worked there handed my a few pairs each of green pants and shirts, one cloth belt, one mesh laundry bag, one brown winter hat, and one pair of black work boots. One of the inmates then instructed me to go into a small utility room off to my left and try on a pair of pants and a shirt to check the size. I flicked the light on to this little broom closet and proceeded to discard my white jump suit in exchange for my new green duds. After I was done changing I noticed a mirror on the far wall and walked over to it to see my new outfit. When I gazed at the mirror is when it all hit me. I said to myself, *"Wow look at me! I look like a real prisoner. The kind I used to watch on TV. Wow! Wow!"* I now looked like everyone else on the compound and this sent an eerie chill up and down my spine. Even more unsettling was my name and number stamped on each of my green pants and shirts. Each pair clearly read *"S. Sharp – 31514-068"* in bold black letters. I finally decided it was time to get out of that little closet. I thanked the inmates in the laundry room for my new clothes and then exited the laundry room.

For the remainder of the day I aimlessly walked around the prison grounds in an endless circle. Towards the end of the day is when my emotions got the best of me. I knew it was not a good idea to display emotions in any prison environment so I quietly walked over to the far end of the compound where there were only a few inmates. I took a seat on one of the picnic benches and let a few loose tears leave their path down the sides of my face. I thought about my family and then plopped my head into my jacket and sobbed quietly for about ten minutes. Separation from family and loved ones is the one thing that hurts the most. I headed back to my bunk shortly after and stared out the window for most of the night.

On my third day my inner strength caught up to me and gave me the power I needed. I told myself in stern words while in the shower, *"I know who I am and there is nothing anyone can do to take that away. No uniform, no prison, nobody will ever take away my dignity, pride, or the true character that defines who I am!"* From that day on I kept my chin up, focused on getting in great physical shape and began my intense studies of the federal justice system.

Two Ways

When it all comes down to the wire there will be two ways which a defendant in a criminal case will be able to reduce an upcoming sentence of imprisonment: either one or more of the charges must be dropped, or the overall offense level, which resulted from the charges, must be lowered. Additionally, there will be only two avenues that a defendant will be able to proceed in a criminal case: He will either decide to take the case to trial and let a jury or judge decide his fate or plead guilty in court to one or more of the alleged charges. Unfortunately, the stats compiled from previous years of federal criminal cases shed a very dim light on those that do choose to go to trial. In total, only about five percent of defendants charged with federal crimes decide to proceed with a trial by jury. Of these cases, a mere twenty-five percent are adjudicated with a not guilty verdict. The remaining seventy-five percent are found guilty on one or more charges. These numbers show that the odds are clearly in the government's favor when going to trial.

This book will focus on the various techniques and arguments which can substantially help reduce a defendant's offense level before and after he is sentenced in federal court. The act of lowering a defendant's overall offense level is referred to as a downward departure. It will be the amount of *"departing"* that is successfully litigated that will essentially determine the total amount of one's sentence reduction. Downward departures can result from a myriad of factors and valid arguments which are allowed to be used in federal court. This is why it so important for all defendants to have some degree of knowledge about the federal sentencing guidelines and mitigating factors that are relative to their case and allowed in federal court.

It is important for anyone to remember that a sentence of imprisonment never ends after the judge remands someone to prison. Even after a sentence of imprisonment has begun there are many sentencing relief tools that any inmate can utilize all the way up to his final day of incarceration. An example of some of these are the appeal, the compassionate release, executive clemency, Rule 35's, RDAP, and the habeas corpus, all of which are explained in this book. The more information and understanding that a person has with his case, the better position he will be in to secure positive results.

The information in the following chapters will clearly identify, analyze, and discuss the various tips, tricks, and techniques that are available to help substantiate the request and subsequent consideration for a downward departure on one's offense level. Learning about these legal strategies will also help a defendant and his family communicate better with legal counsel and maybe open the doors for additional avenues of sentencing relief. Whether one has been recently charged, sentenced, or already imprisoned, the following information will address helpful avenues for each scenario. Before we get started, let's briefly outline some of the important stages of a federal criminal case:

The Investigation

Being on the wrong end of a federal investigation can be one of the most stressful times in a person's life. Going to sleep knowing that the United States government, along with its plethora of federal agents and operatives, is looking into every aspect of one's life is not easy by any comparison. If this same person has a family then the stress and anxiety levels are only that much more amplified.

A federal investigation is usually initiated when the government suspects there may be a violation of federal law. Federal investigations can take months and years to be completed and can involve hundreds of people. Many times a defendant is unaware that he is under investigation until he is handed an indictment and arrested by federal agents. Sometimes though, the defendant is aware of the investigation from the early stages. Whatever the case may be, it is important to remember that lying to a federal agent at any time before, during or after an investigation is a crime in itself and classified as a felony in the U.S. If you are talking to federal agents and lying to them they will likely find out. Additionally, being deceitful will only compound the problems that someone may already be experiencing during a federal investigation.

Another mistake that many people make when subjected to the enormous amounts of stress from an investigation is to begin talking immediately to federal agents. Even if there is nothing to hide, and everyone under investigation is completely innocent, the most important thing to do is to keep silent. Contrary to what many people may think, keeping silent is not in any way a sign of guilt but a show of intelligence pressing the fact that this person wishes to exercise his right to professional counsel before he discusses any facts related to the investigation.

Many times agents will try to make the suspect believe that it is best to talk now and help out. Many times agents try to make the suspect feel like he will get in less trouble if he reveals the truth about the suspected illegal activity. Remember though, the government will use any information you provide against you, your family, or your friends if the need for this arises. Any comments you make at this stage will only make your situation worse whether innocent or guilty. Even if you are completely innocent, it is wise to withhold any information that you wish to disclose until after speaking with a qualified federal criminal defense attorney who specializes in the type of crime that you are the suspect of. For example, don't ever hire a federal defense attorney who is experienced in immigration to handle your drug case. This will certainly work against you! Additionally, remember to have an attorney present whenever talking with federal agents or law enforcement officers. This is important as it will keep federal agents on a level playing field. There are strict laws that govern what can and cannot be done during a federal investigation and a good attorney should be able to keep any unethical, sneaky, or illegal tactics at bay.

Statute of Limitations

One thing that can slide by the defendant, the defendant's attorney and the prosecutor is the statute of limitations. Did you know that there is a statute of limitations that exists on all but the most serious of federal crimes? Yes it is true. All federal offenses except capital offenses, offenses involving terrorism, sex offenses involving a child and a few other big time offenses have a set time limit when formal charges must be filed or else the offense can no longer be prosecuted. This allotment of time is generally five years from the date of the commission of the offense. The federal statute of limitations is governed under 18 U.S.C. 3282 (i.e., Title 18 of the United States Code - Section 3282), and it provides the following: *"Except as otherwise expressly provided by law, no person shall be prosecuted, tried, or punished for any offense, not capital, unless the indictment is found or the information is instituted within five years next after such offense shall have been committed."* Certain other offenses have longer time limits as set forth by 18 U.S.C. 3282. Tax offenses generally have a six year time period before they are exempt for prosecution, and offenses consisting of major fraud (i.e., crimes against the government involving $1,000,000 or more) have a ten year limitation. Offenses committed against banks and financial institutions also carry with them a ten year statute of limitations. Additionally, the statute of limitations for immigration offenses has been increased from five to ten years.

I have been approached by more than one individual while incarcerated who told me that the next time they are prosecuted for a federal offense that they would leave the U.S. and live abroad for five years and then come back. They thought that they would then be protected by the statute of limitations and immune to any prosecution after this time allotment had passed. While this sounded like an interesting plan, it was completely lacking in any research. Therefore I took it upon myself to delve into the legal smorgasbord and find out the answer. Interestingly enough, it only took me one day to uncover the list as shown below which contains a number of offenses that have an indefinite statute of limitations:

- Escape from federal custody. 18 U.S.C. 751.
- Flight to avoid prosecution. 18 U.S.C. 1073.
- Failure to report for sentencing. 18 U.S.C. 3146(a).
- Re-entering the United States illegally after deportation. 18 U.S.C. 1326(a).
- Possession of counterfeit money. 18 U.S.C. 472.
- Regardless of the offense, a person who is a fugitive from justice is not protected by any statute of limitations for that offense. 18 U.S.C. 3290.

Consequently, it is often not the main concern of the defendant's attorney to check the statute of limitations on each and every charge. Therefore a case with a close statute of limitations may go by unnoticed if the defendant himself does not identify the problem. Don't expect the government to jump forward and let a defendant know about any possible statute of limitations problem either. It would ruin their chances to prosecute that individual

Having some general knowledge about the amount of time that has passed since the conviction of prior offenses is crucial for any defendant. The statute of limitations for a particular offense begins running when the commission of the said offense has been completed. For example, if a defendant embezzled money from his company and the statute of limitations for the offense was seven years, then the government would have seven years from the date when the embezzlement offense was complete to bring forth charges. If that defendant continued to embezzle money after the initial act, then the statute of limitations would reset and start to run from the beginning again using the most recent commission of the act as the starting point. Any overacts of a particular offense can also reset the statute of limitations such as when an art thief, who stole million of dollars worth of art twenty years prior, decides to sell some of the stolen art at a later date. This transaction would reset the statute of limitations back to the beginning.

Nonetheless, there have been many federal cases where the defendant walked away untouched due to the excessive amount of time that had passed by since the commission of the allcgcd offcnsc. It is important for anyone who is being prosecuted for a crime several years old to swiftly contact a qualified attorney to determine if the amount of time that has passed exceeds the statute of limitations for that offense. Additionally, the statute of limitations defense must be announced before the start of a trial or the prosecution would be allowed to continue with the trial. To prevail on a statute of limitations defense, the defendant must show that the date of filing of the criminal complaint, information or indictment by the grand jury was beyond the applicable time limit of the statute. Once the trial has begun, it's too late!

The Indictment

When someone is formally charged by the U.S. government for a federal offense, an indictment is often unsealed and its contents made public. A federal Indictment is the charging document which formally makes the allegations against one or more people or entities (e.g., companies, corporations, defendants, etc). The United States Attorney's Office will use the Indictment as a legal document to prosecute a person and the prosecutor will have to prove the elements of the crimes that have been listed in the Indictment. All federal indictments should contain a statement of the facts for the charged offense, and for each charge the Indictment must list the citation of the relevant statute (e.g., 18 U.S.C. 371).

The government must also present their case to a Grand Jury and subsequently have the grand jurors vote in favor of prosecution, therefore making the Indictment valid. Grand jury proceedings are *"secret"* and the only members allowed to attend besides the grand jury members are the attorney for the government, the court reporter and witnesses. Interpreters, if needed, are also allowed to be at the proceedings. Title 18, United States Code, Section 1504, makes it a federal crime to communicate with a federal grand jury regarding an official matter with the intent to influence the grand jury. Therefore, an Indictment may be returned with little or no notice to the defendant. In fact, many defendants don't even know about the indictment until they see it on the news or a friend or family member calls them and tells them about it. After the indictment is unsealed, the defendant will be arrested and held in custody or allowed to remain free either on bond or via the defendant's own recognizance. This largely depends on the seriousness of the charge(s) as well as the nature and characteristics of the defendant. Someone who would be suspected of fleeing the country or committing another offense would obviously be taken into custody, while a bank owner who embezzled $20,000 may never get arrested throughout his entire case. Whether or not to arrest an individual is primarily in the hands of the District Attorney who is handling the case. There are many different districts located across the nation with at least one district in each state. Each district is headed by a District Attorney who is appointed by the President of the United States. The District Attorney reports to the Attorney General and the Attorney General reports to the President.

While the indictment is the most common document for filing formal federal charges against a person, there are two other documents that are also used quite often. These are known as the *"criminal complaint"* and *"criminal information."* With an indictment, the prosecutor must present the facts of the case to the grand jury, the grand jury will listen to the facts, and then they will vote on whether or not there are enough facts to support the charges. The Federal Rules of Criminal Procedure prescribe that a grand jury must have from sixteen to twenty-three members and that an indictment may be issued only if at least twelve jurors concur. Only after the grand jury gives its approval to move forward on the charges, can the indictment be filed and the case prosecuted. But, securing an approval from the grand jury is not as difficult as one would think and the old saying *"You can indict a ham sandwich"* still holds true today.

The criminal information and criminal complaint will still contain the same information as the indictment, but the prosecutor can bypass the grand jury proceedings using one of these alternative avenues for prosecution. Prosecution via the criminal complaint document is commonly used when an arrest warrant is needed or if the prosecution is running up against a time restriction such as a statute of limitations for a particular offense and they need to get the charge(s) filed as soon as possible. The indictment process takes the most time to complete due to the extra preparation needed for the grand jury hearings. Prosecution via the criminal information document is used commonly when the defendant and the prosecutor have reached an agreement in the early stages of a case. In this situation the defendant often agrees to plead guilty usually with some type of plea agreement and the government moves forward by filing the criminal information document. Any time a defendant does decide to plead guilty and give up his right to a trial, he must also agree to sign a *"waiver of indictment."* All criminal cases in federal court involving felony offenses, which are decided via a trial by jury, must be prosecuted with a valid indictment. Only if a defendant signs the waiver and pleads guilty, can the case proceed without a valid Indictment.

Once formal charges are filed, the defendant will be required to appear in court and plead guilty or not guilty. If there is a plea agreement worked out between the defendant and the prosecutor, then the defendant will be required to attend a plea hearing where he will be required to sign the agreement, plead guilty to the charge(s) and agree to the terms of the plea agreement. When a defendant appears in court to plead guilty, the judge can either allow the defendant to remain free on his own recognizance until he is sentenced at a later date or he can set a bond amount that would require the defendant to pay ten percent of the total bond if he wishes to remain free until his sentencing. The judge can also have the defendant held in custody until his sentencing. Of course if the defendant is found not guilty or the charges are dropped then there would be no sentencing date. Nonetheless, it is ultimately up to the judge to make the decision on the defendant's fate. The following is an example of what a typical federal indictment may look like when written by the FBI:

Sample Combination Multi-Count Criminal Complaint,

Affidavit in Support of a Criminal Complaint and Application for a Warrant

UNITED STATES DISTRICT COURT

_____ DISTRICT OF _____

UNITED STATES OF AMERICA,

        v.   CRIMINAL COMPLAINT

JOHN DOE and

JANE DOE

CRIMINAL COMPLAINT

I, the undersigned complainant being duly sworn state the following is true and correct to the best of my knowledge and belief.

[PLEASE NOTE THAT NON-APPLICABLE COUNTS ARE TO BE DELETED}

Count One

From on or about_____ 2009 to the present, in _____ in the _____, defendants did, conspire with each other and with others to devise and participate in a scheme to defraud the United States and the people of the United States of the honest services of JANE DOE and JOHN DOE, in furtherance of which the mails and interstate wire communications would be used, in violation of Title 18, United States Code, Sections 1341,1343, and 1346; all in violation of Title 18 United States Code, Section 1349.

Count Two

Beginning no later than _____ to the present, in _____ in the _____ of _____, defendants JANE DOE and JOHN DOE, being agents of the United States, received federal benefits in excess of $10,000, corruptly solicited and demanded a thing of value, namely, _____, intending to be influenced and rewarded in connection with business and transactions of the United States involving a thing of value of $5,000 or more, namely, the provision of millions of dollars in financial assistance by the United States, including through the Department of XYZ, an agency of the United States, to the _____company or individual_____; in violation of Title 18, United States Code, Sections 666(a)(1)(B) and 2.

Count Three

26 - Reduce My Prison Sentence

From on or about_____ 2009 to the present, in _____, in the _____, defendants JANE DOE and JOHN DOE directly or indirectly, corruptly gave, offered or promised something of value to a public official or person who has been selected to be a public official, or offers or promises any public official or any person who has been selected to be a public official to give anything of value to any other person or entity, with intent, in violation of 18 U.S.C. 201(b)(1)

Count Four

From on or about_____ 2009 to the present, in _____, in the _____, defendants JANE DOE and JOHN DOE being a public official or person selected to be a public official, directly or indirectly, corruptly demands, seeks, receives, accepts, or agrees to receive or accept anything of value personally or for any other person or entity, in return for:

    1.   being influenced in the performance of any official act;

    2.   being influenced to commit or aid in committing, or to collude in, or allow, any fraud, or make opportunity for the commission of any fraud, on the United States; or

    3.   being induced to do or omit to do any act in violation of the official duty of such official or person; Directly or indirectly, corruptly demanded, sought, received, accepted, or agreed to receive in return for being influenced in the performance of any official act 18 U.S.C. 201(b)(2)

2.   From on or about_____ 2009 to the present, in _____, in the _____, defendants JANE DOE and JOHN DOE conspired to commit the murder of the late _____ as well as several thousand other deceased U. S. service members, in violation of Title 18, United States Code, Section 1117.

3.   From on or about_____ 2009 to the present, in _____, in the _____, defendants JANE DOE and JOHN DOE murdered the late _____ as well as several thousand other deceased U. S. service members, in violation of Title 18, United States Code, Section 1111.

4.   From on or about_____ 2009 to the present, in _____, in the _____, defendants JANE DOE and JOHN DOE aided and abetted in the commission of the murder of the late _____ as well as several thousand other deceased U. S. service members, in violation of Title 18, United States Code, Section 1111.

5.   Aided and abetted in a conspiracy to commit the murder of the late _____ as well as several thousand other deceased U. S. service members, in violation of Title 18, United States Code, Section 1117.

6.   Engaged in a conspiracy, to deprive _____ of his rights in violation of Title 18, United States Code, Section 241.

7. Deprived _____ of rights under color of law in violation of Title 18, United States Code, Section 242.

8. From on or about _____ 2009 to the present, in _____, in the _____, defendants JANE DOE and JOHN DOE violated the War Crimes Act of 1996, as amended, Title 18, United States Code, Section 2441.

9. From on or about _____ 2009 to the present, in _____, in the _____, defendants JANE DOE and JOHN DOE conspired to violate the Convention against Torture and Other Cruel, Inhuman or Degrading Treatment or Punishment as implemented by Title 18, United States Code, Section 2340-2340A.

10. From on or about _____ 2009 to the present, in _____, in the _____, defendants JANE DOE and JOHN DOE engaged in a conspiracy to defraud the United States in violation of Title 18, United States Code, Section 371.

11. From on or about _____ 2009 to the present, in _____, in the _____, defendants JANE DOE and JOHN DOE Violated Title 18, United States Code, Section 4, Misprision of a Felony.

I further state _____ and that this complaint is based on the following facts:

Finding the Right Attorney

After charges have been formerly filed, the next important step, if not already accomplished, is to find a qualified attorney. When searching for an attorney for a federal case, it should be noted that there will be thousands of these legal eagles around who would be more than happy to take your ten thousand dollars to defend you. It is important to find an attorney that is well seasoned in the type of federal law that surrounds the alleged charge(s). Additionally, it is essential to retain only an attorney that practices federal law. Often, a defendant will hire the first attorney he finds and then learn that this attorney defends cases in both state and federal court. This is a difference between the procedures, arguments, motions, etc., that are applicable to a federal case versus a state case. If your attorney is practicing both federal and state cases then he will not be as polished and savvy as the same attorney who only focuses his time and profession in the federal genre. Ask around, search online, and make phone calls to find an attorney who practices criminal law in the federal system and has a specialty for your type of offense. (i.e. drugs, taxes, immigration, wire fraud, etc.)

Another little secret to remember when hiring an attorney is to find one who practices in the same district as where one's case is being litigated. Hiring a federal criminal defense attorney in Massachusetts for your federal case in New Jersey is not a good idea, even if you live in Massachusetts. The importance of this is vast and there are some obvious advantages to this tactic. For example, my particular case originated out of Pennsylvania, but I lived in central Florida. Since I lived in Florida and knew nothing about this new world of federal criminal law, I proceeded to find an attorney in the Orlando, FL, area. I also made the mistake of doing little research about qualified attorneys for my case and hired the very first one that I met. This was not a bright move and I paid for it dearly. I hope you can learn by my costly mistakes. To begin with, this attorney made no mention of the possible number of trips that we both would have to make to the Pennsylvania District Court to resolve my case nor how I would be responsible for paying his expenses for each such trip. The next problem was that this attorney practiced primarily in Florida and not in Pennsylvania. He knew none of the judges or prosecutors or anyone from the PA area. The smart thing for me to do at that time would have been to hire an attorney who practiced in the same district as where my case was filed. Then my attorney would have been aware of the procedures of that court, and as an added bonus maybe he would have had past experience working with the judge and/or prosecutor who was assigned to my case. Who knows, he and the prosecutor may have just finished negotiating a favorable plea deal for another defendant just prior to receiving my case, or better yet, maybe this attorney and the prosecutor were friends. Maybe the prosecutor, defense attorney and judge are all friends too! Who knows, but every little bit helps in even the smallest criminal case. If all of them were indeed friends, then this in no way means that a particular defendant will receive a *"get out of jail free card,"* but negotiating a plea bargain between two friendly professionals is surely easier then having the same deal argued out between two intransigent legal competitors.

One should think of the court where their case will be heard as home field. A defense attorney who practices in the same court week after week may have a slight advantage when trying to convince a judge to depart downward on a sentencing guideline. It very well could be the deciding factor when the judge is stuck in the middle of a particular situation. In fact, if an attorney is well liked and well respected by both the judge and the prosecutor, then this will serve as another small advantage for the defendant. Consequently, my attorney who lived and practiced in the state of Florida, and the Assistant United States Attorney prosecuting my case developed a sour relationship from the very beginning. This certainly worked against me in many ways. It got so bad towards the end that another attorney at the law firm had to fill in for phone conversations because there was nothing but yelling and arguing going on. This poor relationship did not help me in any way and even led to a similar relationship between my attorney and the judge. What made the judge have what seemed to be an instant disliking towards him? It seemed like he represented the New York Yankees and we were the Boston Red Sox. The courtroom felt like Yankee Stadium.

Please avoid making the poor decisions I did when it comes time to seek professional counsel (Take your time!) Even if your case is from another state and communication with an out of state attorney is a problem, there are effective methods like video and phone conferencing that can be utilized. Even if the defendant is held in custody, he will still have special privileges when it comes time for communication with his attorney. It is wise to ask the following questions to any prospective attorney before signing any type of agreement or legal retainer.

Private Attorney
Does he defend only federal cases or both state and federal?
How many times has he been to trial?
How long has he been practicing?
Does he practice in the same district court as your case?
Is he experienced in your type of offense?
Does he know the prosecutor and/or judge in your case?
Does he have a good reputation with them?
What are his total costs to defend the case without a trial?

What are the total costs to defend the case with a trial?
Are there any other hidden expenses?

Federal Public Defender
Does he defend only federal cases?
How many times has he been to trial?
How long has he been practicing?
Does he practice in the same district court as your case?
Is he experienced in your type of offense?
Does he know the prosecutor and/or judge in your case?
Does he have a good reputation with them?
Are there any hidden expenses?

To Plea or not to Plea

When someone is charged with a federal offense, the biggest question will often be whether or not they will have their case decided via a trial or plead guilty either with or without a plea deal. As we stated before, very few federal criminal cases ever make it to trial. Of the thousands of cases that are completed every year in federal court, over ninety-five percent of them conclude with some type of guilty plea made by the defendant. Of the remaining five percent of cases that are decided by a jury, only twenty-five percent of those result in a not guilty verdict for the defendant. From these stats alone one can see that even a completely innocent defendant will likely be found guilty on one or more charges if the case is decided by a jury. At trial, the government will always do its best to secure a guilty verdict and this can be done by finding every possible way to cast the defendant in a dim light therefore helping to sway the jury into a guilty finding.

One thing that a defendant has going for him in any federal criminal case though, is that the government has a huge overload of cases to handle every month and it is in their best interest to settle the majority of them as efficiently and swiftly as possible. By doing this, they will be able to free up much needed time to spend on other cases and in turn lighten the load on the court's over congested docket;

plea bargaining is one sure fire way to accomplish this task. Even the judges are completely aware that plea deals are a very important tool to keep things moving along in the federal courts. Due to the never ending flow of new cases and the limited amount of government prosecutors to handle the cases, plea bargaining often has the most potential in the earliest stages of a case. This will usually be when the government has its least amount of time vested in the case, and this can be used to the defendant's advantage. If a plea bargain is in the best interest of a defendant, then it should be talked over with an experienced attorney, ideally before the government allocates substantial time and money for further prosecution of the case. In this situation, the defendant and his attorney should carefully evaluate the facts, details and evidence concerning the alleged charges and then compare the scenarios of the possible sentences, fines, restitution, etc., that may coincide with a guilty plea versus a guilty finding after a jury trial.

One thing that many defendants in a federal case are unaware of is the two level point reduction for acceptance of responsibility. When a defendant pleads guilty in federal court and shows full responsibility for the charged offense(s), the court will usually agree to a two or three point reduction on the total offense level. It will be this new lower offense level that will be used by the judge to determine a proper sentence. There may be other adjustments to the defendant's offense level also, either enhancements or reductions. Longer prison sentences almost always accompany higher offense levels for a defendant, therefore securing the lowest possible offense level will help secure the lowest possible sentence.

The point reduction for acceptance of responsibility usually reduces the defendant's recommended sentence by a handful of months. There is also a provision in the sentencing guidelines that awards an additional one point reduction to the offense level for a defendant's acceptance of responsibility. The factor which determines whether the acceptance of responsibility will reduce the offense level by two or three points will depend on the defendant's total offense level before this point reduction is applied. If the defendant's total offense level is a sixteen or lower then the two point reduction applies, and if the total offense level is greater than sixteen then a three point reduction applies. Why defendants with offense levels under sixteen don't also receive the three point reduction is still a question yet to be answered. There are other factors involved for getting the extra one point reduction for acceptance of responsibility and those should be discussed with a qualified attorney. We talk more about plea bargaining later in this book.

The Pre-Sentence Report

Before someone is sentenced in federal court there will be a special report prepared by the probation department called *"The Pre-Sentence Investigation Report"*; also referred to as the PSI or PSIR. The importance of this report and the significance of the information contained in it can not be stressed enough. The PSI report is used to help make important decisions regarding the defendant such as an appropriate sentence length, amount of fine and/or restitution, place of confinement and other important decisions throughout a defendant's case and resulting sentence. The PSI is a detailed report which will verify the defendant's charge(s), offense level, sentencing guideline range, recommended sentence by probation department, applicable fine and restitution, criminal history, family and education history, medical conditions and much more.

One of the biggest pitfalls that a defendant will likely encounter is the lack of attention by his attorney when it comes to preparing the PSI. Because of this, a defendant should take it upon himself to make sure his PSI is accurate, detailed and fruitful in every aspect. An interview to gather information for the defendant's PSI will be set up by the probation department and completed before the defendant is sentenced. A final draft of the PSI must be furnished to the defendant, the defendant's attorney and the prosecutor no later than thirty-five days prior to the defendant's sentencing date unless an extension has been granted. The defendant and his attorney will then have fourteen days to correct any errors or omissions that are found.

A probation officer will conduct the interview for the PSI, either in person or over the phone, and the interview will take roughly a few hours to complete. The probation officer will often contact doctors, employers, family members and friends of the defendant to acquire additional comments and information that will help the probation officer gather an accurate profile of the defendant. It is important for the defendant to make sure his attorney will be present for the PSI interview and if unable to do so then reschedule the interview to a later date. While being interviewed, it is important for the defendant to be honest and contrite. If the probation officer catches the defendant lying on his PSI then the consequences are often vast and the information furnished to the probation officer by the defendant becomes much less credible. Additionally, a judge will look at this as a greater need for correctional services for the defendant and any chance for a downward departure would likely be mitigated after one is caught lying.

The PSI report will be a useful tool when a downward departure is being sought for the defendant because it holds substantial weight in a judge's decision at sentencing and ultimately can be the deciding factor. Additionally, any positive recommendations that the probation officer lists in the PSI, such as a recommendation for home detention or a specific length of sentence, can be brought up by the defendant's attorney and many time agreed to by the judge regardless what kind of rebuttal the prosecutor makes. The statements made by the probation officer, who acts as a neutral party, are extremely important to any judge at the sentencing. Once again, the remarks and recommendations that a probation officer makes, either in person or on a defendant's PSI, is always taken into serious consideration by the judge at sentencing; this point can not be highlighted enough.

Before the PSI interview is conducted, it is important for the defendant to have a list of positive events and facts that pertain to his life. Things like strong family ties, notable achievements, charitable works, heroic acts, good deeds, stable work history, caretaking and financial responsibilities, etc., should be mentioned and put into the PSI report; the more information showing the good traits of the defendant the better. Additionally, any underlying health problems should be carefully outlined in the PSI. This should include any drug or alcohol dependencies also. If a defendant is anticipating a term of imprisonment and wants get accepted into the RDAP to get up to a year wiped of his sentence, then his drug and/or alcohol abuse needs to be clearly detailed in the PSI report. For more information about time off please see the chapter in this book titled *"Take a Year Off."* The medical condition of a defendant is a substantial factor when determining an appropriate facility that a defendant will be designated to if he is required to serve time in a federal correctional institution. Unique health problems that require specialized treatment and care could very well convince a judge to place the defendant in home detention rather that a prison environment. For more about using the health condition of a defendant as an argument for a reduced sentence please see the chapter in this book titled *"Medical Factors."*

A defendant who does not have an extensive past criminal history and is successful filling his PSI with substantial facts and details showing his otherwise law abiding life and good character, may be able to use this aberrant behavior as one of the arguments to help argue for a reduced sentence. Examples of the successful use of aberrant behavior to secure a reduced sentence are talked about later in this book. The essential elements of a Pre-Sentence Investigation Report and the specific topics that a defendant may be questioned about are as follows:

- **Part 1** - The offense, Charge(s) and conviction(s), Related cases, The offense conduct, Adjustment for obstruction of justice, Adjustment for acceptance of responsibility, Offense level computation;

- **Part 2** - The defendant's criminal history, Juvenile Adjudications, Criminal convictions, Criminal history computation, Other criminal conduct, Pending charges (include if pertinent);

- **Part 3** - Sentencing options, Custody, Supervised release, Probation;

- **Part 4** - Offender characteristics, Family ties, family responsibilities, and community ties, Mental and emotional health, Physical condition, including drug dependence and alcohol abuse, Education and vocational skills, Employment record;

- **Part 5** - Fines and restitution, Statutory provisions, Guidelines provisions for fines, Defendant's ability to pay;

- **Part 6** - Factors that may warrant departure (from sentence guidelines;

- **Part 7** - The impact of plea agreement (if pertinent);

- **Part 8** - Sentencing recommendations;

By law, a defendant can not waive the preparation of the PSI. Additionally, the PSI should always disclose the defendant's total offense level as calculated by the probation officer. This value should be checked for accuracy by the defendant and his attorney. Mistakes do happen, and during an independent survey of federal prison inmates back in 2009 it was reported that over fifty percent of them had inaccurate data on their PSI that was never corrected.

It is equally important to remember that any recommended sentence made by the probation officer, prosecutor, defense attorney, etc., is purely advisory and that the final decision will be up to the judge at sentencing. The judge is required by law to impose a sentence sufficient, but not greater than necessary for the offense(s). There are also several factors that the judge is instructed to use as tools to help determine an appropriate sentence. These factors will also be discussed later in this book.

Once a defendant has received a copy of his PSI he can check what his total offense level is as calculated by the probation officer. From there he will be able to get an idea of what the possible sentencing range will be by taking a quick glance at the sentencing table. Looking at the table, one will see six different criminal history categories across the top. Each category has a corresponding number of points labeled with it (e.g., Category III – 4, 5, 6). These points correspond to the total number of criminal points that a defendant may be responsible for. As one can see, the penalties become substantially harsher with a worse criminal history.

Federal Sentencing Table
(in months of imprisonment)

	Offense Level	I (0 or 1)	II (2 or 3)	III (4, 5, 6)	IV (7, 8, 9)	V (10, 11, 12)	VI (13 or more)
Zone A	1	0 - 6	0 - 6	0 - 6	0 - 6	0 - 6	0 - 6
	2	0 - 6	0 - 6	0 - 6	0 - 6	0 - 6	1 - 7
	3	0 - 6	0 - 6	0 - 6	0 - 6	2 - 8	3 - 9
	4	0 - 6	0 - 6	0 - 6	2 - 8	4 - 10	6 - 12
	5	0 - 6	0 - 6	1 - 7	2 - 8	6 - 12	9 - 15
	6	0 - 6	1 - 7	2 - 8	6 - 12	9 - 15	12 - 18
	7	0 - 6	2 - 8	4 - 10	8 - 14	12 - 18	15 - 21
	8	0 - 6	4 - 10	6 - 12	10 - 16	15 - 21	18 - 24
Zone B	9	4 - 10	6 - 12	8 - 14	12 - 18	18 - 24	21 - 27
	10	6 - 12	8 - 14	10 - 16	15 - 21	21 - 27	24 - 30
Zone C	11	8 - 14	10 - 16	12 - 18	18 - 24	24 - 30	27 - 33
	12	10 - 16	12 - 18	15 - 21	21 - 27	27 - 33	30 - 37
Zone D	13	12 - 18	15 - 21	18 - 24	24 - 30	30 - 37	33 - 41
	14	15 - 21	18 - 24	21 - 27	27 - 33	33 - 41	37 - 46
	15	18 - 24	21 - 27	24 - 30	30 - 37	37 - 46	41 - 51
	16	21 - 27	24 - 30	27 - 33	33 - 41	41 - 51	46 - 57
	17	24 - 30	27 - 33	30 - 37	37 - 46	46 - 57	51 - 63
	18	27 - 33	30 - 37	33 - 41	41 - 51	51 - 63	57 - 71
	19	30 - 37	33 - 41	37 - 46	46 - 57	57 - 71	63 - 78
	20	33 - 41	37 - 46	41 - 51	51 - 63	63 - 78	70 - 87
	21	37 - 46	41 - 51	46 - 57	57 - 71	70 - 87	77 - 96
	22	41 - 51	46 - 57	51 - 63	63 - 78	77 - 96	84 - 105
	23	46 - 57	51 - 63	57 - 71	70 - 87	84 - 105	92 - 115
	24	51 - 63	57 - 71	63 - 78	77 - 96	92 - 115	100 - 125
	25	57 - 71	63 - 78	70 - 87	84 - 105	100 - 125	110 - 137
	26	63 - 78	70 - 87	78 - 97	92 - 115	110 - 137	120 - 150
	27	70 - 87	78 - 97	87 - 108	100 - 125	120 - 150	130 - 162
	28	78 - 97	87 - 108	97 - 121	110 - 137	130 - 162	140 - 175
	29	87 - 108	97 - 121	108 - 135	121 - 151	140 - 175	151 - 188
	30	97 - 121	108 - 135	121 - 151	135 - 168	151 - 188	168 - 210
	31	108 - 135	121 - 151	135 - 168	151 - 188	168 - 210	188 - 235
	32	121 - 151	135 - 168	151 - 188	168 - 210	188 - 235	210 - 262
	33	135 - 168	151 - 188	168 - 210	188 - 235	210 - 262	235 - 293
	34	151 - 188	168 - 210	188 - 235	210 - 262	235 - 293	262 - 327
	35	168 - 210	188 - 235	210 - 262	235 - 293	262 - 327	292 - 365
	36	188 - 235	210 - 262	235 - 293	262 - 327	292 - 365	324 - 405
	37	210 - 262	235 - 293	262 - 327	292 - 365	324 - 405	360 - life
	38	235 - 293	262 - 327	292 - 365	324 - 405	360 - life	360 - life
	39	262 - 327	292 - 365	324 - 405	360 - life	360 - life	360 - life
	40	292 - 365	324 - 405	360 - life	360 - life	360 - life	360 - life
	41	324 - 405	360 - life	360 - life	360 - life	360 - life	360 - life
	42	360 - life	360 - life	360 - life	360 - life	360 - life	360 - life
	43	life	life	life	life	life	life

To help understand the sentencing table better, let's say for example that a person was charged and convicted of possession with intent to distribute a small quantity of marijuana and the total offense level was determined to be an eighteen. This individual had no prior criminal history and therefore had zero criminal history points. His total offense level of eighteen would be appropriated in category one of the sentencing table. By looking under category one of the table, we can see that a sentence of 27-33 months imprisonment is recommended. If no further adjustments, either up or down, are made to the total offense level of eighteen then this range will be the recommended guideline that the judge will consider when he calculates an appropriate sentence.

When sentencing day arrives, the judge will use this recommended guideline in combination with other sentencing factors to help determine a sentence that is sufficient but not greater than necessary for the defendant. Often, the sentence imposed will be somewhere between this recommended guideline. If the defendant is seeking a sentence below this range, then it will be up to him and his attorney to present mitigating factors or legal arguments to the court that will substantiate the request for the reduction of sentence, and thus lowering the overall offense level. Many are unaware of the fact that there are indeed a large number of mitigating arguments and law provisions that can open the door to the possibility of a reduced sentence. We will begin to identify and discuss these in the following chapters.

Criminal History

Anyone having a significant past criminal history when facing new federal charges should be aware of the severe consequences that can result if mistakes are made calculating one's criminal history points. Additionally, attorneys, probation officers, prosecutors and even judges have all made errors when trying to compile an accurate total of one's criminal points. Therefore, it is essential for a defendant with a prior criminal record to be fully aware of the exact past criminal conduct that he has been convicted of as well as any sentences of confinement that were imposed. If an error is made when determining a defendant's total criminal points and this error is not caught before sentencing, then it is possible for the defendant to be hit with a substantially longer sentence than what he otherwise should have received.

Let's take a quick look at how the criminal history categories and point system works. If you look across the top of the sentencing table you will see a total of six different criminal history categories. The categories are numbered from one to six with category one being for first time offenders or offenders with only a minimal criminal past and category six for career criminals. Under each criminal history category there is also a set of numbers. These numbers correspond to the total number of a defendant's criminal history points. For example, if a defendant has a total of three criminal history points then his total offense level will be calculated under category two of the sentencing table. Higher criminal history categories equate to longer sentences and vice versa. A defendant's criminal history points are determined by evaluating all prior criminal conduct that has resulted in a conviction and then applying a formula set forth by the U.S.S.C. (United States Sentencing Commission) to gather an accurate number of points.

As stated in the U.S.S.G. (United States Sentencing Guidelines), *"A defendant's record of prior criminal conduct is directly relevant to those purposes set forth in the Comprehensive Crime Control Act. A defendant with a record of prior criminal behavior is more culpable than a first time offender and thus deserving greater punishment. General deterrence of criminal conduct dictates that a clear message be sent to society that repeated criminal behavior will aggravate the need for punishment with each recurrence to protect the public from further crimes of the particular defendant."* This statement made by the commission clearly calls for a longer sentence each time a person breaks the law. The basic formula used to calculate a defendant's criminal history points goes as follows:

> Three points are added for each prior sentence of imprisonment exceeding one year and a month;

> Two points are added for each prior sentence of imprisonment of at least sixty days not counted in the first part;

> One point is added for each prior sentence not counted in the first or second part of this guideline up to a total of not more than four points;

> Two points are added if the defendant committed the offense while under any criminal justice sentence including probation, parole, supervised release, imprisonment, work release, or escape status;

> Two points are added if the defendant committed the offense less than two years after release from imprisonment;

> One point is added for each prior sentence resulting from a conviction of a crime of violence that has not already been accounted for up to a total of not more than three points;

Using this above formula, it could be fairly simple or somewhat difficult to get an accurate idea of one's total criminal points. This obviously will depend on the complexity and magnitude of one's criminal past. Additionally, the Commission instructs that it will be the total sentence imposed that is used when determining criminal points and not the total time served. For example, if someone was convicted of a crime, either state or federal, then was sentenced to two years imprisonment, and then served only one year of the total sentence, the total to be used for figuring criminal history points would be two years. A defendant with multiple convictions over a long period of time will have the highest probability for an error to occur when determining an accurate total of criminal points. A defendant should work together with his attorney to confirm that an accurate total of criminal points is reflected on the total listed in the defendant's PSI report.

There is a second part to the criminal history point formula that can also result in computation errors. This is the part that defines what types of offenses are actually counted towards a criminal history. For example, disorderly conduct and loitering charges are never counted towards one's criminal history points. Additionally, convictions that occurred more than fifteen years prior to the current offense are also not counted unless the term of imprisonment from that conviction ran into that fifteen year time period. An example of this would be if someone was convicted of drug charges twenty years ago but spent six years in prison as a result of the conviction. Since the sixth year of that prison sentence was only fourteen years prior from the current offense, this offense would now count when figuring out this defendant's criminal history points. Convictions that resulted in a term of imprisonment less than thirteen months are only counted if they occurred within a ten year time period from the date of the current offense unless the term of imprisonment extended within the ten year time limit.

As outlined in the U.S.S.G, section 4A1.2, the following offenses only count toward criminal history points when the sentence imposed was either more than one year probation or a term of imprisonment that exceeded thirty days:

> ➤ Careless or reckless driving;
> ➤ Contempt of court;
> ➤ Disorderly conduct ;
> ➤ Disturbing the peace;
> ➤ Driving without a license
> ➤ Driving with a suspended/revoked license
> ➤ Giving a police officer false information;
> ➤ Gambling;
> ➤ Failure to obey a police officer;
> ➤ Insufficient funds of check;
> ➤ Leaving the scene of an accident;

- Prostitution;
- Resisting arrest;
- Trespassing;

The following offenses are never counted when calculating criminal history points:

- Fish and game violations;
- Hitch hiking;
- Juvenile status offenses and truancy;
- Local ordinance violation;
- Loitering;
- Minor traffic infractions (e.g. speeding);
- Public intoxication;
- Vagrancy;

A few other notable points to remember is that Driving under the influence (i.e., DUI, DWI) is always counted towards criminal history points. Charges that have been dismissed or ones that did not conclude in a guilty finding are never counted nor are offenses charged from a country other than the United States. Tribal offenses and expunged sentences are also not counted towards criminal history points. Most military offenses, except for certain court martial offenses and offenses brought forth by a general, are also exempt towards one's criminal points total.

To see a good example on how one's criminal history can greatly affect the outcome of a sentence, let's compare two defendants, both who have been charged with the exact same offense and both who have different magnitudes of prior criminal conduct, and see how their sentencing guidelines differ. Let's say both defendants have a total offense level of thirteen for their crime. The first defendant had no prior criminal history and therefore no criminal history points. His offense level of thirteen should correspond to the sentencing range under category one of the sentencing table. Under category one, the offense level of thirteen results in a recommended 12-18 month imprisonment. The second defendant has had multiple prior convictions that gave him enough criminal history points to be placed in category five of the sentencing table. With the same offense level of thirteen, this defendant faces a much more severe recommendation consisting of 30-37 months imprisonment. This is approximately a one-hundred percent increase between the two defendants who committed the exact same offense.

Anyone with a basic understanding of how criminal points are tallied up should be able to make a prudent estimation of their own total criminal history points. Any errors that are found should be brought forward immediately therefore allowing time for necessary corrections before one is sentenced.

Plea Bargaining

We could write an entire book just on the subject of plea bargaining and the plethora of techniques and tactics that plea bargains can be negotiated around, but that book would likely be too heavy to hold. As stated before, working out a favorable plea deal is done much easier when both the defendant's attorney and the prosecutor have a good rapport and respect for each other. Having an attorney who is well seasoned in plea deals and the types of offense involved in the plea bargaining is also very beneficial.

A plea bargain (i.e., plea deal) is an extremely useful tool that both the prosecution and the defendant can benefit from. In fact, the majority of federal criminal cases do conclude with some type of plea deal in place. Unfortunately, even innocent people are sometimes forced to sign a plea deal to hedge their financial losses and the chance of being found guilty at trial. A plea deal is often offered by the government and subsequently accepted by a defendant to avoid potential lengthy and costly trials and to help shorten sentencing guidelines. One caveat in the system is the threat of receiving a more severe sentence after being found guilty at trial versus pleading guilty and thus avoiding the need for a trial. In a bizarre way, the reality of facing a harsher punishment by taking a case to trial and refusing to plead guilty bears a slight resemblance to a familiar term - extortion. The truth of the matter though is that the courts also benefit from your guilty plea and not just the government. When a defendant pleads guilty, there is a great deal of time saved due to a significant reduction in the total number of hearings, motions and appearances that would otherwise be required in a lengthy trial. The use of the plea deal greatly helps to clean up backlogged cases in the courts. The government can also allocate its resources better and save substantial time and money when a case is resolved swiftly and efficiently using a plea bargain. It would seem safe to say that everyone; the court, the government and the defendant clearly benefit to some degree when a case is resolved with the effective use of a plea deal.

It is important for anyone facing federal charges to also remember that a plea bargain is not a right of a defendant and some defendants facing federal charges will never have any type of deal offered to them. Whether or not a plea bargain is offered to a defendant is purely the discretion of the government and there are several factors that are used to determine who will be offered a deal. Some of the factors involved in this decision making process are the nature and characteristics of the defendant, history of prior criminal acts, overall strength of evidence, seriousness of the offense, etc. If a plea deal is offered to a defendant, it is important to make sure the agreement is completely understood by the defendant before he signs it. The entire agreement should be discussed with the defendant's attorney and amended as deemed necessary. Seeking an amendment to a plea deal does not guarantee that the government will oblige, but it never hurts to try. Many times the plea bargaining process turns into a game of *"give and take"* and *"cat and mouse"* at the same time. Having an attorney experienced both with plea bargaining and in the area of law that surrounds the alleged charges will serve as a big advantage when the plea negotiating begins.

Here is what a DC Court of Appeals had to say about plea bargains: *"To say that the United States Attorney must literally treat every offense and every offender alike is to delegate him with an impossible task; of course this concept would negate discretion. Myriad factors can enter into the prosecutor's decision. Two persons may have committed what is precisely the same legal offense but the prosecutor is* not compelled by the law, duty or tradition to treat them the same as to the charges. On the contrary, he is expected to exercise discretion and common sense to the end that if, for example, one is a young first time offender and the other older, with a criminal record, or one played a lesser and the other a dominant role, one the instigator and the other a follower, the prosecutor can and should take such factors into account; no court has any jurisdiction to inquire or review his decision."

It will be critical for a defendant and his attorney to determine if a plea deal is favorable enough to accept and sign. In the end, the benefits for the defendant accepting a plea deal will usually involve an agreement for a reduced number of charges or an agreement for lower total offense level for the charges. There is also a type of plea deal not commonly used in federal courts which is a *"binding plea deal."* With this type of plea deal, a specific length of sentence is usually agreed upon by the defendant and the government. This length of sentence is then noted in the written plea agreement and brought forth to the judge to examine and make a ruling on (i.e., accept or reject). Once a judge accepts a binding plea deal, the sentence will then be binding on the court and the judge will be bound by the terms of the agreement and have no option but to impose that sentence exactly as noted in the plea deal. If this type of deal can be negotiated, then it will surely relieve a whole lot of stress and worry that correspond with the pressures of not knowing what one's sentence will be.

Prior to plea bargaining, the defendant's attorney should become familiar with all the pertinent details surrounding the case. The defendant and his attorney should have had multiple meetings before any mention of plea bargaining is even discussed with the government. This attorney should have a good understanding of the defendant's personal background including his family, education, health conditions, military and occupational history. The defendant's attorney should also be aware of any past criminal convictions that the defendant may have. These should be disclosed to the defendant's attorney before he starts negotiating with the prosecutor.

A list of mitigating factors should also be prepared by the defendant's attorney early in one's case so that these arguments can be used to help persuade a better plea deal with the prosecutor. A mitigating factor can be anything that works in the defendant's favor for a reduced sentence such as a sick family member, serious health condition, history of good deeds, rehabilitative efforts, etc. Mitigating factors will be discussed more in detail later in this book.

The defendant's attorney should also be fully aware of the guidelines of the plea deal and should always request to see evidence that supports the alleged charges before the defendant signs any plea deal. Finally, the defendant should have a clear understanding of all personal and legal consequences that will coincide with the acceptance of the plea deal.

The Sentencing Hearing

During the sentencing hearing is when a defendant will learn his fate. The sentencing hearing is a court proceeding where the judge will impose a particular sentence for a particular offense that the defendant has been convicted of. The judge will set a date for this hearing and the defendant must be present for it unless there are extraordinary circumstances that exist that preclude the defendant's presence.

At the beginning of the hearing, the defendant's attorney and the government will once again give a summary of the facts and details of the case. The prosecutor for the government will often ask for a particular sentence during this speech and any other conditions that seem fit for the offense. The defendant and his attorney will have their chance to speak to the court first though. If the defendant has decided to make a speech it should have been memorized previously thus making it appear more genuine than reading from a piece of paper. The speech should be brief and to the point and should clearly cast the impression of remorse and show to the judge that the defendant accepts full responsibility for his actions (No matter what he really feels!). This is not the time to be arguing one's innocence or talking about the raw deal that you got. Any attempt at making these statements will work against a defendant at the sentencing hearing. Additionally, it will be during this time when the defendant's attorney should be well prepared to discuss and highlight any and all mitigating factors applicable to the defendant to help convince the judge into delivering a downward departure. The defendant's attorney should argue for a specific sentence for the defendant and ask the judge if friends and family of the defendant can speak as character witnesses, if they are present at the hearing of course.

During the sentencing hearing, other important issues will be discussed also such as applicable fines and restitution, both of which will be determined during the hearing. Other mandatory requirements for the defendant, such as substance abuse programs, anger management counseling and other programming requirements will also be ruled on during the hearing.

It is also possible that victims of the defendant will speak at the sentencing hearing and express their emotions and feelings to the court. This can often have an aggravating effect on the sentence for the defendant and victim impact statements that are conducted in person have often caused sentences to be longer than average. When victims speak to the judge, it almost always puts more pressure on the judge to impose a harsher sentence.

The hearing will conclude with the judge imposing what he feels is an appropriate sentence for the defendant. Once the sentence is delivered, and if it involves a term of imprisonment, the defendant will either be held in custody or allowed to self surrender to federal prison. When a sentence of imprisonment is handed down the defendant's attorney should be prepared to make every argument to allow the defendant to self surrender. Many times, such as with crimes of violence, self surrendering will not be an option, but the argument to self surrender should always be made regardless.

If the defendant is allowed to self surrender, he will be spared *"diesel therapy."* This is the term used for the enduring transitional time period from the date which one is sentenced to federal prison to the day he actually arrives at his designated institution. This term was created as a result of days, weeks, or even months of smelling diesel fumes from the prison bus that transports an inmate to his final destination. On average, it takes one to four months for a defendant to be designated to a federal institution. It will be during this time that the defendant will be under the custody of the U.S. marshals and likely be moved from prison to prison during this transitional period. This period of diesel therapy is often the worst memory that an inmate has of his federal prison sentence.

A defendant who is preparing for his sentencing hearing should remember to dress properly for this very important event. Dressing in proper attire will show respect to the court and is critical for a proper first impression at the sentence hearing. Tardiness is not something that any judge will have a tolerance for either. Obviously there may be circumstances out of the defendant's control that may cause a late arrival, but every effort should be made so that the defendant and his attorney arrive early to the courthouse and ready for action.

One should also remember that there will be a variety of sentences available for the judge to utilize at the sentencing hearing. A judge can impose conditions of straight probation, home confinement, community confinement (i.e., halfway house), or confinement in a federal prison. He can issue one of these conditions as the total sentence or decide on a combination of the above conditions as part of one's sentence. If a defendant does ultimately receive a sentence of imprisonment, then setting goals, avoiding illegal activities, staying close to family and friends and avoiding negative people will help make any prison sentence more tolerable. After a term of imprisonment is ordered, the defendant's fate as to where he will have to do his time will then be in the hands of the Designation and Security Computation Center (DSCC) in Grand Prairie, Texas.

The Road to Prison

When a defendant is sentenced to a term of federal imprisonment, he will either be held in custody at that time or allowed to self surrender. If the defendant is already in custody at the time of sentencing then it is likely that he will remain so. Whether or not one is allowed to self surrender or not, each defendant will be assigned a security score that will be used to determine one's custody level and thus enable the designation of an appropriate institution.

After the term of imprisonment is finalized, the defendant's paperwork will be forwarded to the DSCC in Texas. A designator will then use a special form called the *"Security Classification Form"* (BP-337) to compute a total security score for the defendant. The final score of this form is used to determine the custody level needed for the defendant. The designator is also required to consider other facts in determining the defendant's placement such as recommendations made by the court, location of the facility, RDAP enrollment, medical needs, public safety factor (PSF) and central inmate monitoring (CIM). The chart below shows the required level of custody for the total number of points that an inmate scored on the Security Classification Form.

Security Level	Total Points Male	Total Points Female
Minimum "Camp"	0-11	0-15
Low	12-15	16-30
Medium	16-23	N/A*
High	24+	31+
Administrative	All**	All**

* Female inmates are designated to minimum, low, high, or administrative custody. There are no female medium security institutions in the BOP system.

** An inmate can be designated to administrative custody for many different reasons such as medical needs, investigative needs, risk for escape, security threat, etc.

The BOP claims that its policy is to attempt to place every inmate within a 500 mile radius of their residence. Unfortunately, this does not always happen therefore a simple recommendation by a judge for placement close to home will never hurt one's chances for a more preferential placement. A simple request for this by the defendant's attorney at the sentencing hearing is often all it takes. It's now time for us to begin exploring the many mitigating factors and circumstances that one may be able to utilize to help reduce a sentence of federal imprisonment.

If you ask what is the single most important key to longevity, I would have to say it is avoiding worry, stress and tension. And if you didn't ask me, I'd still have to say it.   **- George Burns**

2
Reduce my Sentence

The ultimate goal for any defendant at sentencing is to secure the lowest possible sentence for the associated offense(s). As you continue to read this book you will begin to see extraordinary case examples which show how some defendants cleverly argued for downward departures and received sentences well below the advisory guideline minimums. Hundred of hours have been spent locating the following cases and making them available for you to examine and use as documented proof for effective sentencing relief. We will start this chapter by looking at some specific family complications that often coincide with any term of imprisonment and how these complications can be used as mitigating factors to help persuade the court to impose a sentence below the advisory guideline range. It should also be noted here that simple ordinary family ties and responsibilities will usually not be enough to sway a judge into imposing a downward departure. There must be more to the argument than the basic woes and heartaches of losing a family member due to a term of imprisonment. Now let's take a look at what has worked well in the past.

One of the arguments that has proven itself as a powerful mitigating argument is the separation of children from a significant parent when that parent is imprisoned. If the defendant has children, and this defendant plays a significant role in the child's welfare such as with nurturing, parenting, financial support, tutoring and mentoring, and every day care, then this can have substantial value as a mitigating factor. Please note though that an argument like this must be argued heavily and not with the typical five minute debate in front of the judge. Examples of the importance of this parent need to be extensively presented to the court and spotlighted. Presenting significant examples showing a defendant's significant role in the child's life such as proof that the defendant's paycheck is used to support the child, proof that the defendant is needed in society to keep a roof over the child's head, or proof showing how the defendant is an irreplaceable caretaker for the child, can be very effective at sentencing. Additionally, if the child has health problems, then it may be even more important for the defendant to remain in the community to be able to provide care and support for the child.

There are some restrictions though as to who is permitted to use family ties as a valid mitigating argument. A defendant who has been convicted of an offense of kidnapping, obscenity, sexual abuse, sexual exploitation, child abuse, or transportation for illegal sexual activity, is not permitted to use any type of family factors as an argument for a reduction of sentence. Below is a copy of this guideline as seen in the U.S.S.G, section 5H1.6:

"Family Ties and Responsibilities – In sentencing a defendant convicted of an offense other than an offense described in the following paragraph, family ties and responsibilities are not ORDINARILY relevant in determining whether a departure may be warranted. In sentencing a defendant convicted of an offense involving a minor victim under section 1201, an offense under section 1591, or an offense under chapter 71, 109A, 110, or 117, of Title 18, United States Code, family ties and responsibilities and community ties are not relevant in determining whether a sentence should be below the applicable guideline range."

Initially, the above statement may give the indication that these types of arguments are not allowed to be presented in federal court and many times a defendant's attorney may suggest that family arguments will simply be a waste of time, but don't believe him. This attorney may simply be avoiding additional work that will cost him extra time preparing your case.

We would like to direct you back to the above statement and memorize the twenty-eighth word. The word you found is *"ordinarily"* right? Good! This is a very important word in the sentencing guideline. When this guideline was constructed by members of the U.S.S.C, the word *"ordinarily"* was put there for a distinct reason. This word was purposely added to give a judge discretion to make his own decision whether or not a defendant's family hardship is **ordinary** or **extraordinary** in nature. The following cases will prove that the wording in the *"family ties and responsibilities"* provision has allowed judges to impose lower sentences due to a myriad of possible mitigating family factors.

One misnomer that many people still believe is that judges are required to leave their compassion at the front door to the court room. This is entirely not true and furthermore, some judges do have a genuine sense of compassion for a defendant facing a serious family hardship due to incarceration especially when the case involves a first time offender guilty of a non-violent offense.

After deciding if a defendant indeed has family mitigating factors that will support the request for a reduced sentence, it will then be up to the defendant and his attorney to properly and cleverly prepare an impressive argument that will clearly show that a term of imprisonment will cause a substantial, direct and specific loss of effective caretaking or essential financial support to the defendant's family, and that this loss is greater than the ordinary loss from a typical parent being incarcerated. Additionally, this loss of caretaking and financial support should be irreplaceable. There should not be any other reasonable means of providing for the child, or children, such as having the defendant's parent or spouse capable of taking over care and responsibility.

Finally, the defendant's attorney should make it clear to the court that an alternative sentence such as community confinement, home detention, or probation will enable the defendant to properly address the family problems therefore allowing the defendant to provide continued support and care.

Now let's take a look at some real life federal criminal cases involving real defendants who successfully used family factors to substantiate a valid request for a reduced sentence. At the end of each case is a locator code. This locator code can be given to one's attorney so he can pull the case from the public records and reference it as needed.

Single Mother Factor

<u>United States vs. Pena</u> – Defendant Irma Pena was charged and subsequently found guilty of possession with intent to distribute fifty kilograms or more of marijuana. The case was handled in a New Mexico District Court back in the 1990's.

It all started when a United States Border Patrol agent stopped the defendant's car at a security checkpoint near Truth or Consequences, New Mexico, and conducted a routine citizenship check. While questioning the defendant, it was apparent to the agent that she was very nervous. The defendant was notably anxious and clenching the steering wheel to her vehicle and stuttering her speech while answering the agent's questions. The agent asked permission to search the defendant's vehicle to which the defendant reluctantly agreed. During the search of the vehicle, the agent discovered sixty-six pounds of marijuana hidden under the vehicle's rear seat.

The defendant chose to take her case to trial and testified that she and her sister were driving their friend's car that they had borrowed. They were en-route to Belen, New Mexico, when they were stopped at the checkpoint. The defendant then testified under oath that they had no knowledge of the marijuana found under the back seat.

Nonetheless, the jury found the defendant guilty of the charged offense. After the trial ended the judge ordered for preparation of the defendant's PSI report. The PSI data showed that the defendant had no prior criminal history and therefore no criminal history points. It also confirmed the total offense level as an eighteen on the sentencing table. The defendant's offense level of eighteen as seen under category one of the sentencing table shows a recommended 27-33 month range of imprisonment.

The defendant's attorney asked the judge for a downward departure from the advisory guideline range using the defendant's family caretaking and financial responsibilities as the primary mitigating factor. The defendant's attorney then disclosed to the court how the defendant was a single mother with a two month old infant. She held a steady job and used her paycheck to provide support for both of her children. The defendant's oldest daughter also had an infant child that needed the defendant's financial support. The defendant's attorney then made a speech that obviously had an impact on the court. In this speech he firmly got the point across by saying, *"The effects of incarceration would have a devastating impact on these two infants."* The defendant and his attorney had clearly worked hard to prepare this mitigating arguments to convince the judge to reduce the sentence. In fact, the judge fairly swiftly agreed that a downward departure was justified due to the defendant's responsibilities to her family and then made the following statement:

"I find that the defendant's unique responsibility warrants a departure to the established guideline range of 27-33 months, for special circumstances. Mainly, that the defendant is a single parent of a two-month old child and is the sole support for herself and her infant child. In addition, she has been steadily employed for a long time and is providing for the financial support of her sixteen year old daughter, who herself is a single parent of a two-month old child. Therefore, should the defendant be incarcerated for an extended period of time, two infants would be placed at a potential risk. The defendant has no prior record of drug abuse, nor other felony criminal convictions and has held a long term employment. She poses no threat to the public and would be justly punished, sufficiently deterred and adequately rehabilitated by a sentence of probation with community confinement as a special condition. Accordingly, a downward departure to a term of three years probation is appropriate as the defendant does not now need to be incarcerated to protect the public from other crimes."

The defendant then walked out of the New Mexico courtroom with a happy look on her face and a prison free sentence. The government appealed the sentence and an appeals court reviewed the case about a year later finding the downward departure was supported by the defendant's mitigating arguments. The sentence stood for the defendant. The appeals court made this statement during their review of the case, *"The aberrational character of her conduct combined with her responsibility to support two infants justified a departure."* Case Locator - 930 F2d 1486

Separation from Children

United States vs. Brand - Mrs. Brand was convicted in a West Virginia District Court for distributing two grams of cocaine in violation of 21 U.S.C. 841. She pled guilty to a one count indictment back in the 1990's. She was facing a term of imprisonment of multiple years.

At the sentencing hearing, the defendant disclosed her situation to the court. She was in the midst of a bitter divorce with her husband. At the center of this divorce was her two children, ages one and seven. The details of the divorce and the defendant's role and responsibility to her children were also clearly documented on her PSI report.

Contemplating a prison sentence for the offense, the defendant gave testimony to the court telling of how her children were going to be separated during her term of imprisonment. One child would go to live with her previous foster parents while the other would move in with the defendant's mother-in-law. Neither of the two caretakers were able to accommodate both children, therefore the only solution was to separate them.

After the unique circumstances involving the three way separation of the defendant and her children were presented to the court the judge chimed in and said, *"What you tell us here this morning is that in effect, strangers will be taking your two children."* The judge also took note to the defendant's honest attempt to be a good mother and stay employed. He then continued to say, *"the carrying forward of the guidelines range of imprisonment would have a devastating impact upon emotions, mind, and the physical well being, just every aspect, of the two very innocent youngsters to be separated from you."* The judge then departed from the recommended guidelines, used the defendant's family responsibilities as a valid mitigating factor, and imposed a sentence of five years probation.
Case Locator - 907 F2d 31

Reduce My Sentence - 55

Irreplaceable Caretaker

United States vs. Johnson - This interesting case of the U.S. versus Johnson concluded with an appeals court delivering somewhat of a scolding to the government for their vague arguments on appeal.

This case was originally decided in a New York District Court back in the 1990's. The defendant, Cynthia Johnson, was involved in an illegal scheme back in the early 1990's while employed at a Bronx V.A. Hospital. The illegal conduct consisted of falsely inflating co-workers paychecks in return for a kickback of fifty percent of the inflated amount. The illegal operation was discovered and the defendant was subsequently charged with theft of government funds in violation of 18 U.S.C. 641 and bribery in violation of 18 U.S.C. 201. Johnson was found guilty via a jury trial on all but one count.

The total offense level for the charges was a twenty-three. The defendant had no prior criminal history which appropriated the offense level in category one of the sentencing table. A level twenty-three in category one of the sentencing table shows a recommended sentence of 46-57 months imprisonment. The defendant's base offense level was enhanced from a level ten to a level twenty-three to accurately reflect the defendant's conduct during commission of the offense. Two points were added due to the numerous occasions (role in the offense) in which the defendant carried out the offense. Five points were added due to the amount of loss from the scheme which totaled $89,222. Additionally, four extra points were added because the defendant was an organizer of the illegal scheme and another two points were added due to the defendant's obstruction of justice.

When sentencing day arrived, the defendant was facing a lengthy prison term for her conduct. At the hearing, the defendant was able to reduce the offense level by three points on the grounds that the offense conduct represented more of a theft type crime than bribery. Additionally, the total losses were split among other employees who were involved in the offense which reduced the total loss that the defendant was liable for down to $27,973. The defendant was still facing a substantial prison term of 33-41 months with the application of the three point reduction.

It was time for the defendant to present to the court the extraordinary family matters that existed in her life in hopes to warrant a lighter sentence. The defendant's attorney began his mitigating speech. First it was pointed out to the court that the defendant was the sole provider for her three children. Additionally, she was the sole caretaker for these children. These two facts alone, when argued with character witnesses and supporting stories of the defendant's irreplaceable parenting role, can be used as a powerful tool when pushing for a reduced sentence. It was then further made known to the court that the defendant was caring and providing for her oldest daughter's six year old child in addition to her own children. The defendant's son also had two children of his own, ages five and six, and they all were residing with the defendant. The father of the defendant's youngest child who lived in Queens, New York, was unemployed and therefore unable to assist the defendant with any child care finances. The extensive amount time that was required to care for the children was also adequately addressed by the defendant's attorney using a myriad of facts and examples.

The defendant and her attorney painted a clear picture of the significance of her role to the health and well-being of multiple children and how a term of imprisonment would clearly be disastrous to these children. The defendant's attorney concluded by talking about the defendant's personal life; it consisted of no alcohol or drug problems and an emotionally and mentally stable life.

The judge returned a sentence of six months home detention followed by three years of supervised release (i.e. probation). The judge's comments included this statement at sentencing, *"In view of the special circumstances of the defendant - I shouldn't say "defendant" I should say of the "defendant's family," which, as the court sees it, is a family in which the mother is the sole link between the children, the six-month old child, and having the father in Queens who does not contribute to the support of the five and six-year-old children, a 17-year-old boy having a father who does not contribute to his support, and a six-year-old grandchild whom the mother is unable to keep because of circumstances of her having another child, at the age of 21, and living in an institution, I'm going to reduce the level."*

The government was not satisfied with the sentence and swiftly appealed. They based their appeal on the fact that the defendant was not entitled to a downward departure based on family circumstances alone, but the government would soon find out that the basis of their appeal was not a valid reason. The government was wrong!

In the government's appeal they made mention of the language in the sentencing guidelines about family mitigating factors which stated, *"Family ties and responsibilities are not **ordinarily** relevant in determining whether a sentence should be outside the applicable guideline range. - U.S.S.G. 5H1.6"*

The court of appeals reviewed the case, ruled in favor of the defendant, and added these intriguing comments, *"The Sentencing Commission understood that many defendants shoulder responsibility to their families, their employers, and their communities. Disruption of the defendant's life, and the concomitant difficulties for those who depend on the defendant, are inherent in the punishment of incarceration. Extraordinary circumstances, however, are by their nature not capable of adequate consideration. They therefore may constitute proper grounds for departure, policy statement 5H1.6 (Departures based on family ties and responsibilities.) does not alter this conclusion, but simply reinforces what we would have expected in this case."*

Obviously the appeals court was clearly ruling in support of the judge's ruling and in favor of the defendant. These comments clearly validate the use of certain family circumstances to substantiate a downward departure to one's sentence. The appeals court chief judge concluded with this statement that resembled more of a scolding to the government, *"The United States Guidelines do not require a judge to leave compassion and common sense at the door to the court room. The government asks us, on this appeal, to reverse a sentencing judge's exercise of downward flexibility on behalf of an infant and three young children who depend entirely upon the defendant for their upbringing. The United States appeals the sentence, which was imposed pursuant to a thirteen level downward departure for Johnson's family circumstances and for the nature of her offense. We agree with the decision as it was imposed."* The judgment stood firm and the defendant left court with a prison free sentence. Case Locator - 964 F2d 124

Financial / Caretaking Responsibilities

<u>United States vs. Galante</u> - Here is yet another significant case where the defendant used valid family circumstances as a solid basis for a request for a reduced sentence. The defendant, Michael Galante, pled guilty in a New York District Court to one count of possession with intent to distribute heroin.

The events of this case began to unfold when the defendant met with a confidential informant who was wearing a secret recording device. It was during this meeting when the defendant claimed he could get heroin from *"Columbians"* who he knew very well. He also stated that he would make a five thousand dollar profit for brokering the deal. The following week the defendant met again with the informant who he provided a sample of heroin to. The defendant told the informant that he wanted to sell one kilogram of heroin and that the total price delivered would be $95,000 cash. The informant agreed to the deal and a subsequent meeting was arranged to complete the purchase and delivery of drugs. This meeting took place a few days later when the informant came to the defendant's restaurant to complete the deal. The defendant and the informant proceeded to a nearby automobile where an undercover DEA agent showed the defendant the money for the heroin purchase. The defendant then provided the informant with one half the total quantity of heroin. The defendant told the informant that the other half of heroin would be arriving momentarily, at which time the defendant was arrested and taken into custody.

After the defendant pled guilty in federal court, the judge ordered for the probation department to begin preparation of the defendant's PSI. The total offense level, as dictated in the PSI report, was determined to be a twenty-three. The defendant had no prior criminal history, therefore the offense level fell under category one of the sentencing table. This resulted in an advisory sentencing guideline range of 46-57 months imprisonment. On the PSI a prison term of forty-six months was recommended by the probation officer. Any recommendation made by the probation officer in a defendant's PSI report is often used heavily by the judge at sentencing, and many times this recommendation is very close to, or exactly matches, what the judge imposes as the sentence.

At the sentencing hearing the defendant was facing over three years in federal prison for his bad decisions. The defendant's attorney began the hearing by requesting a reduced sentence due to extraordinary family matters. The defendant made it known to the court that he was forty-one years of age and had no prior criminal history. While these facts were certainly not extraordinary they did help to start the speech on a positive note. The defendant's attorney continued to tell the court how the defendant and his wife had been married for over ten years and how they have two children together, ages eight and nine. It was also made known that the defendant had recently borrowed $30,000 to open a pizza restaurant. This restaurant was not doing well and the family was deep in debt. The defendant's significant role in the family was then highlighted. He was the primary provider for his family and held an irreplaceable role. The defendant's wife spoke little English and needed assistance from the defendant for day to day family matters including medical, financial, and general matters. This one fact alone put a lot of pressure on the judge to think long and hard about the dramatic effect that the incarceration defendant would cause to family who did not speak English well. The defendant's family would now be severely challenged with the simple task of communicating with others.

The defendant also provided several character letters to the court written by family and friends. These letters told of how the couple could not afford child care and the how the defendant elected to stay at home on the weekends to care for his children. The letters also told of how the defendant went to extremes to help educate his children. Furthermore, the defendant was a devoted son and helped his mother care for his sick father. The defendant visited his sick father several times per week. He was a good man and the court would clearly see this.

The court was also informed the defendant had no outside sources of financial assistance, including any family members or friends that would be able to pitch in to help out during the defendant's term of imprisonment.

After determining that the defendant's family circumstances were indeed extraordinary, the judge departed downward from the total offense level and imposed a sentence of twenty-four months home detention, five years of supervised release, 225 hours of community service, and a special condition of enrolling in English as a Second Language program. Another lengthy prison sentence was circumvented using unique and compelling family ties and responsibilities. Case Locator - 111 F3d 1029

Single Parent

United States vs. Menyweather – Using the mitigating factor of being a single parent is probably one of the most commonly used family related argument presented to the court during a sentencing. The problem with this argument is that it must be accompanied with extraordinary examples and testimony of how this defendant is irreplaceable and how circumstances take his case truly outside the heartland of a typical case. The average Joe argument that many attorneys make is simply not enough. A defendant should therefore make sure that his attorney is fully aware that his family situation is truly unique, and then supply that attorney with an extraordinary amount of information showing how his removal from society will be, clearly and without doubt, detrimental to the welfare of his children.

Dorothy Menyweather pled guilty in a California District Court to one count of mail fraud back in 2001. The defendant was an employee at the United States Attorney's office in Los Angeles at the time of the offense. She began her employment for the government in 1990. In the year 2000 she was indicted on ten counts of theft of government funds, mail fraud, and wire fraud. She decided to accept a plea deal and plead guilty to one charge of mail fraud admitting that she used government credit cards for personal use. The total amount charged on the cards was between $350,000 and $500,000.

The probation department began preparation of the defendant's PSI. It was determined that the defendant's total offense level was a sixteen. She had no prior criminal history therefore her offense level was placed in category one of the sentencing table. A level sixteen in category one on the sentencing table shows a recommended term of imprisonment of 21-27 months. The defendant would now have to fight hard to remain free from prison.

The very first thing the defendant did at sentencing was produce sworn testimony from a psychologist who evaluated her on previous meetings. The psychologist advised the court that the defendant was suffering from *"severe symptoms of post traumatic stress"* due to the loss of her fiancé when she was five months pregnant. The psychologist then testified that the theft offense was part of a *"manic denial of psychic trauma accompanied by compulsive coping behaviors."* The court was then made aware of the fact that the defendant has been the sole provider and caretaker for her eleven year old daughter.

After hearing of the defendant's difficult life and her importance in the parenting role of her child, the judge made the decision to depart downward eight levels from the original offense level of sixteen. This brought the offense level down to a level eight and the new recommended term of imprisonment was now 0-6 months. The defendant was also now eligible for probation and home detention because of the new offense level. The judge imposed a sentence of five years probation which included forty days of jail time. The court also ordered a condition that would allow the defendant to serve the jail time on consecutive weekends therefore allowing her to continue supporting her child. Additionally, the defendant was ordered to pay restitution of $435,918 and perform community service.

It was apparent that then defendant's decision to have her psychologist appear in court and testify in her behalf was a beneficial and important factor in the resulting sentence. The psychologist was able to deliver a firm diagnosis showing the defendant was suffering from multiple conditions and that these conditions largely contributed to her commission of the offense.

The government was not satisfied with the psychologist's testimony or the lenient sentence that was handed down. They appealed the sentence and waited about one year for an appeals court to review the case. The appeals court reviewed the case and remanded it for re-sentencing only because the district court did not give its reasons for *the "direction and the degree of departure."*

When the court departs from a recommended sentencing guideline, either upward or downward, the judge must furnish a *"statement of reasons"* that justifies his decision to depart downward. Since the judgment lacked this legally required *"statement of reasons"* the case was remanded for re-sentencing.

At the re-sentencing the judge reaffirmed his previous sentence of probation and forty days of jail time and this time cited his statement of reasons for departure as *"post conviction rehabilitation"* of the defendant.

In the end, the government appealed this case several times possibly due to some sort of judicial pique but to the best of our knowledge the judge continued to hold firm on his sentence and the sentence stood. Case Locator - 431 F3d 692

Abusive Spouse

United States vs. Manasrah - In this case the defendant successfully argued for a reduced sentence using the real threat of losing her children to an abusive husband.

The defendant, Inam Manasrah, pled guilty in a Wisconsin District Court to one count of wire fraud. The fraud consisted of an illegal coupon scheme which began back in 2002. The total amount of loss the defendant was responsible for totaled $120,000. She was facing over one year in federal prison for the offense.

At the sentencing hearing the defendant's attorney brought forth several family arguments to be used as mitigating factors to the charged offense. The defendant's attorney first brought attention to the fact that she had six children ranging from ages two to sixteen. The defendant, her husband, and their children resided in a two bedroom apartment in a low income apartment complex. Their five oldest children all slept in one room while the youngest child slept in a crib in the defendant's bedroom. Both the defendant and her husband were employed but their income combined was under two thousand dollars per month and not nearly enough to support a family of eight.

Next, the defendant herself began to discuss the circumstances of her marriage. She told the court how she came to the United States from the West Bank and how her marriage was arranged. Her husband was very abusive physically, emotionally, and verbally. This abuse extended onto the children also. The defendant told the court of how wives, from the culture where she came from, were required to stay with their husbands regardless of what their relationship was like. As a result, the defendant abided by her culture and stayed with her husband regardless of the abuse. She continued to disclose stories of the many times when her husband would yell and hit her and the children. He would call all of them *"ugly and stupid"* and never hesitate to slap the children at any time.

The defendant then brought forward a dramatic fact that would help her greatly show the court why a non-prison sentence was needed. The defendant made it known to the court that her abusive husband was planning to move back to the West Bank and take the children along with him if she were to go to prison. He accused the defendant of dishonoring the family and promised to leave with the children if she were imprisoned.

The judge weighed all of these facts and valid arguments and decided to sentence the defendant to three years probation including six months of home detention. Here is what the judge stated regarding the defendant's non-prison sentence, *"The defendant's situation is compelling. If she is incarcerated her six minor children will be left with an abusive father who has vowed to take them away. If Munir (the husband) carried out this threat the children, who are American citizens, would be separated from the only caretaker they have known and removed from the only country they have known. In addition, the defendant might not see her children again or, if she followed them to the West*

Bank, she might not be able to return to the United States. Even if Munir did not take the children to the West Bank, the record shows that the children's safety would be endangered if they were left solely in his care. Munir is not capable of caring for them, and there is no other person who could do so. The defendant's brother, who lives in the United States, has eight children of his own and cares for the defendant's ill mother. The woman who cared for the children when the defendant was initially detained on this charge has since been implicated in the coupon scheme and is not a reliable caretaker. The defendant's other living sibling resides in the West Bank. The defendant's mother can not take care of the children because she is ill. Thus, imprisonment would cause both defendant and her children to suffer inordinately. Their circumstances are extraordinary, far worse than those faced by a defendant-parent and her children in the usual case."

It is clear in this case that the judge showed compassion for the defendant due to the threat of her losing her children to an abusive husband and possibly never seeing them again. The defendant had a well polished argument that was presented with extraordinary details. Her testimony helped to draw a large amount of attention to her family crisis and put overwhelming pressure on the judge at sentencing to give serious thought about the ramifications that a prison sentence would have on the defendant's children. A judges order for the defendant to head off to prison would inherently threaten the loss of her children, the inability for others to provide full time care for the children, and the emotional impact on the children. The end result would be a non-prison sentence for the defendant.

Case Locator - 347 FSupp2d 634

The previous case examples demonstrate the powerful use of significant types of family circumstances that can be used during the pre-sentence and sentencing phases of a defendant's case. As one continues to read through this book, these real life case examples should help identify common situations that can be used to mitigate otherwise prison rich sentences.

Remember, it will be a well thought out, creatively prepared plan of attack, ideally consisting of one or more mitigating factors, that will portray a defendant in such a way that a sentence below the recommended guideline range would clearly be sufficient enough but not greater than necessary to provide just punishment. A defendant should work diligently with his attorney and create this plan of attack using as many mitigating arguments as possible and applicable, and many which are disclosed in this book.

The sentencing guidelines are advisory in nature in this "Post-Booker" era. The case of the United States versus Booker changed the way that federal courts and judges operate. Before the "Booker" ruling in 2003 the sentencing guidelines were mandatory and a judge was not allowed to sentence an individual outside the recommended guideline range. What this essentially means now is that a judge, who listens to extraordinary mitigating arguments from a defendant, will have the power to depart downward and impose a lighter sentence. In a "Post Booker" world the judge has more control over what sentences he can impose, whereas in the "Pre Booker" world the judge would be required to impose a sentence within the recommended guideline range that the offense level dictated.

The magnitude of the downward departure should commensurate with the magnitude of the defendant's mitigating factors. If a solid argument is made, and the court understands the reasons why the defendant committed the offense, such as a bad decision where the defendant needed money, or maybe the offense clearly defined a display of aberrant conduct, and the court is fairly certain that the defendant would not commit the same offense again, then good results can happen.

There are no solutions when you are focused on the negative.
— **Byron Pulsifer**

3
Medical Factors

The next formidable avenue that can help convince a judge to impose a reduced sentence, and one that carries substantial weight when determining an appropriate sentence for a defendant is the medical condition of a defendant or a member of the defendant's family, the latter being slightly less valuable during sentencing.

Downward departures for documented health problems are a valid and effective means to induce a lower sentence. Anyone who has been charged with a federal crime and has one or more serious health problems should bring those forward to their attorney immediately to discuss the possible options for a downward departure. Obviously, the severity and type of health condition will play a factor when determining one's sentence. For example, a defendant should not anticipate a lower sentence because he gets colds more frequently than usual and uses a special herbal cold medicine that is not available inside of federal prison. The actual health condition must be substantial in nature, either physically or mentally, and must be documented well. In many instances a defendant's doctor or health specialist will furnish testimony either in person or through written documents confirming one's adverse health condition. If a defendant's health condition can not be documented in some way by testimony other than that from the defendant himself, then it would likely not hold much weight when arguing for a reduced sentence.

The sentencing guidelines, pursuant to 5H1.4, state this about the health condition of a defendant, *"Physical condition or appearance, including physique, is not ORDINARILY relevant in determining whether a departure may be warranted. However, an extraordinary physical impairment may be a reason to depart downward; e.g., in the case of a seriously infirm defendant, home detention may be as efficient as, and less costly than imprisonment."*

Therefore, if an individual's health problems require specialized care and treatment, and the required treatment can not be afforded reasonably and effectively by the Bureau of Prisons, then a judge will be forced to consider other punishment options such as home confinement, community confinement, or a combination of both.

Remember though, the statute says, *"extraordinary physical impairment"* and it will ultimately be the decision of the sentencing judge to determine what qualifies as *"extraordinary."* Each and every medical condition should have its own unique set of circumstances and facts. A judge will use all of these to help determine an appropriate sentence. The facts surrounding the offense will also be important with respect to the argument for a reduced sentence. For example, if someone robbed a bank at gun point and then stole a getaway car that was occupied by a pregnant woman, who was subsequently thrown out of the car by the defendant, this person will likely not get any type of lenience at sentencing despite the fact that he needs a liver transplant.

One other point to note regarding those with intense medical needs is the lack of facilities to properly care for an individual requiring specialized treatment. Federal Medical Centers (FMC) are otherwise known as federal prison hospitals. There are only a few of these type institutions in the federal prison system and they are all severely overcrowded. If it is probable that a defendant's health condition will ultimately place him in one of these FMC institutions, then the judge should be reminded of this overcrowding problem at sentencing.

If a defendant with health issues is sentenced to a term of imprisonment, he will be classified by the BOP with a corresponding medical score. This medical score, which determines what medical type institution will serve the inmate's medical needs, combined with the inmate's security score, will be the primary factors for determining an appropriate correctional facility.

The BOP medical scoring system has a total of four levels. Level one institutions are for inmates who are in good overall health and in need of only emergency type care. Level two inmates will have some type of health issues such as asthma or high blood pressure that is only in need of periodic checks and otherwise under control. Inmates are classified as level three when their health problems are more severe and require frequent monitoring and medication such as high blood pressure that requires medication and frequent checks, serious asthma conditions, etc. Inmates who are classified as level four are assigned to one of the BOP Federal Medical Centers. These FMC's are best suited for inmates who would be otherwise required for inpatient placement in a hospital if not incarcerated.

The BOP also contracts with nearby community medical facilities for additional outpatient medical treatment for inmates. Level one institutions are furthest away from these medical centers, usually an hour or more away. Level two institutions are within one hour of an outside medical center and level three institutions are usually located adjacent to one of the FMC's.

Medical treatment inside of a federal institution is not of the same quality and care that is found on the outside. The obvious reason for this is the amount of experience that the BOP medical staff has and their overall credentials. The bottom line is that top notch doctors and nurses with more skills and experience will usually be found at notable hospitals around the nation and not working for the BOP. Additionally, the pay that these individuals receive is considerably less than what a reputable hospital would pay on the outside. Others problems in the system are the amount of time that it usually takes to have a medical problem checked out and diagnosed. This is largely due to large number of inmates per each assigned doctor and medical assistant in the federal institutions.

One caveat for a defendant having a medical condition that requires specialized care is the chance of being sent to one of the Federal Medical Centers that just may be located hundreds of miles away from the defendant's home, if in fact a term of imprisonment is imposed. Once again, these details should be carefully discussed with the defendant's attorney before any plan of action is made. Of the many hundred medical problems that have been used in court to help secure a lighter sentence, the ones that have worked the most effectively are the conditions that require some type of special test or treatment that the BOP does not have any reasonable ability to administer. Now let's look at a few real cases to see what arguments have worked in the past.

United States vs. Rioux - In this case the defendant, Alfred Rioux, was convicted via a jury trial for extortion in a Connecticut District Court back in the late 1990's. The defendant was a sheriff in Hartford County and also the head of the *"sheriffs association."*

The *"association"* was a private organization that many deputies and special deputies belonged to. These individuals paid annual dues to the organization for their memberships. The defendant used his position to threaten deputies who did not pay their dues. He threatened to suspend or terminate any deputy that did not pay his annual dues or purchase tickets to the association's fund raising events.

After the trial the probation department prepared the defendant's PSI report and concluded at a total offense level of twenty-four. This former sheriff, who made some bad decisions, was now facing a recommended sentence of imprisonment of 51-63 months for his conduct. His offense level was also enhanced four points from the base level of twenty due to his leadership role in the offense.

At the sentencing hearing the defendant argued for a reduction of sentence on multiple grounds. First, it was discussed that the defendant did not deserve the four point enhancement on his offense for being the leader of the illegal operation. The defendant's attorney argued that his client inherited this role and that the illegal conduct was in place long before he was appointed to the position of *head of the association*. The court agreed to this and proceeded by lowering the offense level by four points resulting in a level twenty. Looking at the sentencing table, we can see that even with a level twenty under category one of the sentencing table, the recommended prison sentence was now 33-41 months. The defendant was still facing a considerable prison term.

Next came the mention of the defendant's health condition. The defendant had undergone a kidney transplant some twenty years prior but his transplant still required for him to undergo regular doses of medication and have **special blood tests** performed. Remember how we mentioned the significance of any medical condition requiring special equipment or testing that the BOP could not reasonably provide? Well, these tests were confirmed to be necessary by the defendant's doctor and they were also not readily available through BOP medical services.

The defendant and his attorney did their research before the sentencing hearing by calling various BOP staff and gathering information about the BOP's capability to treat him properly and perform these critical tests as required. Preparing for the sentencing hearing with this information was very clever by the defendant and his attorney. This was also a substantial mitigating factor for the judge to consider.

With all the facts on the table at sentencing, and even with the recommended sentence of 33-41 months imprisonment, the judge made the prudent decision to impose a sentence consisting of three years probation including six months home confinement and five hundred hours of community service.
Case Locator - 97 F3d 648

United States vs. Collins – This particular case demonstrates the effective use of one's health issues as an argument for a reduced sentence and thus the outcome of this case was very favorable for the defendant.

Back in the mid 1990's the defendant, James Collins, pled guilty in federal court to one count of cocaine distribution. The total amount of cocaine involved in the offense was between 200-300 grams. Being convicted of large quantities of cocaine such as in this case often leads to ten or more years in prison. The defendant's offense level for the offense was a twenty-eight. The defendant also had prior convictions therefore his offense level was placed in category four of the sentencing table. This resulted in a recommended 151-188 months of imprisonment.

Prior to the sentencing hearing the defendant's attorney filed a motion for downward departure. This motion asked the court for lenience due to the defendant's age, health, and the fact that his prior drug conviction close to ten years ago. The government subsequently opposed the defense's motion for the downward departure and it was apparent, due to the intransigence between both parties, that they would have to battle it out at the sentencing hearing.

During the sentencing hearing the judge listened to the defense and then the prosecution. The defendant's attorney talked extensively about the mitigating factors that were involved with his client's case. The defendant and his attorney highlighted the fact that he was sixty-four years old at the time of sentencing and not a threat to society in any way. His health issues that required frequent monitoring included heart disease, high blood pressure, and arthritis. Written testimony was submitted by the defendant's doctor and other health specialists.

At the end of the sentencing hearing, the judge ruled in favor of the defendant and made the decision to reduce the defendant's sentence from a possible sixteen years imprisonment substantially downward to forty-two months of confinement. With good time credit and possible admittance into the BOP residential drug program (RDAP), this man could be walking out of prison after just two years compared to a previously recommended sentence of sixteen years.

How did this happen? Well it is likely that the defendant's age combined with the extensive amount of written testimony from several doctors and health experts painted a clear picture for the judge showing that a lengthy term of imprisonment for this individual could be a punishment "greater than necessary" and thus imposed the forty-two month term.

<u>United States vs. Norris</u> - The defendant, William Norris, was convicted in a Indiana District Court on thirteen counts of wire fraud, five counts of mail fraud, and eleven counts of assisting in the unauthorized reception of cable service. Another co-defendant, James Gee, was also convicted of ten counts of wire fraud and one count of conspiracy. Both Norris and Gee were found guilty after going to trial.

This case was interesting because one of the defendants who had no adverse health conditions was sent to prison for thirty-seven months while the other, who had valid mitigating health issues, was successful obtaining a non-prison sentence.

Both defendants were involved in a business that specialized in cable descramblers. They would purchase special chips and subsequently install these chips in cable boxes. These cable boxes would then be sold to customers.

Both defendants were facing several years of imprisonment due to the charges.

At the sentencing hearing Norris wisely provided several hundred pages of medical records to the court which documented his cardiovascular (i.e., heart) problems. The defendant's cardiologist also prepared a video presentation which was played at the sentencing hearing. The video talked extensively about Norris's heart problems and gave testimony of how the defendant required special medical care and frequent scheduled visits for his health condition. It was made clear to the court that high levels of stress could be lethal to the defendant and thus a term of imprisonment could literally kill this individual.

The government responded by obtaining a letter from the Bureau of Prisons that claimed they had the ability to handle the defendant's medical issues. The defendant's attorney then cleverly argued back to the court the fact that the BOP letter was nothing more than a generic form letter that trumpeted the BOP's ability to handle medical conditions of all kinds. It made no specific mention of the individualized medical care that the defendant required. This clever argument showed a lack of effort on the part of the government to precisely show to the court that this defendant would truly be afforded proper care while in the custody of the BOP. This was another great job done by the defendant and his attorney.

The judge sided with the defendant and proceeded to reduce Norris's sentence due to his valid health arguments. He considered the defendant's mitigating health conditions extraordinary enough to impose a non-prison sentence of thirty-seven months of home detention. The fact that the government spent little, if any time giving attention to the defendant's medical condition, and that they did little research to determine if in fact he would be properly cared for while in custody of the BOP, was a major factor in this sentence. Additionally, the generic letter used to show the court that the defendant would be cared for properly hurt the government further and was likely a big factor in the judge's decision to depart downward.

Case Locator - 226 F3d 903

74- Reduce My Prison Sentence

<u>United States vs. McClean</u> - This particular case involved the illegal drug smuggling of heroin into the U.S. The defendant was a Nigerian man who pled guilty to smuggling more than one-hundred grams of heroin into the U.S. As serious of a crime this was, there is always a chance for a successful outcome, especially considering the defendant's health problems.

The defendant was originally caught with 857 grams of heroin during his passage through J.F.K. Airport in New York. He was a citizen of Nigeria with no financial assets and the father of four children ranging from two to eight years of age. They all resided in Nigeria with the defendant and his wife. The defendant held a steady job as a sales clerk in his home country. He also suffered from Polio and had a crippled leg as a result of the disease. He walked with crutches and it was likely that he would need to use them for the rest of his life for walking.

With a guilty plea to the 857 grams of heroin the defendant would be facing a mandatory ten years behind bars. The government though, while negotiating a plea deal, agreed to lower the base offense level to represent a lesser amount of 80-100 grams of heroin in return for guilty plea. This guilty plea would save the government much time and money from having to prepare for the trial of a non-citizen of the U.S. The defendant agreed to the plea deal, and as a result the new offense level was lowered to a twenty-six.

Because of the defendant's acceptance of responsibility, the court also agreed to lower the offense three additional points to a twenty-three. The defendant was still facing 46-57 months of recommended prison time for this new offense level and needed an obvious miracle to avoid a term of imprisonment.

The defendant and his attorney prepared their effective arguments which primarily included the defendant's health issues. The defendant hoped that these would be accepted by the court as unique and extraordinary enough to warrant a lighter sentence.

At the sentencing hearing the defendant's attorney began his presentation to the court. He began by talking extensively about the defendant's health condition. It was made known to the court that the defendant, due to his Polio disease, had to walk with crutches everywhere he went. It was also made known to the court that the defendant would be required to walk with crutches for the remainder of his life.

It was then pointed out in a clever move by the defense that the defendant had been using metal crutches for most of his life and was only comfortable walking with the metal type. He had tried previously on numerous occasions to walk with wooden crutches but they never suited him properly and were very uncomfortable to get around on. The defendant would likely become immobile if given a set of wooden crutches to use. The many times he failed with the wooden version was also discussed.

The court was then advised of the fact that the BOP would not allow the defendant to use metal crutches while incarcerated in a federal institution because they could be easily substituted as a weapon for inmates to use. The court was also informed of the multiple attempts, while in custody awaiting sentencing, that the defendant's crutches were stolen by other inmates and used as weapons. The difficulty for the defendant to get around and perform basic daily tasks while incarcerated, such as going to the bathroom and getting through the lunch line, were also discussed in detail. The defendant's attorney gave detailed examples of how his client had extreme trouble surviving in the prison environment during his pre-trial days.

The judge considered the defendant's arguments extraordinary enough to substantiate a reduced sentence and proceeded to reduce the defendant's sentence below the recommended guidelines. The judge reduced the defendant's guideline sentence of five years down substantially to thirty-three months of imprisonment. Although not as lucky as some of the other defendants in this book, this defendant was still successful in shaving off close to half of the recommended sentence and almost seven years less than the original ten year mandatory sentence.

With good time credit and possibly extra time secured in a halfway house this man could essentially walk out of prison in as little as one-and-a-half years. He will also have a second chance at life much quicker compared to the original threat of facing ten years in a federal prison. This individual will not be eligible for the RDAP because he is not a citizen of the United States. Case Locator - 822 FSupp 961

76 - Reduce My Prison Sentence

<u>United States vs. Tocco</u> - The case of Tocco versus the U.S. is another good example of how a defendant's health condition and charitable deeds worked to secure a lighter sentence. Back in the late 1990's the defendant was charged in a twenty-five count indictment for a variety of illegal activities. The illegal conduct included extortion, illegal lotteries, loan sharking, and illegal investments. The defendant took his case to trial and was found guilty on racketeering conspiracy and Hobbs conspiracy charges. He was acquitted on all remaining charges.

During preparation of the defendant's PSI report it was confirmed that the total offense level was a twenty-two. Since the defendant did not have any prior criminal history, the recommended term of imprisonment, as shown in the sentencing table under category one was 41-51 months. The defendant was facing four years in a federal prison.

At the sentencing hearing the defendant's attorney argued for a lower sentence using the defendant's health condition, age, and the deteriorating health of his wife. To begin, the defendant's age of seventy-two was made known to the court. Then the defendant's ill health was brought forward and highlighted. The defendant suffered from coronary disease and hypertension. His wife was also in poor health and was in constant need of the defendant's assistance.

After these arguments were spotlighted and discussed in great detail, the defendant's charitable works and good deeds were brought to the attention of the court. These mitigating factors were presented in a package that would give the judge an enormous amount of information displaying why the defendant should be spared a term of imprisonment. The defendant was also hoping that the mention of his good intentions would make the court consider his health conditions with a greater magnitude.

He was involved in many charities that the court was made aware of such as the Rotary Club and many church organizations. Various letters written by representatives of the charitable organizations were submitted to the court several days before the sentencing via a sentencing memorandum to confirm the defendant's good works.

At the end of the defendant's plea for a reduced sentence the judge paused and then sentenced Mr. Tocco to one year and one day in community confinement (i.e., halfway house). The defendant was able to dodge a prison sentence using the extraordinary arguments that defined his life.

Doing time in a halfway house is much less restrictive than in any federal prison. Most individuals are allowed to hold a job in the community and travel to and from that job as one's work schedule dictates. The rules that govern the halfway house are also less restrictive than any federal institution. Residents are usually allowed to leave the halfway house for trips to the store, church visits, medical appointments, and other privileges. After several weeks of being at the halfway house, and after securing a job in the community, residents are also allowed to go home on weekend passes anywhere from twelve to forty-eight hours in duration. Most residents ultimately end up serving the end of their sentence in home confinement. This avenue is much less stressful than any term of imprisonment and allows individuals to continue supporting their family while serving out the sentence. Case Locator - 200 F3d 401

United States vs. Johnson – In this particular case, a physician was convicted in a Michigan District Court on nine counts of distribution of a controlled substance and four counts of mail fraud. A description of the charges were as follows: "*On August 12, 1993 defendant Keithley Johnson, a medical doctor, was named in a 58 counts of a 111 count indictment charging him and his medical partner, Dr. Tejinder Uppal, with various crimes. Following a lengthy jury trial, the defendant was convicted on nine counts of distributing pharmaceuticals outside the course of professional practice and for no legitimate purpose, in violation of 21 U.S.C. 841(a)(1). Defendant was also convicted on four counts of mail fraud, in violation of 18 U.S.C. 1341.*"

After the trial, the judge ordered preparation of the defendant's PSI report. It was determined that the defendant had no prior criminal history and his offense level of fourteen was appropriated under category one of the sentencing table. The recommended term of imprisonment for Johnson was 15-21 months for the conviction.

At the sentencing hearing the defendant successfully used his medical conditions as the primary argument for a

78 - Reduce My Prison Sentence

reduced sentence. What this defendant and his attorney did cleverly to help his argument was obtain a letter from the defendant's doctor that confirmed a condition of imprisonment would be detrimental to his health. The defendant's doctor confirmed in the letter that the defendant was suffering from a variety of health disorders including hypertension and ulcers.

The defendant also began seeing a psychiatrist for an unknown amount of time before his sentencing hearing. The defendant's psychiatrist submitted a letter to the court that claimed the defendant was under his care and was suffering from depression. These letters would have significant weight to the judge when deciding on the proper sentence for the defendant.

Any time a defendant has an extraordinary condition, either mentally or physically, the judge must give the condition serious consideration when deciding to place one in a prison environment. When these conditions are further backed up by letters and testimony from the defendant's health care specialists, it will only increase the level of consideration deemed necessary to decide on a suitable sentence. These letters clearly made it known to the court that this defendant would not be able to adapt well in prison and his health would be greatly jeopardized. The letters also made it clear that this defendant was suffering from an additional mental problem consisting of depression that required frequent therapy.

The judge concluded by departing downward on the recommended guideline sentence of 15-21 months imprisonment using the defendant's mental and medical condition as the basis for departure. The judge agreed that the sixty-five year old defendant had *"a number of medical problems that suggest it would be less expensive to the taxpayers and the public interest would be better served if he were confined in a community correction center where he could have his medical treatment locally rather than under the aegis of the Bureau of Prisons."* The judge likely relied heavily on the two letters submitted by the defendant. Mr. Tocco was sentenced to twelve months in a halfway house and fined $40,000 for the offenses.

Case Locator - 71 F3d 539

After reading the last few cases one should begin to see the types of health and medical arguments that can help sway a judge into delivering a reduced sentence. One of the strongest arguments that a defendant can bring forward when seeking a reduced sentence is a medical condition that involves some type of specialized treatment or testing that is not readily available through the federal prison system. A good example of this was the case mentioned earlier that involved a defendant who proved his health condition warranted special blood tests. The clever argument used by the defendant who needed metal crutches worked surprisingly well also to secure a reduced sentence.

Being creative, but candid and contrite when arguing for a reduced sentence can surely pay off when the arguments presented to the court are true and unusual compared to the circumstances of a typical case.

BOP medical facilities do not have all the bells and whistles that a patient might find in a state of the art medical treatment center outside the prison system. Anyone having an illness or medical condition that requires specialized treatment and monitoring should have his attorney promptly contact the appropriate BOP representatives to discuss the individual needs of the defendant for proper survival while incarcerated in the federal system. We use the word survival here because this is the word that should be used in front of the judge at sentencing. Whenever a situation arises that raises a doubt about the ability of the BOP to properly care for an individual, terms like "survival in prison" will serve well in court.

Whether it is special testing and treatment, special medicine, or special counseling required by the defendant, if the BOP is unable to fully meet the medical needs of the defendant, then this should have a huge impact on the outcome at sentencing.

Statements and sworn letters from doctors and additional health care specialists should be gathered together to further back up the defendant's health claims. Even if the BOP claims it can satisfy the needs of a particular person, those needs may be extraordinary enough to warrant a reduction of sentence and therefore should be spot lighted and exemplified during the sentencing hearing.

As stated in 5H1.4 of the U.S.S.G., *"in the case of a seriously infirm defendant, home detention may be as efficient as, and less costly than imprisonment."* Now let's look at a few more cases demonstrating the successful use of one's health condition as a mitigating factor for a reduced sentence.

<u>United States vs. McFarlin</u> - In this federal case, the defendant, James McFarlin, pled guilty to one count of conspiracy to distribute 102 grams of cocaine. The court proceedings took place in an Arkansas District Court back in 2007. The defendant was facing up to ninety-seven months in federal prison for the offense.

The defendant was originally charged in 2005 with a twenty-five count indictment for possession with intent to distribute Alprazolam (i.e., Xanax) and cocaine. In 2006 an additional charge of witness tampering was added to the indictment. Both the defendant and the government eventually came to a mutual agreement where the defendant agreed to plead guilty to one count of conspiracy to distribute cocaine.

At the sentencing hearing, the defendant was facing seven to eight years of prison time for the guilty plea. During the hearing, the defendant's attorney brought forward the defendant's age and health problems as the primary argument for a lighter sentence.

The defendant was fifty-six years of age at the time of sentencing. His medical condition involved prior open heart surgery that was performed in 2005. In 2007 the defendant required graft bypass surgery on his leg to help with his ongoing heart condition. Asthma also aggravated the defendant's heart problems and as a result he was required to have frequent monitoring of his condition. The defendant was taking at least eleven different prescription medications and had a rigid daily schedule for administrating the medicine.

During the months before the offense and leading up to the sentencing, the defendant also revealed that he had become addicted to his pain medication and that this addiction contributed significantly to his criminal activity. Stories about the defendant's ongoing addiction and his need for pain medicine were disclosed to the court.

The judge accepted the defendant's mitigating factors at sentencing and adopted them as his "statement of reasons" for his reasons for a downward departure. The judge then imposed a sentence of three years probation and the defendant was able to avoid a lengthy term of imprisonment. Case Locator - 535 F3d 805

United States vs. Sherman - In this case, the defendant successfully used his severe obesity to help secure a non-prison sentence. The defendant, Keith Sherman, was convicted in a Illinois District Court for possession of a sawed-off shotgun in violation of 26 U.S.C. 5861. He pled guilty to the single charge via a plea agreement back in the mid 1990's. Because of the corresponding offense level of fifteen, the defendant was facing a recommended 18-24 months imprisonment as shown under category one of the sentencing table.

At the sentencing hearing the defendant requested a downward departure using his asthma and obesity as the primary argument. The defendant had limited documentation to show any extent of medical treatment he had received for his health conditions, therefore leaving the court with only the defendant's sworn testimony to take into consideration.

The defendant gave his own testimony to the court that he was more than 100 pounds overweight and also suffered from asthma. He also advised the court that due to his obese condition combined with his asthma he had difficulty breathing after even the slightest amount of physical activity. The court questioned the defendant on his lack of effort to seek treatment for his health conditions, and in response to this the defendant advised the court that he had no health insurance and was unable to afford any type of health care for his conditions. The defendant also made it known to the court that he suffered from arthritis in his ankles and knees and that the pain from the arthritis made it impossible for him to exercise to lose weight. The defendant then expressed great concern about his

82 - Reduce My Prison Sentence

vulnerability if sent to prison with regard to his inability to defend himself should an altercation occur.

The defendant's detailed testimony, regardless of the lack of documentation from any health experts confirming his medical conditions, still forced the judge to consider the defendant's lack of ability to move around easily, his lack of ability to defend himself in a prison environment, and his overall vulnerability to other inmates, when deciding on an appropriate sentence for the defendant.

After hearing all of the defendant's mitigating arguments, the judge agreed to reduce the defendant's offense level downward by five levels. This lowered the total offense level from a fifteen to a ten. The judge used the *"appearance of the defendant"* as a determining factor when imposing the sentence and proceeded to give the defendant a non-prison sentence consisting of one year of home detention followed by two years of probation. Case Locator - 535 F2d 602

4
Other Mitigating Factors

At the sentencing hearing is where a defendant will learn his fate. It is during this hearing when the defendant and his attorney must bring forward all viable mitigating factors and argue these to the judge in hopes for a lighter sentence. The ultimate goal is to present relevant factors relative to one's case and life that are accepted by the court as valid mitigating arguments, and then cast these mitigating factors in a spotlight to show their uniqueness and extraordinary value. This is done in an effort to make one's case appear *"outside the heartland"* of a typical case with similar conduct. When a defendant is successful showing to the court that his case is *"outside the heartland"* then good things can happen on sentencing day.

Many defendants will be able to identify mitigating factors that do apply to their case simply by reading this book, but it will be those who work diligently with their attorney that will likely receive the most favorable results. The ultimate goal for anyone charged with a crime is to stay out of prison. Presenting enough unique and extraordinary mitigating factors for a judge to consider has enabled many to do just that.

What is a mitigating factor? The definition of *"mitigate"* is to make less severe, intense, or painful. Therefore, a mitigating factor in court is a characteristic, circumstance, trait, or condition of a defendant that can be used to counter the charged offense(s) and lessen the resulting punishment. The mitigating factor is the *"good"* while the charged offense is the *"bad."* What a defendant needs to do is provide as much mitigating *"good"* as possible so that some of, or even all of the *"bad"* can be neutralized. In the end of any sentencing hearing, if the judge is sufficiently convinced that a defendant's mitigating factors are extraordinary enough to warrant a downward departure from the total offense level, then he will almost always act accordingly and reduce the sentence.

The United States Sentencing Commission is responsible for determining the legal language of what mitigating factors can be used as valid arguments for a defendant. A description of these can be found in the United States Sentencing Guidelines manual. The sentencing commission has also determined that there is a list of criteria that is not considered valid to be used as mitigating arguments in court. The following seven factors are classified as irrelevant and invalid for use as mitigating arguments when seeking a reduced sentence: **race, sex, national origin, creed, socio-economic status, lack of guidance as a youth, and religion**. Aside from these seven factors, the door is wide open for any argument that may be unique and extraordinary pertaining to the defendant's life or offense that may warrant a downward departure at sentencing.

With that being said, the sentencing commission has identified some of these mitigating factors in the guidelines manual. The following list of mitigating factors is not an all inclusive one and should not be accepted as such. These are simply some of the more common areas that a defendant and his attorney will explore in hopes for a reduced sentence. It is imperative for a defendant to work with his attorney and be creative with his case bringing forth the "*unusual*" facts and details. Once again, extraordinary facts and circumstances will often bring extraordinary sentences.

The below list of mitigating factors and the cases that follow will serve as good examples to show the types of arguments that have helped defendants secure reduced sentences. Hopefully as one continues to read through this book the wheels will start to turn and extraordinary circumstances will begin to appear related to one's case.

This chapter lists several examples of federal cases, all in which the defendants were facing lengthy prison sentences and all that concluded with very unique results – mostly non-prison results. The list of mitigating factors which is recognized in the U.S.S.G. manual is as follows:

5H1.6 - Family Ties
5H1.1 - Age
5H1.2 - Education
5H1.3 - Mental and Emotional Conditions
5H1.4 - Physical Condition
5H1.5 - Employment Record
5H1.11 - Charitable Good Deeds - Military Contributions

Other Mitigating Factors - 85

5K2.10 - Victim's Conduct
5K2.11 - Lesser Harms
5K2.12 - Coercion and Duress
5K2.13 - Diminished Capacity
5K2.16 - Voluntary Disclosure
5K2.19 - Post-Sentence Rehabilitation
3E1.1 - Acceptance of Responsibility
3B1.2 - Mitigating Role
5K2.20 - Aberrant Behavior

It is important also to mention that most of mitigating factors listed above come with a variable impact. What we mean by variable impact is that there is no set value for the level of sentencing adjustment that a judge has to abide by when he decides on a reduced sentence due to one of these mitigating factors. These types of mitigating arguments that a defendant will use are different than other types fixed sentencing adjustments that are mentioned in this book. For example, when a defendant has shown an acceptance of responsibility to the court and met this requirement pursuant to 3E1.1 of the sentencing guidelines under *"acceptance of responsibility,"* the result is an award of a fixed reduction of either two or three points deducted from the defendant's total offense level. Additionally, these fixed point adjustments are often decided on before the sentencing hearing and are usually confirmed on the defendant's PSI report. Then they are either accepted or rejected by the judge at the sentencing hearing. When a defendant successfully uses a mitigating argument such as one from the list above there will be no set award amount that the judge will have to follow, therefore the amount of the offense level reduction awarded by the judge is flexible (i.e., The judge could award a two point reduction or a twelve point reduction!).

With a *"fixed points"* downward departure such as a defendant's acceptance of responsibility the process may evolve like this:

1) The defendant pleads guilty to a federal charge pursuant to a plea agreement;

2) The defendant's attorney and the prosecutor have agreed that the defendant will be awarded with the acceptance of responsibility two point reduction. (This was negotiated before the defendant signed the plea agreement.);

3) The two point offense level reduction is listed on the defendant's plea agreement and then factored into the total offense level;

4) The defendant pleads guilty at the plea hearing and signs the plea agreement;

5) The probation department conducts an interview with the defendant and prepares the PSI report;

6) During preparation of the defendant's PSI report the probation officer also confirms that the defendant qualifies for the "acceptance of responsibility" two point reduction;

7) The probation officer prepares the defendant's PSI and calculates the defendant's total offense level factoring in the two level point reduction for defendant's acceptance of responsibility. The new offense level and adjusted sentencing range is also calculated and listed on the PSI report;

8) The defendant is sentenced at the sentencing hearing at which time the judge will review the defendant's PSI report and see on it that everyone (i.e., defendant, government, probation department) has agreed on the defendant's eligibility for the two point offense level reduction;

9) At the sentencing hearing the judge confirms the defendant's eligibility for the two point reduction for his acceptance of responsibility and imposes a sentence using the adjusted offense level as shown on the defendant's PSI report;

This is often how offense level adjustments work when there is a fixed value involved. Sometimes though, the prosecutor and/or the probation department will not agree to a specific offense level adjustment. When this happens, it will usually come down to sentencing time to battle it out in front of the judge. A case will proceed much smoother when the defendant's attorney, the prosecutor, and the probation officer who prepares the PSI report are all on the same page.

So remember, the aforementioned list of mitigating factors, except for 3E1.1 and 3B1.2, have no fixed value for the number of points that an offense level can be reduced. The judge can elect to depart one level or ten levels on a particular sentence. This will depend on the nature and applicability of the defendant's arguments. This is why it is so imperative to identify every possible mitigating argument which can be helpful towards a defendant's defense and then present them effectively to the court.

As an example of this variable impact, let's say that a particular defendant was facing a federal charge for wire fraud. He has never been in trouble with the law and is a stable hard working father and sole provider and caretaker for his four children. He has been taking care of his dying mother for two years and has some health problems of his own including an addiction to alcohol and gambling that was part to blame for his criminal conduct. In this particular case the defendant has identified several mitigating arguments for his case. When presented effectively to the court, a reduced sentence is possible.

The problem here is that even if the prosecutor and probation department agreed with the defendant's attorney on the validity of the mitigating factors, there is no definitive procedure to determine the amount of points in which the total offense level should be reduced. In situations like this, the defendant, through his attorney, will usually make a suggestion to the court for a specific number of points that the overall offense level should be reduced by. This request is usually submitted in the defendant's pre-sentence memorandum as well as any motion filed by the defendant's attorney for a downward departure. The final decision though will be ultimately up to the judge at sentencing.

Age

One of the very first items that the defendant should look at is his age. The age of a defendant can be a beneficial factor when argued in court. The argument of one's age is usually bundled in the defendant's complete mitigating package and never usually argued alone to request a reduced sentence.

While an elderly person will usually have a better chance arguing for a reduced sentence, there have been cases where younger individuals, such as a defendant under eighteen years of age, have used the age factor to help secure a lighter sentence. Here is what the sentencing guidelines say about using a defendant's age as a mitigating factor:

AGE - (U.S.S.G. 5H1.1) "Age may be a reason to depart downward in a case in which a defendant is elderly and where a form of punishment such as home confinement might be equally efficient as and less costly than incarceration."

If a defendant is considered elderly and infirm then this should be used as a mitigating argument to the court. The following is a prime example of how a defendant successfully argued for a lower sentence using his age and physical condition.

<u>United States vs. Baron</u> - The defendant, Mr. Baron, pled guilty to bank fraud in a Massachusetts District Court back in the mid 1990's. A summary of the case goes as follows: *"In the mid-1980's, apparently during a downturn in the economy, Baron was in need of cash to save his business. He turned to other banks, concealing the fact from his main bank - the State Street Bank. He arranged an annual "flip" transferring corporate debt to himself in order to show that the company owed nothing. Baron also caused false documents to be prepared by employees for false orders worth hundreds of thousands of dollars. On May 1, 1992, Baron signed two notes to the State Street Bank for one-and-a-half million and one million dollars respectively. By the end*

of 1992 the company had defaulted on the loans and the bank lost more than $2,500,000 as a result."

While computing the total offense level for the fraud charge, thirteen points were added for the amount of loss, which was estimated at $2,500,000 - $5,000,000. The total offense level was calculated at an eighteen. Under category one of the sentencing table the defendant was faced with 27-33 months of imprisonment.

At the sentencing hearing, the defendant and his attorney focused on several mitigating factors. It was first made known to the court that the defendant was seventy-six years of age at the time of sentencing. His life expectancy, as documented by his doctor, was 7.39 years. This life expectancy figure caught the attention of the judge and likely held significant weight at the hearing. Any time a defendant's age is classified to be in the final quarter of the average life expectancy - over sixty being a good age to use as the starting point - then this argument should be brought up at sentencing.

When a judge hears testimony approximating the remaining years left in one's life it can have a huge impact on the resulting sentence. In this particular case the defendant's doctor issued a written statement claiming that the defendant had only about seven years of life left. Obtaining this figure was a brilliant move by the defendant and his attorney. The health condition of the defendant was discussed next. The defendant had his pituitary gland removed due to cancer several years prior. The defendant then talked about his battle with cancer and how it has affected his life over the years.

The judge then commented on the defendant's arguments as follows: *"defendant's medical condition was unstable and made him susceptible to rapid deterioration to life-threatening situations from such ordinary factors as stress and exposure to common germs, stress from imprisonment could trigger a physiological reaction that would be difficult to control, and home detention was less expensive and more efficient than incarceration."*

At the end of the sentencing hearing, the judge weighed all of the facts and proceeded to sentence the defendant to one year of probation including six months of home confinement. Here is what the judge said to conclude his

sentence, "The best policy considerations can be unnecessarily cruel when applied rigidly and without exception to individual human beings. Some offenders would be destroyed by a term in prison. There are defendants for whom prison incarceration makes no sense."
Case Locator - 914 FSupp 660

<u>United States vs. Davis</u> - The defendant in this case, William Davis, applied for, and subsequently received a line of credit for approximately $1,500,000 for his company Fries Correctional Equipment. The company soon after defaulted on the loan and the bank filed a civil action against the defendant and his company. About the same time, the defendant and his wife filed for bankruptcy. The government conducted a short investigation into the defendant's actions about a year later and followed up with a letter sent to the defendant advising him of the criminal investigation and likely prosecution that would follow due to his conduct involving the fraudulent line of credit.

Shortly after this notice, the defendant was indicted on fraud charges. He decided to take his case to trial which ended with the defendant found guilty on two counts of bank fraud. The defendant was sentenced to thirty-three months imprisonment for conviction. His attorney did little, if anything, to fight for his freedom at the sentencing hearing and now he was facing the next few years in federal prison. He filed a timely appeal as to the sentence in hopes to change the outcome. About a year later, using a new attorney and a new version of the sentencing guidelines, the defendant brought forward some valid arguments to substantiate his request for a reduced sentence. His appeal was based on ineffective counsel who did not represent the defendant properly.

The defendant and his new attorney argued the mitigating factors to the court in what seemed to be an effective presentation. The mitigating arguments used were the defendant's age, which was seventy years old at the time of the sentencing, as well as the defendant's good behavior. The defendant gave testimony to the court telling of how he was getting older and had decided to retire and move closer to his family and his grandchildren for the last chapter in his life. This successful presentation about the defendant's age and family ties helped sway the judge into delivering a lighter sentence. The judge accepted the defendant's arguments for age, family ties, and aberrant behavior. He then decided to depart downward on the overall offense level and imposed a sentence of twelve months of home confinement and two days jail time.

Charitable Works

Using a defendant's good deeds and charitable works seems to be most effective when prepared in a *"package deal"* where the defendant has other potential mitigating factors to argue in front of the court such as family caretaking, financial responsibilities, ill health conditions, sick family members, aberrant behavior, etc. Here is what the sentencing guidelines mention about charitable works and military service:

CHARITABLE WORKS - GOOD DEEDS - MILITARY/PUBLIC SERVICE (U.S.S.G. 5H1.11) - "Military, civic, charitable, or public service; employment-related contributions; and similar prior good works are not ORDINARILY relevant in determining whether a departure is warranted."

Now let's look at some significant cases that clearly demonstrate how this argument can be of substantial value when argued successfully in front of a judge.

United States vs. Crouse - The defendant in this case, Edward Crouse, pled guilty to interstate shipping of adulterated orange juice. The defendant had no prior criminal history and it was determined that his total offense level was a nineteen. He was facing a recommended prison sentence of 30-37 months.

The primary mitigating argument used to ask for a reduced sentence was the good acts performed by the defendant. The defendant also made sure that all of his charitable works were listed in his PSI report for the judge to read.

At the sentencing hearing, the judge heard about the defendant's substantial involvement with multiple church organizations as well as his involvement with other notable charitable organizations such as the Rotary Club and the United Way. The defendant also helped out at his local hospital on several occasions. These arguments held weight during the sentencing hearing and the defendant was successful using these mitigating factors to secure a non-prison of twelve months home confinement. This case did not end there though and took an interesting turn of events on a legal roller coaster.

Initially, the government was not satisfied with the non-prison sentence, subsequently filed an appeal, and wanted this individual to serve time behind bars. The appeals court reviewed the case and remanded it for re-sentencing citing the fact the defendant's charitable works were not considered extraordinary considering the circumstances and his position as a prominent businessman. Remember the mitigating arguments presented to the court must be extraordinary in nature to allow for a reduction of one's sentence. The District Court received the case back for re-sentencing and this time the judge imposed a new sentence that did indeed contain a term of imprisonment - eighteen months to be exact - but still substantially below the recommended guideline range of 30-37 months.

Now it was the defendant who was unhappy with his new sentence of imprisonment and proceeded to file his own appeal. The defendant's attorney swiftly prepared the defendant's appeal and submitted it to the courts. This appeal made it all the way to the Supreme Court where it was once again remanded for re-sentencing ruling that a statement of reasons was not given by the judge after the prison sentence was imposed. The District Court once again received the case for yet its third sentencing and this time the judge imposed the exact same sentence as the first time around. The sentence of twelve months home confinement was once again handed down. This time the judge cited, *"that a significant departure based upon good works...is in fact merited."*

One again, the government was not satisfied with the non-prison sentence, but because the judge gave a valid *"statement of reasons"* for its departure the government elected not to appeal the case again and the sentence finally stood firm. The defendant's formidable arguments concerning his good deeds likely helped sway the judge into delivering the non-prison sentence.

Any time a judge hands down a sentence below the recommended guidelines, the defendant should ask his attorney to make sure the judgment has a valid *"statement of reasons"* submitted with it. The judgment and *"statement of reasons"* is filed with the court usually within a few days after the sentencing. This *"statement of reasons"* explains the reasons why the judge departed below the recommended guidelines. This explanation is required by law, and without it, a particular case could be remanded on appeal for a re-sentencing. Case Locator - 145 F2d 786

Victim's Conduct

Below is what the U.S.S.G. states about using the conduct of a victim as a mitigating factor in court:

5K2.10 Victim's Conduct - "If the victim's wrongful conduct contributed significantly to provoking the offense behavior, the court may reduce the sentence below the guideline range to reflect the nature and circumstances of the offense. In deciding whether a sentence reduction is warranted, and the extent of such reduction, the court should consider the following:

1) The size and strength of the victim, or other relevant physical characteristics, in comparison with those of the defendant;

2) The persistence of the victim's conduct and any efforts by the defendant to prevent confrontation;

3) The danger reasonably perceived by the defendant, including the victim's reputation for violence;

4) The danger actually presented to the defendant by the victim;

5) Any other relevant conduct by the victim that substantially contributed to the danger presented;

6) The proportionality and reasonableness of the defendant's response to the victim's provocation;

Victim misconduct ordinarily would not be sufficient to warrant application of this provision in the context of offenses under Chapter Two, Part A, Subpart 3 (Criminal Sexual Abuse). In addition, this provision usually would not be relevant in the context of non-violent offenses. There may, however, be unusual circumstances in which substantial victim misconduct would warrant a reduced penalty in the case of a non-violent offense. For example, an extended course of provocation and harassment might lead to a defendant to steal or destroy property in retaliation.

<u>United States vs. Tsosie</u> - Here we have a case that clearly illustrates the successful use of the victim's conduct as a mitigating factor. This was the case of the United States vs. Jimmy Tsosie. Back in the early 1990's the defendant, Mr. Tsosie, drove home after working at his day job and found a note from his wife telling the defendant that she was taking their children out to visit her sister and was planning on staying the night. The next morning the defendant went to his sister-in-law's house to look for his wife only to discover that she and their children were not there.

The defendant proceeded to search around town all day for his family with no success. Later that afternoon the defendant saw his wife's van on the highway and attempted to flag it down. The van sped up quickly without reason. The defendant soon after caught up with the van and attempted to pull it over. The van eventually pulled over to the side of the road and the defendant then pulled his vehicle in front of the van. As the defendant exited his vehicle, he saw a man sitting in the passenger seat of the van. He immediately recognized the individual as a man that the defendant's wife had been having a long time affair with. As the defendant approached the van, the man opened the door and exited the van quickly. A fight ensued and both men wrestled on the ground for a brief moment.

The man from the van, Stephen Arnold, had been romantically involved with the defendant's wife for a long time. Arnold was the larger of the two men and was able to break away from the fight and flee on foot. The defendant grabbed a survival knife from his vehicle and proceeded to chase Arnold over a fence and into an open field. Arnold saw that the defendant was catching up to him and removed his belt from his waist in an attempt to fight back.

Arnold was successful in hitting the defendant in the face with his belt and the defendant was successful swinging his knife causing several superficial wounds on Arnold. The fight continued until Arnold raised his leg and was subsequently cut deep with the knife. After the defendant was able to push Arnold off of him he noticed a large amount of blood coming from Arnold's knee.

The defendant, stunned over the amount of blood, drove to a nearby trading post and asked the cashier to call the police and have them send an ambulance. He then returned to the site of the incident and found Arnold laying there bleeding badly. The defendant attempted to use a towel to stop the bleeding but it was too late and Arnold died before the ambulance arrived almost an hour later.

The defendant pled guilty to voluntary manslaughter and was facing four to five years imprisonment for the offense. The defendant and his attorney decided that this was the right time to try and use the "victim's conduct" as a mitigating factor. At the sentencing hearing, the defendant's attorney argued that due to the larger size of the victim and the obvious advantage in physical strength there was an inherent disadvantage to the defendant when the fight occurred between the two. Since the defendant was also a non-violent individual, the argument of aberrant behavior was also used at the sentencing. The defendant's attorney asked for a substantial downward departure using the victim's conduct and the aberrant behavior of the defendant. The judge agreed that the mitigating arguments were extraordinary enough to warrant a reduced sentence and proceeded to sentence the defendant to four months in a halfway house.

The government appealed the sentence and about a year later the court reviewed the case and agreed that the downward departure for the mitigating factors was warranted. Here is what the appeals court stated: *"We find that Arnold's conduct contributed significantly to provoking Tsosie's offensive behavior. Arnold's conduct consisted not merely of having an affair with Tsosie's wife but also of being in a vehicle with Tsosie's wife the day after she took her children away and gave a false excuse about her whereabouts. Tsosie, who believed the affair with Arnold was over, was surprised and angered. Further, in the ensuing fight, Arnold took off his belt and hit Tsosie on the nose with it and actively participated in affray during which his leg was stabbed."* The victim's conduct was used successfully as a mitigating factor to avoid a potentially long prison term. Case Locator - 14 F3D 1438

Diminished Capacity

Using a defendant's reduced mental capacity as a mitigating factor will take a substantial amount of supporting documents and testimony to convince a judge that a reduced sentence is warranted. Successful use of this argument has often involved a mental evaluation by a psychologist who can provide proof that the defendant was clearly suffering from mental challenges during the commission of the offense.

Testimony and letters from doctors, family members, friends, and people known in the community to help to back up the diminished capacity argument are often helpful to a judge in determining the magnitude of the defendant's mental condition. In the next two cases we will see the successful use of this argument and its powerful effect on a sentence. Next is a copy of the sentencing guideline for this argument:

Other Mitigating Factors - 97

5K2.13 Diminished Capacity - "A downward departure may be warranted if:

1) The defendant committed the offense while suffering from a significantly reduced mental capacity;

2) The significantly reduced mental capacity contributed substantially to the commission of the offense. Similarly, if a departure is warranted under this policy statement, the extent of the departure should reflect the extent to which the reduced mental capacity contributed to the commission of the offense."

"However, the court may not depart below the applicable guideline range if (1) the significantly reduced mental capacity caused by the voluntary use of drugs or other intoxicant; (2) the facts and circumstances of the defendant's offense indicate a need to protect the public because the offense involved actual violence or a serious threat of violence; (3) the defendant's criminal history indicates a need to incarcerate the defendant to protect the public; or (4) the defendant has been convicted of an offense under chapter 71, 109A, 110, or 117, of title 18, United States code."

<u>United States vs. Cockett</u> - On November 30, 2000, a jury found Cockett guilty on twenty-one counts for aiding and assisting in false tax returns. The defendant, Virginia Cockett, was a nurse at the Grace Ross Medical Center in Detroit, Michigan. While employed at the hospital the defendant met several individuals who came to the medical center seeking care for their children. The defendant became friends with many of these people and offered to save them money on their tax returns. This offer extended beyond the hospital and throughout a short period of time several individuals sought the help of the defendant.

Cockett then began to help each of these people by inflating figures and entering false information on their tax returns. She requested one-half of the refund received by each individual as compensation for the time spent preparing the return. She also neglected to sign her name on any of the returns as the preparer. The IRS eventually caught up with the defendant and charged her in a twenty-two count indictment for her illegal conduct.

Shortly after being indicted, Cockett began to see psychologist on a weekly basis. The psychologist evaluated her and determined that the defendant was suffering from intermittent immobilizing depression over the past fifteen years. The doctor also stated that the defendant was somewhat naive, rigid, and had difficult being insightful about her own situation. Prozac was prescribed for the defendant.

The court subsequently ordered a psychological evaluation of the defendant to determine her competency to stand trial. A neutral doctor performed the evaluation. The doctor concluded that the defendant was suffering from moderate to severe depression. There was a delay in the start of the trial until the defendant was more competent.

After the trial was complete, a pre-sentence report was ordered. The probation department determined that the defendant had no prior criminal history and that her total offense level was a fourteen. This resulted in a recommended sentence of 15-21 months imprisonment.

A week before the sentencing the defendant filed a motion requesting a downward departure on the recommended sentence due to her diminished capacity and mental condition at the time of the offense. This request was filled pursuant to the sections 5K2.13 and 5H1.6 of the U.S.S.G. Included with this motion were letters from both of the defendant's psychologists regarding their evaluations. The defendant greatly benefited from the information contained in these letters. Inside one of the letters, the psychologist stated, *"On the basis of my interviews with Mrs. Cockett, it appeared to me that although she engaged in illegal behavior, she could not consider herself to have been a conscious and willful law-breaker. Her image of herself is of a person who helps others, rather than a person who takes advantage of them."*

The other psychologist, Dr. Abramsky, stated, *"I have never found that the defendant Ms. C. understood that she actually did something wrong and her denial of responsibility is not a conscious, manipulative or practiced one."* The judge weighed in all the testimony and proceeded to impose a sentence of two years probation on each count to run concurrently. Case Locator - 330 F3D 706

United States vs. Sadolsky - This case is a great example of how the mitigating argument of *"diminished capacity"* can help a defendant. This argument was used successfully by Sadolsky in relation to a gambling addiction that led to fraud charges.

The sentencing commission has made it clear that a gambling addiction is not a valid argument when seeking a reduced sentence under section 5K2 of the sentencing guidelines which includes the diminished capacity provision. However in this case the defendant cleverly used the *"diminished capacity"* argument successfully by showing to the court that the circumstances were unusual and extraordinary and outside the *"heartland"* of a typical case.

This case is not about the reduced sentence that the defendant received but more to show how this argument may be able to help others with cases involving similar circumstances.

In this case the defendant, Michael Sadolsky, pled guilty to computer fraud in a Kentucky District Court in 1999. Sadolsky was a carpet manager at Sears Roebuck & Co. Over a short period of time he was able to devise a plan to access the company's computers and issue himself credits for merchandise that was never returned. The total amount of loss to Sears amounted to $39,477.

The illegal activity was initially uncovered by one of the store managers when the defendant executed a fraudulent credit to his Visa card using one of the store's cash registers and another sales associate's pin number.

Sears reported the incident to the U.S. Secret Service in Louisville, Kentucky for further investigation. When the defendant was interviewed he immediately confessed to the illegal conduct. He was subsequently charged in a seven count indictment in violation of 18 U.S.C. 1030.

Both parties agreed to an offense level of twelve. Since the defendant had no prior criminal history the recommended sentence was 10-16 months imprisonment. The defendant and the government also agreed that there were several arguments that would be left until the sentencing. One of these arguments was the defendant's claim that he committed the offense while suffering from a state of *"significant reduced mental capacity,"* also known as "SRMC," as a result of his gambling addiction. The probation department did not make any recommendation for downward departure on the PSI regarding the mental capacity argument, but did agree that the offense level was a twelve under category one of the sentencing table.

At the sentencing hearing the defendant's attorney began by calling upon three witnesses to reference the defendant's SRMC based on his compulsive gambling. He called on the defendant himself, his wife, and a member of Gambler's Anonymous (GA). Each person then offered up testimony that appeared inline to portray someone with SRMC.

The judge ultimately agreed that there was enough information disclosed to support the defendant's claims of having SRMC and proceeded to reduce the defendant's offense level. The defendant was given a sentence of five years probation, a seven-hundred dollar assessment, and restitution of $39,477.

The government appealed the sentence claiming that the defendant was not entitled to a reduction under 5K2 regarding his claim to have suffered from SRMC. An appeals court reviewed the case about a year later and upheld the sentence. The defendant had won the case successfully using *"significant reduced mental capacity"* (SRMC) as the primary basis for his request for a reduced sentence. The district court agreed to this and subsequently the appeals court agreed also. This was a huge victory for the defendant and for anyone with a case involving similar circumstances.

What made the appeals court rule in favor of the defendant? To begin, the district court granted the departure under 5K2.13 after finding that the defendant's *"capacity was sufficiently impaired to be able to control this particular kind of behavior."* In 1998 the U.S.S.C. added the term *"significantly reduced mental capacity"* to the sentencing guidelines as shown below:

"SRMC" means the defendant, although convicted, has a significantly impaired ability to:

A) understand the wrongfulness of the behavior comprising the offense or to exercise the power of reason; or

B) control behavior that the defendant knows is wrongful;

Another important point about using this argument is that it does not have to be proven that there was a direct link between the defendant's SRMC and the crime charged. Interestingly, other courts have also concluded in similar ways and granted downward departures to defendant's who were compulsive gamblers and who committed crimes not related to gambling, but more importantly, crimes motivated by the defendant's gambling addiction.

One factor that substantially helped the defendant prove that his crime was committed due to his suffering from SRMC was the testimony from William Thomason, a prominent member of Gambler's Anonymous. Mr. Thomason testified about his own experiences with a gambling addiction. His testimony was extremely credible due his twelve years of participation in the GA organization. Mr. Thomason was also the chairperson at one of the weekly GA groups in and around his home. Thomason was also very familiar with the defendant and had spoken with him many times prior to the offense regarding his gambling addiction.

During the sentencing hearing another important piece of information was disclosed to the court. The defendant's attorney cited a section in the Diagnostic and Statistical Manual of Mental Disorders which is considered the standard text of the American Psychiatric Association. In that section it was made known to the court that pathological gambling was listed in the manual as an **impulse control disorder**. This fact likely helped to convince the judge that the defendant's SRMC mitigating factor did in fact warrant a sentence below the recommended guidelines. Case Locator - 234 F3D 945

Rehabilitative Efforts

Rehabilitative efforts have been used in court many times to support the request for a reduced sentence. As we take a closer look at the language set forth in this guideline statement, we will immediately see a loop hole with the word "Post-sentencing" that is used.

5K2.19 Post-Sentencing Rehabilitative Efforts - "Post-Sentencing rehabilitative efforts, even if exception, undertaken by a defendant after imposition of a term of imprisonment for the instant offense are not an appropriate basis for a downward departure when re-sentencing the defendant for that offense. (Such efforts may provide a basis for early termination of supervised release under 18 U.S.C. 3583 (e)(1)."

The guideline clearly mentions only *"Post"* rehabilitative efforts of a person and makes no mention of a defendant who has successfully demonstrated *"Pre-Sentencing"* rehabilitative efforts or *"Post-Arrest"* efforts.

The following case was argued in a clever and prudent manner. Here the defendant, Mr. Decora, successfully argued for a reduced sentence due to his *"Post Arrest"* rehabilitative efforts completely circumnavigating the guideline restriction that clearly mentions only *"Post-Sentencing."*

<u>United States vs. Decora</u> - Here is a case where the judge returned a sentence substantially below the guidelines after some interesting mitigating details were presented to him. In the late 1990's the defendant, Mr. Decora, pled guilty in a South Dakota District Court to one count of assault with a deadly weapon. The defendant's problems began one night after being out drinking with friends. On the way home the defendant was observed speeding and subsequently passed an undercover officer using the *"no passing zone"* of the road. The off-duty officer radioed ahead to another officer who was on duty at the time.

Both officers followed the defendant to his home. When the defendant exited his vehicle he proceeded to walk

Other Mitigating Factors - 103

towards the officers. The officers instructed the man to place his hands on the patrol vehicle. The defendant put his hands on the patrol car for only a brief moment and then decided to remove them without permission. The officers then placed the defendant in handcuffs to further restrain him. As the officers proceeded to escort the defendant to the back seat of the patrol car, the defendant lifted his legs and kicked one of the officers who was sitting in the front of the car. The defendant's leg struck the officer's head.

The officers then extracted the man from the patrol car and a brief struggled ensued.

The defendant was indicted on federal assault charges. After pondering the thought of taking the case to trial, he agreed to plead guilty to one count of assault. The defendant pled guilty at the plea hearing and the PSI was prepared by the probation department. The probation department concluded that the total offense level was a twenty-one under category one of the sentencing table. The defendant did not have any prior criminal history. A level twenty-one in category one of the sentencing table shows a recommended prison sentence of 37-46 months.

During the sentencing hearing the defendant's attorney would use his client's *"post-rehabilitating"* efforts as a powerful mitigating factor. The defendant had an alcohol abuse problem and this clearly was a factor in the offense conduct. Unfortunately, the sentencing guidelines do state that alcohol dependence is not a valid argument that a defendant can use as a mitigating factor. The only hope the defendant had to have his sentenced reduced would be to show the judge the extent of the defendant's *"pre-sentence"* efforts to treat his alcohol problem.

During the sentencing hearing the defendant's attorney disclosed the fact that the defendant had a serious alcohol dependency problem and that alcohol played a large part in the defendant's conduct on the night of the arrest. It was shown to the court that the defendant, while free on bond, successfully completed an extensive in-patient treatment program for his alcoholism disease. He also participated in an alcohol after-care program, and attended regular meetings of Alcoholic's Anonymous. This was substantial documentation showing the defendant's sincere efforts to treat his disease.

The sentencing judge listened to all the facts and details about the defendant's efforts and this was enough for him to impose a sentence below the recommended guidelines. The magnitude of the defendant's post-arrest actions substantiated his request for a reduced sentence and subsequently the judge reduced the sentence to three years probation as opposed to the recommended three years of prison time. The judge also required the defendant to continue with substance abuse programs and to submit to random drug tests by the probation officer, but the smart and sincere efforts of the defendant had earned him a prison free sentence. Case Locator - 177 F3D 676

Aberrant Behavior

Aberrant behavior is a common mitigating factor that is used in court to try and reduce a defendant's sentence. Many times this argument is simply not enough to get a judge to budge on a downward departure because so many offenses committed by first time offenders do have some degree of aberrant conduct involved.

For example, if a defendant and his attorney are contemplating the use of this argument to try and get some sentencing relief, then it must be supported by extraordinary details of the defendant's otherwise very productive, law abiding, family oriented, and hopefully very charitable life.

5K2.20 Aberrant Behavior - "Except where a defendant is convicted of an offense involving a minor victim under section 1201, an offense under section 1591, or an offense under chapter 71, 109A, 110, or 117, of title 18, United States Code, a downward departure may be warranted in an exceptional case if:

1) The defendant committed a single criminal occurrence or single criminal transaction;

2) The occurrence or transaction was committed without significant planning;

3) The occurrence or transaction was of limited duration;

4) The occurrence or transaction represented a marked deviation by the defendant from otherwise law-abiding life;

The court may NOT depart downward pursuant to this policy statement if any of the following circumstances are present:

1) The offense involved serious bodily injury or death;

2) The defendant discharged a firearm or otherwise used a firearm or dangerous weapon;

3) The instant offense of conviction is a serious drug trafficking offense;

4) The defendant has either of the following :

A) more than one criminal history point;

or

B) a prior federal or state felony conviction, or any other significant prior criminal behavior, regardless of whether the conviction or significant prior criminal behavior is countable under Chapter Four of the sentencing guidelines;

United States vs. Blackwell - In this case the defendant, Tracy Blackwell, entered a guilty plea to conspiracy to possess with intent to distribute fifty grams or more of cocaine base (crack). The defendant was originally arrested at a Greyhound Bus terminal in the District of Columbia after agents found more than three hundred grams of crack cocaine in her backpack during a trip to New York with her boyfriend. The defendant told police that her boyfriend made the drug purchase and then gave her the drugs to carry in her backpack. She agreed to a plea deal shortly after her arrest.
 The defendant's total offense level was a thirty-two under category one of the sentencing table. She had no prior

criminal history. The resulting recommended range for imprisonment was a hefty 121-151 months. The defendant could be gone from society for as much as twelve long years. At the sentencing hearing the defendant's attorney used aberrant behavior as the main mitigating factor. Here is the successful arguments that were used to mitigate the potential long prison sentence.

"Defendant, a twenty-seven year old black woman, is the single mother of six young children. The children range in age from four to ten years old, and the youngest has eye problems, and needs medical care. Five of the children presently live with the defendant's mother, whose high blood pressure and heart condition make it difficult for her to continue caring for her grandchildren.

The facts also disclose that the defendant has no criminal history and no history of violent behavior, drug, or alcohol abuse. The defendant remained employed while out on release and was not re-arrested. Moreover, defendant's family members are law abiding, stable people with no known criminal history. Defendant's mother is fifty-four years old, worked her entire life, was never on public assistance, and raised her family in the church. Defendant's two oldest brothers are also employed." We can conclude from the defendant's otherwise law abiding life that this act is clearly one of aberrant conduct, but was this enough for the judge to initiate a downward departure?

Another very important factor in this case is the wording in the defendant's PSI. The probation officer who prepared the PSI inserted wording that stated he agreed the offense was an aberration in the defendant's life. This was a huge plus for the defendant. She now had the probation officer, a neutral body, telling the court in his own words that this offense clearly represented an act of aberrant behavior.

The judge handed down a sentence of fifteen months to be served in a halfway house. The defendant avoided jail time and would still be able to work and stay connected with her family while serving the fifteen months of community confinement. Despite the large amount of cocaine that was found upon the defendant, the solid presentation of mitigating facts involving her family and own personal past behavior enabled her to dodge a prison sentence.

United States vs. Martinez - This case represents an excellent example of the use of family ties and a single act of serious, but also aberrant behavior. Would this argument be enough to convince a judge to depart downward in another otherwise lengthy prison sentence? Here the defendant had an obvious addiction to gambling and pled guilty to armed robbery of a casino in a New Mexico District Court back in 1996. The events unfolded as shown next:

"One day, while off duty, Mrs. Martinez gambled at the casino and hit a $25,000 jackpot. The casino gave her a choice of receiving the payoff in cash or in the form of a check. Mrs. Martinez chose a check because she was concerned about having a large sum of cash in her possession. The Cities of Gold Casino issued a check to Mrs. Martinez, but put a "stop payment" order on the check before Mrs. Martinez was able to deposit it two days later, by that time taking the position that Mrs. Martinez was not permitted to gamble at the time she won her large jackpot. The casino then terminated Ms. Martinez' employment. Since then she has been unemployed for a period of eight months, possibly the longest gap in her forty-one year work history. Unfortunately, because of her age and felony conviction, her prospects for future employment are dim." Mrs. Martinez then gave her own testimony of the events that transpired that evening as follows:

"Her financial matters and gambling addiction would get the best of her. One night after several hours of gambling at another casino Mrs. Martinez arrived home only to keep thinking about how bad her finances had become. We pick up the story now from the mouth of the defendant herself, "After I got back home, I kept thinking about how bad my financial circumstances were, and how much money I owed, my mind kept rehashing the Cities of Gold Casino incident when they refused to pay me my rightful jackpot winnings. My mind kept racing back and forth to all the negative and unpleasant things brought on by my compulsive gambling. I kept thinking about my three loving adult sons who throughout their entire lives have brought me nothing but joy with no disgrace whatsoever. My church came to my mind. A feeling of shame and disgrace overcame me. I thought of my beloved mother who I had recently lost.

108 - Reduce My Prison Sentence

I had taken care of my mother for over forty years and I felt I was utterly shattering the precious memories of her upbringing. The dreaded thought of how I spent the money I had to pay on her funeral expenses that dreadful night at the Cities of Gold Casino when I lost all my money to win the $25,000 jackpot. It was all just unbearable. I felt miserable. I felt suicidal. I just could not cope with it anymore. I wanted out of my whole misery.

I took a gun and one shell from a drawer where it has been kept for years and years. I put the gun and the shell, along with a light rain jacket (it was threatening rain), in the car trunk and got started to Santa Fe, hoping that I could, as in the past, lose myself completely in the gambling but I just couldn't shake my headache and depressed feelings so I decided just to go on with my plans for Santa Fe.

As I approached Santa Fe I decided to head out to the Villa Linda Mall on the south end of town. I thought I could just walk around and try to focus on how I might be able to change my life. I walked the mall for a good while trying to concentrate on what I could possibly do to change my life for the better but it seemed that the more I thought, the worse everything seemed with no apparent solution. I went back to my car and sat there for a good while just watching people go back and forth and could not help but admire and envy those that appeared to be so happy and in control of their lives.

I drive to Rosario Cemetery feeling extremely miserable, knowing what my intentions were. When I got there, I took the purse with the gun and shell from the trunk. I sobbed for quite a while. I prayed that God would forgive me for all of my actions.

My thoughts raced to my three sons, my youngest grandson, my two sisters. I suddenly realized none of them deserved the misery that I would cause them by committing a suicidal act. I could not do this to them. I did not want to leave them. I love them all so very much! I decided to head back home.

I drove heading back to Espanola, my home town. As I approached the Camel Rock Casino I decided to stop and use the restroom and check the dinner buffet line. The minute I walked in I was overcome with such overwhelming emotions I hated myself for being there again. I went back to my parked car. It was there in my car that I felt the horrible hatred towards all Indian Casinos overcome me.

I just decided to go in and take their money as they had been taking it from me for all these years. I took the purse with the gun from the trunk, left the shell behind. I put on some gloves that I had left there all winter. I hurriedly wrote a note to the effect that I wanted a bundle of $100's and one bundle of $50's and put the note in the purse with the gun.

I drove the car up to the front of the casino and I remember much traffic congestion and it seemed like people everywhere. I felt sick and trembling. I parked the car and got out, went inside the casino, stood in line for a cashier, showed the note, got some money, walked out feeling like any second a shot would go though me. As I attempted to open the car door, I felt I was going to collapse. I dropped the purse, picked it up and some of the money fell out. I backed up and drove off. I drove a few miles before I had to stop because I became very sick to my stomach and felt like I was going to pass out. I proceeded to drive home. How I got there I don't know. I remember walking in my home, putting the money in a drawer and then I was sick again."

After Mrs. Martinez pled guilty in federal court, the probation department prepared her PSI. It was determined that the total offense level for the crime was a twenty under category one of the sentencing table. Mrs. Martinez was facing 33-41 months in federal prison for her actions.

While negotiating the plea agreement, both the defendant's attorney and government agreed that there were grounds for a downward departure. The defendant's attorney filed a Motion for Downward Departure with the court and in response the government replied, *"The United States believes there are grounds for departure from the applicable guidelines pursuant to U.S.S.G. 5K2.0."*

At the sentencing the defendant's attorney argued for the reduced sentence using the defendant's aberrant behavior. He discussed her age, sixty-two at the time of sentencing, her flawless employment record, her family ties, and strong family bond, the fact that her emotional suffering contributed to her gambling addiction, and the fact that she would likely be the target of abuse while incarcerated due to her age and meek physical stature.

The fact was then argued that this criminal act, while serious in itself, was truly an act of aberrant conduct, and completely outside the normal realm of the defendant's true character and personality. The defendant's life was discussed extensively during the sentencing hearing and concluded without opposition from the government regarding the request for a reduced sentence. The judge concurred and imposed a sentence of five years probation including six months of home confinement and restitution to the casino. Case Locator - 978 F Supp 1442

Coercion and Duress

5K2.12 Coercion and Duress - "If the defendant committed the offense because of serious coercion, blackmail, or duress under circumstances not amounting to a complete defense, the court may depart downward. The extent of the decrease ordinarily should depend on the reasonableness of the defendant's actions, or the proportionality of the defendant's actions to the seriousness of coercion, blackmail, or duress involved, and on the extent to which the conduct would have been less harmful under the circumstances as the defendant believed them to be. Ordinarily coercion will be sufficiently serious to warrant departure only when it involves a threat of physical injury, substantial damage to property, or similar injury resulting from the unlawful action of a third party or from a natural emergency. Not withstanding this policy statement; personal financial difficulties and economic pressures upon a trade or business do no warrant downward departure."

We can conclude from the above guideline statement that an offense that was the result of blackmail or coercion can be grounds for a reduced sentence. Additionally, if the defendant was under extreme duress at the time when the offense was committed, then this could also warrant a downward departure. Even coercion from law enforcement agencies can be the cause for a reduced sentence under this provision. This next case demonstrates how this mitigating factor was argued perfectly.

<u>United States vs. Juarez</u> - Here is a case where the defendant used the coercion of the government to

Other Mitigating Factors - 111

successfully argue for a lighter sentence. This case unfolded in an Arizona District Court back in the 1990's. The defendant, Joe Juarez, and his brother, were convicted of the sale of firearms and possession of unregistered silencers. The defendant and his brother were involved in an illegal operation where they sold firearms and silencers at swap meets in and around the Casa Grande area in Arizona.

The operation was initially uncovered when the government questioned an individual who they had arrested due to possession of an assault-type MAC 11 firearm. While being questioned, the man described the individuals whom he had made the purchase from. Shortly after, the government sent two agents to a Casa Grande swap meet to look for defendants. The agents found the Juarez brothers who were tending a booth where several firearms and silencers were available for sale. The undercover agents began to question the defendants about the weapons. The agents asked the two if they could convert some of the weapons into fully automatic. They also asked about purchasing a silencer. The defendants were reluctant to answer but told them that they knew a friend that could convert the weapons to fully automatic and that they would have to fill out paperwork in order to get a silencer. The agents continued the conversation with the defendants and left the swap meet with their phone number.

The agents followed up with a phone call and set up a meeting where they claimed they wanted to purchase some weapons. The two agents met the defendants in the parking lot of a department store and purchased a MAC-11 semi-automatic firearm. One of the agents told the defendants that he was a felon and was not allowed to carry a firearm. The defendants told the agents that the gun could not be traced back to them so there was no need to worry.

About two months later, the agents returned to the swap meet to find the defendants again. This time they questioned them again about making a fully automatic MAC-11. One of the brothers conceded this time and told the agents that it would cost five hundred dollars for the conversion plus the cost of the gun. The defendants soon after finished the conversion and then setup another meeting in the department store parking lot to make the sale. It was here that the two were arrested and subsequently charged with the crimes.

A ten count indictment followed and the defendant's attorney was told by the government, "*You may wish to consider that your client and his brother will have to plead guilty very quickly or I will consider filing additional charges against your client for the matters contained in the supplemental reports that I gave you.*"

The defendants rejected the plea offer, proceeded to take the case to trial and were found guilty of all but one of the charges. The defendants now were faced with several years in federal prison. It is interesting to note that the original indictment only contained seven charges but then returned a superseding ten-count indictment after the two refused the government's plea agreement.

Before the sentencing hearing took place the defendant's attorney argued to the court that the government committed outrageous conduct by targeting them even though the government had no evidence that any one of them was engaged in criminal activity. The defendants claimed that the government's actions, after their very first contact with the defendants, fit the description of outrageous conduct. At the sentencing hearing, the court also agreed that a downward departure was appropriate because "*the conduct of this investigation, although not amounting to entrapment, was sufficiently coercive in nature as to warrant a downward departure under Guideline 5K2.1.12.*"

The judge concluded by sentencing the defendants to six months home detention, five years probation, and one hundred hours of community service. The government filed a timely appeal and the appeals court also ruled in favor of the defendant. Case Locator - 992 F2D 896

Lesser Harms

A reduced sentence could be warranted for types of crimes that are overstated by the charging offense or those offenses where a defendant commits a crime to avoid a perceived greater harm, such as a mercy killing. While a murder was still committed, the reasons for it were to

Other Mitigating Factors - 113

prevent the victim from causing greater harm in the future. Examples of crimes in which the seriousness of them are grossly exaggerated by the charged offense, would be an antique collector, who had in his collection a machine gun back from World War II, or a school teacher who possessed a controlled substance for display in a drug education class. While the above two examples are in violation of federal law, there was no underlying intent or conspiracy to cause harm with these items. Here is the legal description for "Lesser Harms."

Lesser Harms 5K2.11 – "Sometimes a defendant may commit a crime in order to avoid a perceived greater harm. In such instances, a reduced sentence may be appropriate, provided that the circumstances significantly diminish society's interest in punishing the conduct. For example, in the case of a mercy killing. Where the interest is punishment or deterrence is not reduced, a reduction in sentence is not warranted. For example, providing defense secrets to a hostile power should receive no lesser punishment simply because the defendant believed that the government's policies were misdirected.
In other instances, conduct may not cause or threaten the harm or evil sought to be prevented by the law proscribing the offense at issue. For example, where a war veteran possessed grenade as a trophy, or a school-teacher who possessed controlled substances for display in a drug education program, a reduced sentence may be warranted.
A simple approach to determining if a specific crime may fall under the lesser harms policy statement would be to determine if the offender possessed an item, that violated a federal law, but its possession was not for an unlawful purpose." The next case is another great example that clearly shows how this argument can be used effectively.

United States vs. Buffalo - The defendant, Michael Buffalo, was arrested for driving while intoxicated after a night of drinking. While being arrested, police officers noticed a twenty-two caliber rifle on the floor of his vehicle. The rifle had a shortened barrel and was unloaded.

114 - Reduce My Prison Sentence

The defendant pleaded guilty in a South Dakota District Court to one count of possession of an unregistered firearm in violation of 26 U.S.C. 5861(d). At the sentencing, Buffalo successfully argued that his crime clearly fell under a lesser harms category. During the sentencing hearing, the defendant testified that the gun was used to shoot skunks, weasels, and raccoons that had been killing his chickens. He further stated that these animals would hide in crawl spaces in the shacks that were next to his house. The defendant claimed that he sawed off the barrel of the gun to make it easier to hunt the animals in the crawl spaces. He testified under oath that this was the only purpose for the weapon.

The defendant's attorney asked for a downward departure under U.S.S.G 5K2.11 for lesser harms. The defendant's attorney also talked about the defendant's strong family ties and responsibilities as well as his favorable employment record and good standing the community. The judge returned a sentence of three years probation with additional conditions requiring alcohol treatment. The defendant was facing up to two years in federal prison and was able to use the several mitigating factors to sway the court into a non-prison sentence. The government was not satisfied and appealed the sentence.

An appeals court reviewed the case about a year later and upheld the sentence. The defendant was able to walk away from court a free man. The appeals court commented on the case as follows:

"At sentencing, the district court based its departure from the guidelines range when the defendant's "conduct does not cause or threaten the harm or evil sought to be prevented by the law proscribing the offense at issue." The district court concluded a downward departure was justified under 5K2.11, after finding that Buffalo did not use the gun in a violent offensive way and that Buffalo's actions were not the kind of misconduct and danger sought to be prevented by the gun statute.

The district court observed that although Buffalo had the gun in his van, the gun was not loaded and there was no ammunition in the van or in Buffalo's possession. The district court also noted that there was no evidence that Buffalo ever brandished the gun or used it in a threatening way, Buffalo

Other Mitigating Factors - 115

had no criminal record, and Buffalo's use of a weapon to shoot animals did not pose any quantifiable risk of accidental harm to others because he lived in a remote area of the reservation.

The district court refused to infer a criminal motive from the nature of the single-shot bolt-action .22. As for the harm targeted by the gun statute, the district court decided the law is meant to protect people from crime and violence, and not to protect predatory animals or restrict the lawful use of weapons."

We can see from even the appeals court's comments that the argument of *"lesser harms"* can put significant weight on a district court to seriously think about the defendant's intent with respect to the charged offense. It the true intent does not fall in line with the charged offense then an argument using the 5K2.11 *"lesser harms"* statement policy may be able to help reduce one's sentence. Case Locator - 47 F3D 60

<u>United States vs. Nunez</u> - This case is an excellent example of how a crime was committed to help prevent a potentially greater harm, that greater harm being a health issue with another individual. This case opened the doors to the broad use of the lesser harms argument. In the 1990's the defendant, Francisco Nunez, was deported from the United States. He was an illegal alien. He returned later that year to help assist his girlfriend who was pregnant with his child and was in need of surgery. He was arrested shortly after authorities became aware of his unauthorized presence back in the United States. Nunez pleaded guilty to illegal reentry in violation of 18 U.S.C. 1326(a)(b). He was now facing a recommended 57-71 months imprisonment for the offense.

At the sentencing the defendant's attorney argued that the defendant committed the offense to prevent a greater harm. This was described as the harm to his girlfriend and unborn child if proper care was not given to her. The defendant insisted that his return to the United States was *"to be responsible for my children."* This put a lot of pressure on the judge to give long thought into the proper sentence for the defendant.

The judge said this at the defendant's sentencing, *"The court is of the opinion that I should not impose a fifty-seven month sentence on this defendant. This defendant did not commit any crimes except for illegal reentry, and he is going to be deported. I am not naive enough to believe that once he is deported he will not come back again, but neither do I believe that once he is deported the government of the United States would be well served by supporting a man in prison for four and one-half years who did nothing more than come back to see his children and assist in the birth of another child. That is just beyond me to do. The court makes a finding that it should depart from the 5K series of the guidelines manual, specifically, 5K2.0, 5K2.11, and 5K2.13.*

In addition to that, the Court believes that 5K2.11 is impacted. It indicates to the Court and to the readers of the guidelines that sometimes the defendant may commit a crime in order to avoid a perceived greater harm. In this instance, the Court finds as factual matter that the defendant perceived that his woman was in grave danger of physical harm, and as father he was responsible for making certain that she received medical care. In that kind of instance, I think that, and so find, a reduced sentence may be appropriate because I believe the circumstances diminish society's interest in punishing his conduct in the case."

The judge then departed from the possible six year prison sentence and imposed a sentence of eight months imprisonment with two years of supervised release. This defendant, who had a prior drug conviction, which was the cause of his initial deportation, came very close to avoiding prison completely due to the true intent of his conduct.
Case Locator - 91 F3D 826

Risk of Abuse in Prison

<u>United States vs. Parish</u> - This next case shows how a defendant used the risk of being abuse in prison as an effective argument against a long sentence of incarceration. The defendant in this case pled guilty to two counts of possession of child pornography back in 2001 in a Montana

District Court. The defendant, Robert Parish, was employed by a company in Bozeman, Montana. In 1999 Parish was terminated from his place of employment as a result of spending too much time on the internet while at work, and also because of abuse of the company's travel allowances. The defendant turned in his laptop computer shortly after losing his job.

While another employee was cleaning out the hard drive one day he noticed images of child pornography. There were multiple images on the hard drive and the employee decided to turn the laptop over to the local police for further investigation. The FBI soon became involved in the investigation. They uncovered over nine thousand images on the defendant's hard drive in which thirteen-hundred contained images of child pornography.

The defendant was subsequently arrested and put in custody. The agents seized the defendant's new laptop from his possession. On this laptop there was also evidence of child pornography as well as emails which involved communication with a fifteen year old female high school student in North Carolina.

The defendant reached an agreement with the government to plead guilty to the two counts of possession of child pornography. His total offense level was a twenty under category one of the sentencing table.

During the interview for preparation of the PSI report the defendant and his attorney tried to convince the probation officer to recommend a downward departure within the report. They had no such luck with this attempt though. The defendant then asked to be examined by the clinical psychologist who was the director of the sex offender treatment unit at the Missoula Regional Prison. The doctor examined the defendant and then testified at the sentencing hearing in the defendant's behalf. This would be the testimony that the defendant needed to help get a reduced sentence. The doctor testified that the defendant's conduct was less culpable than the other ten patients he was treating for the same problems and also the likelihood of recidivism was minimal at best. The defendant's wife, father-in-law, and mother-in-law also testified on the defendant's behalf. The doctor also stated at the sentencing hearing that the defendant's conduct was *"outside the heartland"* of the offense.

The government then presented testimony that told of the multiple graphic images of children who appeared to be only six years old or close to that age. The government also brought attention to the emails found on the defendant's computer as well as some icons on his desktop that served as shortcuts to the pornographic sites.

After the government concluded its testimony the judge called on the doctor once more. The judge then asked the doctor if the facts that he just heard from the government changed his view at all. The doctor once again stated that the defendant's conduct was *"outside the heartland"* of the offense."

During the sentencing hearing a lengthy amount of time was also used talking of the defendant's susceptibility to abuse while in prison. The defendant had a reserved stature and a low key demeanor. The nature of his offense would play a large factor in prison and his life would likely be at risk. The defendant's risk for abuse in prison was effectively compared to one of a police officer who lost his job and then subsequently was sentenced to prison for assaulting a woman.

With all the mitigating arguments now in the court's hands it was time to impose a sentence, one sufficient but not greater than necessary for the offense. The defendant was facing a recommended 33-41 months imprisonment. The defendant's PSI from the probation department did not recommend a downward departure either. A recommendation in the PSI on the defendant's behalf surely would have helped the judge sway in favor of a lighter sentence.

In the end the judge came back with a split sentence for the defendant. It was ordered that the defendant spend eight months in prison and eight months in home confinement. The defendant came close to dodging a prison sentence completely and the eight months of incarceration will surely go by quicker than a sentence of forty-one months. Without the testimony from the psychologist, or the discussion of how this man's safety will be severely jeopardized, a much longer sentence would have likely resulted. Case Locator - 308 F3D 1025

Acceptance of Responsibility

One of the easiest ways to reduce one's offense level and lighten a sentence is the utilization of the sentencing provision for acceptance of responsibility. A defendant who demonstrates an acceptance for their wrong doing can receive a two or three point reduction on his overall offense level. After a defendant pleads guilty and has met the requirements for *"acceptance of responsibility,"* and the government does not object to it, then the probation department will usually agree to it also and calculate the total offense level with the point reduction included.

Regardless if the government or the probation department disagrees with the defendant's eligibility to this point reduction, the final decision will be that of the judge at sentencing. Most of the time this point reduction will be negotiated with a plea deal and mentioned in the *"terms"* of the deal. This is just another important piece of the puzzle that a defendant should consider to help determine whether or not to plead guilty or take a case to trial. Most of the time a judge will deny that a defendant has accepted responsibility for his conduct when the defendant proceeds to trial and thus not entitled to the point reduction. Below is what the sentencing guidelines say about a defendant's acceptance of responsibility:

A - Two Point Reduction - *"If the defendant clearly demonstrates acceptance of responsibility for his/her offense, decrease the offense level by 2 levels."* A defendant can also qualify for a three point reduction but there are additional requirement for this as set forth in U.S.S.G 3E1.1;

B - Three Point Reduction - *"If the defendant qualifies for a decrease under subsection (a), and the total offense level prior to this operation is greater than sixteen, and upon motion of the government stating that the defendant has assisted authorities in the investigation or prosecution of his own misconduct by timely notifying authorities of his intention to enter a plea of guilty, thereby permitting the* *government to avoid preparing for trial and permitting the government and the court to allocate their resources efficiently, decrease the offense level by one additional level."*

The above guideline means two things. First, anyone can qualify for the two point offense level reduction if they demonstrate a clear acceptance of responsibility for their conduct. A plea of guilty is usually the first indication that a defendant has accepted responsibility and will often help the defendant receive the reduction of two points off his offense level provided he has truthfully admitted the conduct compromising of the offense and not denied any wrongdoing.

For the defendant to qualify for the additional one point reduction, he must cooperate with the authorities, give up the option of a trial by jury, and have a total offense level of sixteen or greater before this deduction is applied. Taking a case to trial could disqualify a defendant for any relief under this statute but once again this depends on the individual circumstances. A defendant that drags a case out via trial forcing the government to prove its case, and only admits acceptance for his actions after being found guilty, would likely not receive any deduction under this guideline.

Defendants that plead guilty are more likely to receive the two or three points deduction because most people who plead guilty have already terminated the illegal conduct associated with the offense and shown other acts that define an acceptance of the wrongdoing, such as voluntarily surrendering to authorities and providing restitution to victims. These actions help display the defendant's acceptance of responsibility and secure the award of a points deduction. An exception to this rule would be with a defendant who pleads guilty to a charge of obstruction of justice. Since this offense in itself already shows a un-acceptance for criminal conduct, the defendant would likely not qualify for the point reduction.

This is one method of reducing a sentence before the actual sentencing hearing. If a defendant can reduce his overall offense level by two or three points then this can wipe several months off his sentence. This *"acceptance of responsibility*" award is also a legal caveat that lures defendants into signing a plea deal or pleading guilty, otherwise risking the loss for the chance to get the points deduction because of going to trial or delaying the case for long time.

Ultimately, it will be up to the defendant's attorney to confirm the applicability of the statute with the government during plea negotiations, during preparation of the PSI, and in front of the judge at sentencing. If all parties agree on the two or three point reduction then this will reflect on the defendant's PSI when the probation department calculates the total offense level.

Mitigating Role

Depending on a defendant's role in the offense, a reduction in the offense level may be warranted. The sentencing guidelines contain a section that specifically addresses downward departures for defendants who were minor participants in the offense. Consequently, there is also the possibility for an upward departure in one's offense level if the defendant played a leading role in the offense. Below is a copy of the guideline as it reads in the U.S.S.G:

"Based on the defendant's role in the offense, decrease the offense level as follows:

A) *If the defendant was a minimal participant in any criminal activity, decrease by four levels.*

B) *If the defendant was a minor participant in any criminal activity, decrease by two levels.*

In cases falling between (a) and (b), decrease by 3 levels."

There is no secret strategy to successfully using this sentencing guideline. A defendant and his attorney should thoroughly outline all the facts and details of the offense and determine if this guideline applies.

The guideline also states that there must be more than one participant for a defendant to be eligible for a *"mitigating role"* adjustment. Additionally, if the defendant was part of a group who all participated in the offense conduct, the number of participants who were charged or convicted of the offense is irrelevant for application of this guideline. For example, if the defendant proves he was part of a group, even though he was the only individual charged with the offense, he may still qualify for an adjustment due to his minimal or minor role in the offense.

There are two different parts to this guideline: The first part lowers the offense level by four points for minimal participation in the offense conduct. The second part lowers the offense level by two points for minor participation. Under the guideline, a minimal participant is defined as one who committed the offense without having much knowledge or understanding of the activities of others and overall structure and operation of the illegal enterprise. If the defendant does not qualify under the above description, but is still considered less culpable than the other participants, then he would qualify under a minor participant. An example of someone who would likely qualify for this reduction would be a messenger or delivery man in a drug ring. If this individual was unaware of the scope of the illegal operation and merely took a package from point A to point B, then he may qualify under this guideline and be eligible for a sentence reduction.

This guideline application will depend on the facts that surround the defendant's conduct during commission of the offense. If the defendant does feel that his conduct clearly constitutes a downward departure under this section then it will be up to the defendant's attorney to argue the supporting facts in front of the judge. The prosecution will either agree or disagree to the argument but the final decision is that of the judge. If the defendant's attorney can convince the probation officer to apply the *"mitigating role"* adjustment in the defendant's PSI report, then this will help influence the judge's decision at the sentencing hearing.

5
The 5K1 Motion

Nobody likes to be called a snitch or thought of as one, but a so called snitch can have a lot to gain in a criminal case. If you or someone you know has been charged with a federal crime that involves multiple people then its best to keep silent until that person has had ample time to consult with professional counsel. Once again, the best advice is to keep silent until the time comes to disclose pertinent information. Any information that you may have may be of important negotiating value and this should be discussed with a qualified attorney as soon as possible.

There is a provision in the United States Sentencing Guidelines referred to as the *"5K1,"* formally known as *"5K1.1 - Substantial Assistance to Authorities."* This statute allows the government to file a motion with the court when a defendant has provided substantial assistance in the investigation or prosecution of another person. This motion advises the court of the nature and magnitude of the defendant's assistance and subsequently requests some degree of leniency on the defendant's sentence. The amount of leniency depends on several factors that the judge must factor in his decision at sentencing time. These factors are listed below as follows:

1) The court's evaluation of the significance and usefulness of the defendant's assistance, taking into consideration the government's evaluation of the assistance rendered;

2) The truthfulness, completeness, and reliability of any information or testimony provided by the defendant;

3) The nature and extent of the defendant's assistance;

4) Any injury suffered, or any danger or risk of injury to the defendant or his family resulting from his assistance;

5) The timeliness of the defendant's assistance;

Here is what the sentencing commission states about the 5K1 statute: *"A defendant's assistance to authorities in the investigation of criminal activities has been recognized in practice and by statute as a mitigating sentencing factor. The nature, extent, and significance of assistance can involve a broad spectrum of conduct that must be evaluated by the court on an individual basis. Latitude is, therefore, afforded to the sentencing judge to reduce a sentence based upon variable relevant factors, including those listed above. The sentencing judge must, however, state the reasons for reducing a sentence under this section. The court may elect to provide its reasons to the defendant in camera and in writing under seal for the safety of the defendant or to avoid disclosure of an ongoing investigation."*

Should a defendant ultimately decide not to cooperate or assist authorities with an investigation, then this can not be used against that person as an aggravating sentencing factor. Being offered a 5K1 deal and then refusing to assist will not cause one's sentence to be any harsher than if that same person was never offered the 5K1 deal.

The government is the only entity that can offer a 5K1. Additionally, the greatest chance of receiving a 5K1 proffer is usually in the early stages of one's case. If that defendant has valuable information about particular offense or offenders, then he may decide to disclose the details to the government in return for some degree of sentencing relief.

Most of the time, it will be the defendant that has already worked out a plea deal who is offered a 5K1. The government will likely not offer a 5K1 to a defendant who decides to fight and drag a case through trial forcing the government to allocate much of its time and resources proving the defendant's guilt.

Before the 5K1 is agreed to, the defendant's attorney should make sure that none of the information supplied by the defendant will be used against him for additional charges; this is important! A defendant does not want to reveal facts about other possible illegal conduct, not known about by the government but relevant to the charged offense, unless there is a written agreement not to hold the defendant responsible for the information that is furnished.

Early in one's case is when the possibility of a 5K1 should be discussed with a qualified attorney. If the defendant is pleading guilty via a written plea agreement, then the details of the 5K1 should be clearly listed in the plea agreement. The defendant and his attorney should make sure that the details of the 5K1 are written up exactly as agreed upon. He should never begin any assistance with the government until the plea agreement and pertinent facts about the 5K1 have been thoroughly reviewed for accuracy.

The sentencing hearing will likely be held at the conclusion of the defendant's period of assistance or after the government has determined that enough information has been supplied and the defendant's assistance is no longer required. There have been cases though where a sentencing hearing has been delayed months and even years to allow the defendant to continue assisting authorities with a particular investigation. When this happens a simple *"motion to continue sentencing"* is filed with the court that asks the judge to extend the sentencing date.

Once the sentencing day does arrive, and the government has filed the 5K1 motion, the judge will review the previous five factors to determine how much of a downward departure the defendant should be entitled to for his assistance. The court will also hear testimony from the government concerning their view of the extent and usefulness of the defendant's assistance. Several months, and many times, even years, have been wiped off one's sentence due to the 5K1 motion.

Next, we will review several cases showing examples of reduced sentences that resulted from a defendant's assistance to authorities and the subsequent filing of a 5K1 motion by the government. Before we do this, we want to caution anyone who decides to become a *"rat"* or *"snitch."* Yes, there are plenty of high profile cases that talk of how this guy or that guy *"got away with murder."* Yes, there are also those that decide to snitch in fear of being sent to prison for a long time and for other reasons, but remember this, anyone labeled as a *"rat"* will not be well respected in prison. There have been many instances where a particular snitch has been injured or even killed as a result of telling on others.

Luckily for snitches though, the federal government has a program in place that segregates a snitch from his co-defendants and other inmates that may pose harm. This is done through Central Inmate Monitoring or CIM. Defendants who are involved in cases involving multiple people (i.e., co-defendants) who have been indicted on the same charges are protected in prison from having physical and social contact from each other. The CIM system is especially helpful for co-defendants who have testified against other members of an illegal organization. The CIM program utilizes different prison institutions for each co-defendant and also for any inmates who may pose a safety risk to each other.

Whatever a defendant should decide to do in his case, it should first be discussed with a qualified attorney extensively before deciding anything. There have been instances where the government proffered a 5K1 to a defendant, the defendant accepted the 5K1 and assisted authorities, and then the government refused to file the 5K1 motion with the court claiming that the degree of assistance was not adequate. Although this does not happen that often, it does happen. When a defendant is put in this predicament he will be forced to argue to the court that he kept his end of the agreement and provided whatever information he knew. In a situation like this the defendant's attorney could still request a downward departure under what is known as a "5K2" guideline. This guideline, if accepted by the court, will allow for a downward departure without the requirement of a government motion, which is mandatory for a sentencing reduction under 5K1. If a defendant is unlucky enough to have this happen, he should talk it over with his attorney and explore the 5K2 options. Now let's look at some real cases where a 5K1 motion has helped secure a reduced sentence.

<u>United States vs. Dominquez</u>: In this case involving *"substantial assistance"* the judge decided to give the defendant a second chance in life. The defendant, Ms. Dominquez, entered a plea of guilty in a New York District Court to one count of conspiracy to distribute more than 500 grams of cocaine in violation of 21 U.S.C. 846. Back in

2004, the government charged the defendant along with fifteen others in a large drug distribution ring. The cocaine distribution ring was centered in Rome, New York. Members of the conspiracy gathered large quantities of cocaine and crack cocaine and sent it to the Rome location to break down into smaller quantities and prepare for distribution.

The defendant entered into a plea agreement with the government and was offered a 5K1 in return for a lighter sentence. The defendant proceeded to assist authorities with vital knowledge of the illegal activity and agreed to testify against some of the co-defendants. The defendant was held in custody the entire time until he was sentenced. The defendant also had a prior conviction for possession with intent to sell a controlled substance. This previous conduct was handled in a state court and resulted in a sentence of five years probation.

During preparation of the defendant's pre-sentence report, it was determined that the defendant, due to her prior conviction, was liable for three criminal history points. There was one point added due to her prior conviction and an additional two points added because she was on probation when she committed the most recent offense. It was determined that her past conduct put her in category two of the sentencing table. Her base offense level was a thirty-two and this was agreed upon by all parties. The offense level was reduced by three levels for the defendant's acceptance of responsibility and then by an additional four levels for the defendant's minor role in the offense. The resulting total offense level was a twenty-five.

As an additional aggravating factor, due to the substantial quantity of drugs related in the charges and due to the fact that the defendant had a previous drug charge, Ms. Dominquez was facing a mandatory minimum sentence of twenty years. The applicable mandatory minimum of ten years was hence doubled because of the defendant's prior conviction. If we look at the sentencing table we can see that a level twenty-five under category two of the chart yields a recommended sentence of imprisonment of 63-78 months. Unfortunately, this advisory guideline would be trumped by the mandatory 240 month mandatory minimum sentence that applied. The only hope for the defendant to receive a lighter sentence, and one under the mandatory minimum, would be for the government to file a motion for both the 5K1 and also under 18 U.S.C. 3553(e) to allow the judge to disregard the mandatory minimum when determining the defendant's sentence. The 5K1 would allow the judge to impose a sentence under the advisory guideline of 63-78 months and the 18 U.S.C. 3553 motion would permit the judge to essentially throw out the twenty year mandatory minimum. The only other solution for the mandatory minimum would be if the defendant met the requirements of the *"safety valve."* Since she had more than one history point from a prior conviction though, she was ineligible to qualify for *"safety valve"* relief.

The defendant and her attorney made a prudent move and filed a sentencing memorandum three days before the sentencing. The memorandum stated that the defendant had been confined for over a year due to her current offense. It then talked of how the defendant had virtually turned her life around while locked up. She made good use of her time and held a positive attitude towards post-arrest rehabilitation during her confinement at Montgomery County Correctional Facility. The defendant's attorney noted that she enrolled in several academic courses, held a steady job position in the prison laundry department, and started a women's group which focused on making better life choices. Included in the memorandum were no less than fourteen letters from family members, members of the community, and co-workers which explicitly characterized the defendant as a hard working, capable, and generous person with the benefit of a close network of family and friends who have stood by her and will continue to stand by her and help her stay *"straight"* when she returns home. The memorandum concluded with a request to impose a sentence at the low end of the guideline. This would have resulted in a sixty-three month sentence.

Two days before sentencing, the government filed its memorandum, and with it, a motion under 5K1 for the defendant's substantial assistance and a motion under 18 U.S.C. 35553 (e) to allow the judge to impose a sentence disregarding the mandatory minimum of twenty years. The government also based their calculations on an offense level of thirty-three and recommended a sentence to the judge of 151-188 months imprisonment. The government stated that a sentence in this range "would be reasonable and appropriate based upon all the relevant sentencing factors." The defendant's attorney then filed a supplemental memorandum on the same day in response to the government's motions for downward departure under the 5K1 and 18 U.S.C. 3553 (e) which was filed earlier in the day. The memorandum was written to show that the defendant fulfilled every request asked of her by the government. She exposed herself and her family to substantial risk of injury due to her cooperation. The memorandum concluded with a request for further downward departure based on the magnitude of her cooperation.

At the sentencing, the government conceded that the defendant was remorseful and also that she did indeed have a very supportive family. The government also argued that the extent of her participation in the offense, as well as her prior convictions, were pertinent factors to be considered in determining the correct sentence. The government then asked the court, "to resist the urge to go well below the guideline range because there are factors that come into this case which indicate that she should have learned her lesson, and she did not."

As somewhat of a negative blow to the defendant the government prosecutor made this statement with respect to the assistance provided, "I absolutely did not need her, but we did it anyway, and we gave her a break in that regard." The government concluded stating that they thought the defendant's participation in the criminal activity was greater than reflected in the charge. The defendant spoke to the court briefly and stated, "I am very sorry for the actions that I have chosen in my life. I know if given the chance again, I would make the right decisions, and I want to make the right decisions."

It was now time for the judge to make his decision. Here is how the judge addressed the defendant, "I don't find that your involvement is substantial as the government indicated, but you were involved." The judge then told the defendant that without the government's motions the twenty year sentence would have been required and, "I would have absolutely no discretion in this matter." The judge continued, "Now that the motion has been made, I have discretion to sentence you as to what I feel would be fair and reasonable under the circumstances. I have reviewed and considered all the pertinent information including but limited to the pre-sentence investigation report, submissions by counsel, the factors outlined in 18 U.S.C. 3553, and the sentencing guidelines." The judge then put a smile on the defendant's face. He imposed a sentence of *"time served"* for the previous 464 days spent in confinement and eight years of supervised release. The judge also required the defendant to participate in a substance abuse program and to perform community service. Case Locator - 521 F3D 149

<u>United States vs. Repking</u> - The defendant, Mark Repking, a former bank president, pled guilty in an Illinois District Court to one count each of filing a false tax return and making false entries in bank records. These charges were in violation of 26 U.S.C. 7206(1) and 18 U.S.C. 1005.

The defendant founded the Liberty Bank in Alton, Illinois, back in 2002. During his tenure at the bank he drew up false documents showing that a friend of his had borrowed $350,000 from his bank. Repking's friend asked the defendant to do this so he could expand his construction business. The defendant and his friend continued the scheme by creating false bank records to conceal the conduct. The pair then began cashing checks on the false account causing a large overdraft condition. In addition to this, the defendant was skimming funds from the bank for personal use.

Eventually the government initiated an investigation into the bank's activity. When the defendant became aware of the government's investigation he quickly resigned from his position. He was questioned by authorities and agreed to enter into a plea agreement and cooperate with investigators in exchange for the possibility of a reduced sentence under the 5K1 guideline. During the investigation, the government determined that, in addition to the illegal bank activity, the defendant failed to report his year end bonuses to the IRS resulting in unreported income of approximately $240,000.

It was determined that the defendant had a total offense level of twenty-two under category one of the sentencing table. This offense level gave a recommended range of 41-51 months imprisonment for the defendant. The pre-sentence report estimated total losses to be $976,046.

Shortly before sentencing, the defendant's attorney filed a sentencing memorandum that requested a reduced sentence. He based this request on his charitable works and submitted several letters written by family members and friends telling of the defendant's good deeds. At the sentencing hearing the primary focus was on the nature and extent of the defendant's assistance to the government. The government, prior to sentencing, filed a motion for 5K1 and asked the court to impose a twenty-four month prison sentence for the defendant's conduct. The defendant's attorney presented the facts and details of the defendant's assistance to the judge. This included his extensive cooperation with the investigation and the investigation of his friends, assistance with information on an unrelated tax investigation, consent to be barred from future FDIC participation, and consent to forfeit $100,000 in addition to his restitution.

During the sentencing hearing, when the judge asked the defendant why he committed the offenses, the defendant replied, "*Success came to me too early in life. I have a problem pleasing people and I take full responsibility for my actions.*" The defendant continued on by accepting and showing full responsibility for his conduct to the court. The judge then announced that while he was initially planning on a harsher sentence, the defendant's allocution had changed his mind. A sentence was imposed consisting of six months home detention, one day imprisonment, nine-hundred hours of community service, $100,000 in fines and a forfeiture of $75,000. Case Locator - 467 F3D 1091

United States vs. Christenson - The defendant in the case was convicted via a guilty plea to conspiracy to distribute 500 grams of methamphetamine. The penalties for any crime involving "*meth*" are severe and the defendant was facing twenty years in federal prison for the conviction. The defendant made the decision to cooperate with the government in exchange for a 5K1 agreement as set forth in the defendant's plea agreement. The defendant assisted the government and offered up information involving the investigation and prosecution of others who were also involved in the illegal conduct. The defendant also clearly admitted her involvement with the conspiracy and testified in front of a grand jury. She continued her assistance by offering to complete a controlled purchase of drugs. These controlled drug purchases put the defendant's safety in jeopardy especially if something went wrong with the drug purchase. This magnitude of assistance by the defendant was important during the sentencing hearing and is one of the determining factors used by the judge when determining an appropriate sentence reduction for 5K1 assistance.

When the sentencing day came, the government spoke and requested only a mere ten percent reduction in the defendant's sentencing guideline range. The result of this would have only been about two years off the recommended twenty year prison term. The defendant's attorney argued for a better deal and gave the court precise details of how it was the defendant's assistance that led authorities to additional arrests. Her level of cooperation was deserving of much more than ten percent. Her attorney finished off his testimony making it known to the court that his client's assistance put her in imminent danger and her life was at stake while assisting the government with undercover controlled purchases of illegal drugs.

The judge evaluated the extent, truthfulness, and usefulness of the defendant's assistance and returned with a sixty month prison sentence for the defendant, seventy-five percent less than the recommended guideline. The government was not happy with the sentence and appealed it to a higher court. About a year later an appeals court reviewed the case and ruled in favor of the defendant. If the defendant is able to get placement in the federal RDAP, receive good time credit, and obtain six months or more in a halfway house, she could very easily walk out of federal prison after two to three years. Case Locator - 403 F3D 1006

United States vs. Coyle - The defendant, Ms. Coyle, was convicted in an Iowa District Court of conspiracy to distribute methamphetamine. The defendant agreed to cooperate with the government in return for a 5K1.

The defendant immediately began to work undercover making controlled purchases of illegal drugs and testifying in court against other suspects involved in the conspiracy.

At the sentencing hearing, the government spoke of the extent of the defendant's cooperation. The defendant's attorney also made it known to the court that due to the extreme nature of assistance supplied, there were numerous threats made to her and her family. Judges will sometimes calculate a greater sentence reduction when the defendant encountered additional risks and threats while assisting authorities. Unfortunately, due to the seriousness of the defendant's offense, she was facing eleven to fourteen years in a federal prison.

The government filed the 5K1 motion before the sentencing and asked the court for only a fifteen percent sentence reduction. The defendant's attorney countered that request with his own request for a fifty percent sentence reduction. The government did file two important motions in the defendant's behalf though. They first filed the motion for 5K1 which would allow the judge to impose a sentence under the recommended guideline range of eleven to fourteen years. Additionally, since the defendant was subject to a ten year mandatory minimum prison term, it was imperative for the government to also file a motion pursuant to 18 U.S.C. 3553 which would also allow the judge to impose sentence without regard to the ten year mandatory minimum sentence.

Remember, so often in drug cases there will be a total offense level that dictates a certain advisory sentencing range and also a mandatory minimum sentence that applies depending on the quantity of drugs charged in the offense. In any case where the defendant has both sentences to deal with, it is important that the government files both motions (i.e., 5K1 and 18 U.S.C. 3553 motions) to allow the judge to reduce the sentence as he sees fit. See the section in this book titled *"Getting Around Mandatory Minimums"* for more information on the safety valve and mandatory minimums.

In this case, the government did indeed agree to file both motions; the 5K1 and the 18 U.S.C. 3553 with the court. During the sentencing hearing, the judge commented with the following remarks, *"Based on my evaluation of the substantial assistance you have provided using the five factors set forth in United States Sentencing Guideline 5K1.1, I am going to reduce your sentence to thirty-six months."* The defendant was able to obtain seventy-three percent reduction in her sentence and will likely walk out of prison after about two years with good time credits applied and some time in a halfway house. Case Locator - 429 F3D 1192

United States vs. Livesay - The defendant, Mr. Livesay, was a businessman who was indicted for fraud in 2007. The offense conduct involved a one billion dollar fraud scheme that was eventually exposed and discovered by authorities. The defendant pled guilty to the charges and was facing a possible fifteen years behind bars. His total offense level as calculated by the probation department was a twenty-eight. The defendant had no prior criminal history. The sentencing table as shown in category one showed a recommended sentence of 78-97 months imprisonment.

The defendant was offered a 5K1 and decided to assist the authorities. During the time between the defendant's plea hearing and the sentencing hearing, substantial assistance was provided regarding information on the illegal fraud scheme. The defendant provided much useful information about the illegal activity and the government subsequently filed the 5K1 motion with the court prior to sentencing. At the sentencing hearing, the judge imposed a sentence consisting of home confinement with probation. The defendant was able to dodge a potentially long prison sentence and continue on with his life.
Case Locator - 409 F3D 105

United States vs. Burns - In this case, the defendant was still given a heavy prison sentence but he was originally facing thirty years to life in prison. In 2005 the defendant, James Burns, pled guilty in an Iowa District Court to one count of conspiracy to manufacture and distribute fifty grams or more of methamphetamine. Until the defendant pled guilty to the charge, the government's intention was to seek a life sentence due to the defendant's extensive criminal past. With the guilty plea also came a government request for a downward departure via a 5K1 motion and a motion under 18 U.S.C. 3553(e) to allow sentencing under the mandatory minimum.

The total offense level called for thirty years to life imprisonment for the defendant. If he should be sentenced to life then there would be no chance for parole as parole has been abolished in the federal system. The defendant, soon after his arrest, began to supply substantial information to the government about several groups who were involved in the manufacturing of methamphetamine. The defendant also assisted by testifying before a grand jury two times.

At the sentencing hearing, the government asked the judge for only a fifteen percent sentence reduction. The result still would have been a twenty-five year prison sentence for the defendant. Luckily, because of the defendant's substantial assistance, the judge rejected the government's request for the fifteen percent reduction and proceeded to impose a sentence that was sixty percent less than the recommended guideline. This still resulted in a twelve year prison term but when compared to life in prison this was a huge victory for the defendant. The 5K1 greatly helped this defendant avoid life in prison.

The judge gave his statement of reasons as to the sixty percent reduction as follows, *"I am going to use 360 months as a starting point. In this case I specifically find under the 5K1 factors, factor number 5, the timeliness of the defendant's assistance. The defendant was exceptionally timely in this case. My understanding is he started cooperating as soon as he was arrested. To me that's exceptional timeliness. Factor number 4 does not apply, any injury suffered or danger of risk, because I have not heard anything beyond that. Number three, the nature and extent of the defendant's assistance. In this case, based on the representations of the United States assistant US attorney I find that the defendant provided every single bit of information he knew, so the extent of the defendant's assistance could not be greater in the sense that he provided every single bit of information he knew. Now for some reason which the government refused to disclose, they only recommended fifteen percent. The government refuses to indicate how any one of the five 5K1 factors affect the fifteen percent recommendation. Having taken into consideration the fact that the defendant scores very highly on the second factor, the third factor, and the fifth factor, I am going to reduce the defendant's sentence substantially in this case."*

With good time credit and possibly admission into the Residential Drug Abuse Program (RDAP), this individual will have a second chance at life and be out of prison in as little as eight to nine years. This surely is more tolerable than waking every day with a life sentence. Case Locator - 438 F3D 826

United States vs. Pearce/Chapman - In this particular drug case, the two defendants decided to plead guilty to conspiracy to distribute cocaine and also offer assistance to the government in return for a 5K1 motion. The charges for the offense involved an undercover purchase of one-quarter kilogram of cocaine that the defendants sold for $4500. One of the defendants brokered the deal while the other brought the cash and picked up the drugs. They were both arrested after the deal was made with an undercover agent.

The two defendants soon after provided assistance to the government regarding their case and other cases being investigated. In the 5K1 motion, the prosecution stated that the level of assistance provided by the defendants was *"instrumental in assisting law enforcement agents in a particular investigation which resulted in the arrest of another individual who will be prosecuted in either federal or state court."*

The total offense level for each defendant was a twenty-nine. Both individuals had an extensive past criminal history which earned them enough criminal history points to have their offense level placed in category six of the sentencing table. They were each facing 151-188 months in federal prison. During the sentencing hearing, the defendant's attorney pointed out that both defendants had assisted the government for over seven months in the investigation and prosecution of others. The defendants also made several controlled purchases of drugs during this period. They were both known as good fathers and husbands who got caught up in the wrong business. It was further made known to the court that over ten years had passed since a previous offense was committed by either defendant.

The judge considered the level of assistance provided by the defendants to be substantial and the amount of time spent assisting the government to be extraordinary. Their assistance led to additional arrests and this was a factor when calculating any sentence involving a 5K1. He handed down a split sentence to the defendants consisting of five months imprisonment and five months in a halfway house.
Case Locator - 191 F3D 488

United States vs. Johnson - The defendant in this case was facing a possible twenty years to life in federal prison for narcotics trafficking. Mr. Johnson pled guilty in a South Carolina District Court to possession with intent to distribute fifty grams or more of crack cocaine. As part of the plea agreement, the defendant agreed to assist in the ongoing investigation of the importation and distribution of controlled substances and other related offenses. He began his cooperation shortly after being indicted and continued helping while free on bond. The defendant assisted authorities by completing multiple controlled purchases of crack cocaine from other dealers. The assistance provided by the defendant led to the arrest of four additional individuals.

At the sentencing hearing, the defendant's attorney used the extensive amount of assistance provided by the defendant as the primary argument for a reduction sentence. The judge departed from the recommended guidelines and imposed a sentence of eighty-four months imprisonment. This sentence would enable the defendant to possibly walk out of prison in as little as four years when factoring in good time credits, possible placement in the RDAP, and several months in a halfway house.
Case Locator - 393 F3D -466

When fate hands us a lemon, let's try to make lemonade.
> - **Dale Carnegie**

6
Getting Around Mandatory Minimums

Federal drug charges carry with them some of the stiffest penalties around causing prison overcrowding at an alarming rate. Yes, of course we must try our best to keep deadly drugs away from our children and off the street, but sentencing procedures under federal laws for even the most minute quantity of narcotics are harsh at best.

In 2010 we saw the second amendment to the *"crack cocaine"* sentencing guidelines. This amendment changed the triggering threshold amounts for the mandatory minimum prison terms for crack cocaine. This is a small step in the right direction to address the many problems involving the federal prison system. We all know drugs are dangerous, potentially deadly, and addicting in many cases, but locking someone up for ten years after a typical first time, non-violent drug offense is surely not the answer to the war on drugs. If you or someone you know has been unfortunate enough to have been busted by the feds for a drug offense, and this is the first offense, then there is a statute in the federal system which may be able to help when facing a mandatory minimum sentence for the charge.

A mandatory minimum sentence, also called an MM, is a sentence for specific federal offenses where a judge must impose at least the length of sentence that the *"minimum"* dictates. For example, if someone got pulled over by a law enforcement officer and was subsequently caught and charged with federal possession with intent to distribute six grams of cocaine, that person would be subject to an MM sentence of five years. If the charge though was only for simple possession then the mandatory minimum would not apply. With the charge of possession to distribute, the judge would be forced to sentence the individual according to two sentencing guidelines in this case: the first being the mandatory minimum sentence of the five years; the second being the total offense level for the specified charge(s).

For example, let's say John Doe had a total offense level of fifteen for a drug offense in which he was also facing a mandatory minimum of sixty months. The judge would have these two guidelines to consider when sentencing John. First, he would look at the guideline offense level of fifteen. If the defendant had no criminal history then a level fifteen on the sentencing table under category one would give a recommendation of 18-24 months imprisonment. The judge would then look at the mandatory minimum, if any, and consider the length of that term. In this case the judge would have no choice but to impose a sentence of at least sixty months due to the application of the mandatory minimum. If there was no mandatory minimum, or if the defendant was able to use a statute to circumvent the mandatory minimum, then the judge would be able to impose a sentence using the guideline range of 18-24 months. If the defendant could use a sentencing provision to nullify the mandatory minimum then he would have a great shot at an eighteen month sentence or less compared to the mandatory five year sentence. Well, there is indeed two possible remedies available to a defendant facing a mandatory minimum sentence, both which we will discuss in this chapter.

There is another scenario to this situation though. What if this defendant had both an offense level and mandatory minimum that applied to the charge, but the length of the mandatory minimum term was less than the low end of the offense level? For example, let's say that the defendant had an overall offense level of twenty-six on the sentencing table that recommended 63-78 months. The defendant was also facing a mandatory minimum sentence of five years. In this particular case the judge would likely impose a sentence using the highest guideline (i.e., 63-78 months). The judge would impose a sentence using the offense level of twenty-six since the advisory guideline of 63-78 months imprisonment is higher than the mandatory minimum of five years (sixty months). In this particular case the mandatory minimum term would not become an aggravating factor in the sentencing unless the judge was planning on imposing a reduced sentence under the mandatory minimum but was unable to because of it.

With that said, there will be only two ways to get around a mandatory minimum sentence. The first is with the help of the government. In this situation the government would file a motion pursuant 18 U.S.C. 3553(e) that would instruct a judge to impose a sentence without regard to any mandatory minimum sentence. This type of motion is commonly used in combination with a 5K1. The second method which a defendant can qualify to get around a mandatory minimum is called the *"safety valve."* The *"safety valve"* sentencing relief provision is only available for drug offenses. This provision is not applicable for other types of offenses like fraud, tax evasion, bribery, etc. Additionally, a defendant must meet certain criteria to be eligible for the *"safety valve"* and these will be discussed shortly.

Before we discuss these requirements, we want to briefly talk about the specific quantities of narcotics that do trigger the mandatory minimum sentences. As set forth in Title 21 of the United States Code, a person will be subject to a five year mandatory minimum sentence of imprisonment if he has been charged with any of the following:

5 or more grams of cocaine
100 or more grams of heroin
10 or more grams of PCP
1 or more grams of LSD
100 or kilograms of marijuana
100 or more marijuana plants
5 or more grams of methamphetamine

That same person would be subject to a ten year mandatory minimum sentence for the following quantities of narcotics:

50 or more grams of cocaine
1 or more kilograms of heroin
100 or more grams of PCP
10 or more grams of LSD
1000 or more kilograms of marijuana
1000 or more marijuana plants
50 or more grams of methamphetamine

Upon a second conviction for a similar offense, these mandatory minimums double, and for those who have two or more convictions the mandatory minimum sentence can be as harsh as life in federal prison.

Now, anyone who has been charged with a federal drug offense, who is facing a mandatory minimum sentence, needs to swiftly determine if they do indeed qualify for the *"safety valve."* Your attorney may or may not know the requirements of the *"safety valve"* off the top of his head but we will guess that he won't. Some attorneys who do not practice in the area of federal drug laws will not even be aware that this statute exists. This is why it is ever so important to find an attorney experienced in federal criminal law and in the subject of law that is related to the charged offense(s).

For a defendant to be eligible for the *"safety valve"* there are five requirements by law that the defendant must meet. Let's use our friend John as an example. John was facing a sixty month mandatory minimum sentence for his federal offense. In order for John to get around this mandatory minimum he must meet the following five requirements for *"safety valve"* eligibility;

First, John must have not more than one criminal history point. If John has no prior convictions or prison sentences then he is good to go on this part. In order to have more than one criminal history point John would likely have to have been convicted of a felony and spent some time in prison within the last ten years.

Second, there must not have been any serious bodily harm or death associated with the offense. If there was any harm inflicted on anyone during the commission of the offense then this would disqualify that person from qualifying for the safety valve.

Thirdly, John must not have possessed a weapon or used violence in connection with the offense. This violence could have been in the form of a verbal threat or actual physical harm.

For the fourth requirement, John must not have been an organizer, leader, supervisor, or manager of others who were involved in the offense, nor must he be engaged in any continuing criminal enterprise. A continuing criminal enterprise, loosely defined, is a business that involves the distribution and sale of illegal drugs operated by five or more individuals. This operation must also make substantial income to qualify as a criminal enterprise.

The fifth and final requirement for John to qualify for the safety valve would be for him to provide to the government all information he has concerning the offense. This does not mean he will have to testify against others or make undercover drug purchases. He only must disclose the information he has about the charged offense and relevant conduct. This information must be furnished at some time no later than the sentencing hearing.

If John meets all of the requirements for this statute then it will surely help him at sentencing any time when a mandatory minimum applies. After it has been determined that John is eligible for the safety valve it will then be up to John's attorney to make sure the prosecutor and the probation department are also in agreement with John's eligibility. If there is disagreement as to the defendant's eligibility then these arguments will be resolved at the sentencing hearing. It will be at this hearing also when John's attorney will argue for a particular sentence or sentence range for John with the benefits of the safety valve factored in to the equation. Once the judge has agreed to the defendant's safety valve eligibility he will then have the ability to impose a sentence without regard to the once mandatory minimum term of imprisonment.

There is one caveat to the safety valve though. The guideline states that if the offense committed was punishable by a minimum statutory sentence of at least five years, and that person qualifies for the safety valve, then the minimum offense level must be no less than a seventeen. This rule applies to everyone facing a mandatory minimum sentence. What does this mean for John? Well, John's offense level will actually now be increased from the original ten to a seventeen on the sentencing table. Regardless of the fact that the judge will be able to overlook the minimum mandatory sentence of five years for John's offense, he must still use the overall offense level to determine his sentence. Now though, that offense level has been increased to a seventeen. What can John do to get that offense level reduced further? There may still be help ahead that John can use to his advantage.

144 - Reduce My Prison Sentence

John passed up a trial by jury and decided to plead guilty to the charge. Due to the fact that John accepted full responsibility, pled guilty, and disclosed all information known to him about the offense, he would be eligible for a two point reduction for his acceptance of responsibility. We talked about the offense level reduction for *"acceptance of responsibility"* back in chapter four of this book.

Now, with the addition of the two point reduction, John's total offense level will be back down to a fifteen. Looking at the sentencing table, we can see that an offense level of fifteen in category one gives a recommendation of 18-24 months imprisonment. This would be the recommended sentence range for John and many times the judge will hand down a sentence in this range. It will then be up to John and his attorney to find other ways to help reduce his sentence even further. John should work with his attorney and bring any and all ideas and mitigating arguments forward to help obtain an even lower sentence. If all else fails and John is sentenced to eighteen months imprisonment, with good time credit and some halfway house time he would most likely walk out of prison after ten to twelve months. This is a huge difference when compared to the five year mandatory minimum sentence that once lurked. A copy of the safety valve guideline as set forth in the U.S.S.G is shown below:

§5C1.2. - Limitation on Applicability of Statutory Minimum Sentences in Certain Cases (i.e., SAFETY VALVE)

(a) Except as provided in subsection (b), in the case of an offense under 21 U.S.C. § 841, § 844, § 846, § 960, or § 963, the court shall impose a sentence in accordance with the applicable guidelines without regard to any statutory minimum sentence, if the court finds that the defendant meets the criteria in 18 U.S.C. § 3553(f)(1)-(5) set forth below:

(1) the defendant does not have more than 1 criminal history point, as determined under the sentencing guidelines before application of subsection (b) of §4A1.3 (Departures Based on Inadequacy of Criminal History Category);

(2) the defendant did not use violence or credible threats of violence or possess a firearm or other dangerous weapon (or induce another participant to do so) in connection with the offense;

(3) the offense did not result in death or serious bodily injury to any person;

(4) the defendant was not an organizer, leader, manager, or supervisor of others in the offense, as determined under the sentencing guidelines and was not engaged in a continuing criminal enterprise, as defined in 21 U.S.C. § 848; and

(5) not later than the time of the sentencing hearing, the defendant has truthfully provided to the Government all information and evidence the defendant has concerning the offense or offenses that were part of the same course of conduct or of a common scheme or plan, but the fact that the defendant has no relevant or useful other information to provide or that the Government is already aware of the information shall not preclude a determination by the court that the defendant has complied with this requirement;

(b) In the case of a defendant (1) who meets the criteria set forth in subsection (a); and (2) for whom the statutorily required minimum sentence is at least five years, the offense level applicable from Chapters Two (Offense Conduct) and Three (Adjustments) shall be not less than level 17.

Now that you have a general idea about the requirements for eligibility of the safety valve and how it can help a defendant facing a mandatory minimum prison sentence, let's take a look at some real life cases where the safety valve was used to reduce one's sentence. Anyone facing federal drug charges that involve a mandatory minimum sentence should carefully examine each of these following cases to see just how valuable the safety valve sentencing relief provision of the law can be.

United States vs. Hendricks - This case is a great example of how the safety valve provision helped to give someone a second chance at life. Mr. Hendricks, the defendant, entered a guilty plea in a Iowa District Court for possession with intent to distribute crack cocaine. The defendant had a prior felony drug conviction which made this offense punishable by a mandatory minimum twenty year prison sentence.

The defendant and his attorney went to work to find some type of resolution to this harsh sentence. For the defendant to qualify for the safety valve he would have to have no more than one criminal history point. Luckily, the probation department, who prepared the defendant's PSI, concluded that Mr. Hendricks did only have one criminal history point from his prior conviction, therefore meeting the first part of the safety valve requirement.

It was also confirmed that Mr. Hendricks did not use violence or threats of violence, did not possess a firearm or other dangerous weapon, nor was there any serious bodily injury or death that resulted from the drug offense. He also was not classified as a leader or organizer of any other people in connection with the offense and agreed to offer any and all information about the offense to the government before his sentencing hearing. The government also agreed that the defendant met all requirements set forth in the safety valve provision as well as the probation department.

After the defendant disclosed the information about the offense to the government, the requirements for eligibility of the safety valve were then satisfied. The defendant could now be sentenced according to his offense level, which was a twenty-five, and without regard to the mandatory twenty year prison sentence.

At the sentencing hearing, the defense attorney argued for a lenient sentence and was able to help convince the judge to hand down a sentence that shaved 164 months off the once mandatory twenty year sentence. The defendant walked out of court with a fifty-six month term of imprisonment. With good time credit, possible acceptance into the residential drug program (RDAP), and maximum placement in a halfway house, Mr. Hendricks could easily walk out of prison in as little as three to four years.

Case Locator - 171 F3D 1184

United States vs. Martinez - The defendant, Gabriel Martinez, was charged along with his son in a two count indictment for conspiracy in violation 21 U.S.C. 846 and possession of cocaine with intent to distribute in violation of 21 U.S.C. 846. The father and son owned a trucking company in California which was being used to transport illegal narcotics. Through the assistance of a confidential informant, a meeting was arranged between the two defendants and an undercover DEA agent to discuss transportation of some cocaine. The undercover agent posed as a Latin drug king and offered to pay the defendant three hundred dollars for each kilogram of cocaine that the defendants transported for him. The undercover agent and the defendant scheduled the first load of drugs to be transported to San Francisco, CA. The estimated total amount to be moved was one hundred kilograms. The defendant and his son agreed to make the delivery and the defendant's son proceeded to the pre-arranged address to pick up the shipment. After the cargo was loaded into the defendant's trailer the defendant's son was arrested. Shortly after, the father was also arrested and held in custody. They were then charged in the two count indictment.

    A trial took place in a California District Court where the defendant and his son were found guilty of both charges. Since their intentions were to transport approximately one hundred kilograms of cocaine, and this is the quantity of drugs they were charged with in the indictment, the total offense level was calculated to be a thirty-six. The defendants did not have any prior criminal history therefore the offense level as seen under category one of the sentencing table called for a recommended prison sentence of 188-235 months. Worse yet was the twenty year mandatory minimum sentence that applied to the defendants due to the large quantity of cocaine involved in the offense.

    The safety valve is the only law provision without needing a government motion that will allow a judge to disregard a mandatory minimum sentence in a drug offense. Luckily, the defendants did meet the requirements set forth for the safety valve provision and the judge now could impose a sentence using the offense level guideline rather than twenty year mandatory minimum that was applied.

Since the offense level was so high though, both defendants were still facing a recommended guideline range of 188-235 months imprisonment.

It was now time for the defendant and his attorney to gather up every possible mitigating factor to substantiate a downward departure from the offense level. Multiple mitigating arguments were presented to the judge at the sentencing hearing. The defendant's attorney used a number of factors such as aberrant behavior, roles in the offense, entrapment by the government, and acceptance of responsibility to help secure a lower sentence for the defendants.

At the sentencing hearing, the court did acknowledge the eligibility of the safety valve for each defendant. The defendant's attorney then began his arguments to try and lower the offense level. He first discussed the defendant's minor roles in the offense and how they were nothing more than delivery drivers for the drugs. It was also argued that the defendants should receive a reduction in the offense level because their offense conduct did not involve any leadership or management roles. The defendant's attorney argued for a two point reduction in the offense level because the defendants had nothing to do with the original transaction and were only brought into the deal after all the transactions and arrangements were made.

Next up was the argument of entrapment. The defendant argued that he was clearly entrapped by the undercover DEA agent. The judge commented, *"Drug agents can decide, apparently without any supervision by anybody to negotiate with somebody for an ounce, a pound, a kilo, 100 kilos, a million kilos of substance, of course, if the defendant bites at the bait, then that amount chosen by the drug agent will determine his drug sentence."*

The argument of aberrant behavior on behalf of the defendants came up next. Aberrant behavior is the appropriate name for any type of conduct a person exhibits that falls outside the norm for that person's typical behavior. The court can depart downward when aberrant behavior is proved. The defendant's attorney argued that there was no clear evidence showing either defendant was part of any type of ongoing criminal enterprise or other

Getting Around Mandatory Minimums - 149

illegal acts, therefore falling in the category of aberrant behavior.

Then came the request for a downward departure for the defendant's acceptance of responsibility. Here is the judge's response to that, *"The defendant qualifies for a three point reduction under the first prong of 3E1.1(b), as he had timely provided information to the government concerning their involvement in the offense."*

These arguments required substantial time and effort by the defendant's attorney to prepare an effective presentation. Additionally, a stack of supporting documents, prepared by the defendant's attorney was used at the sentencing hearing to substantiate the request for a reduced sentence. It was also likely that the defendant did a lot of work in this case contributing vital information to warrant a reduced sentence. In the end, the judge reduced the offense level by ten points and sentenced the defendant and his son to sixty-three months imprisonment. The hard work of the defendant and his attorney helped wipe off the approximately fifteen years of prison time. With good time credit, possible admittance into the residential drug program (RDAP), and a few months of halfway house placement, the defendants could be out of federal prison after two to three years. Case Locator - 993 FSUPP 766

United States vs. Clavijo - In this case the defendant, Mr. Clavijo, was convicted in a Florida District Court on his plea of guilty to conspiracy of possession with intent to distribute marijuana, and possession of marijuana. The defendant worked in two grow houses which were the target of the investigation. There was also a third grow house that was also part of the investigation but the defendant did not perform any work at that location. During the search of the third grow house, a shotgun was found and seized as evidence. The defendant claimed he had no knowledge of this shotgun and again stated that he only worked in the two other grow houses and not the grow house where the weapon was found.

After the plea hearing, the judge ordered for the PSI to be prepared. During the preparation of the defendant's PSI, the probation officer came to the conclusion, using the broad language for what legally defines "*possession,*" that the defendant was accountable for *"possession of a firearm."* This caused the defendant to receive a two level enhancement to his base offense level. This enhancement, along with the wording in the PSI that described the defendant as being in possession of a firearm would make him ineligible for any sentencing relief under the safety valve guidelines..

Additionally, due to the fact that the defendant's charges involved more than 100 marijuana plants, he would be subject to a minimum mandatory sentence of five years imprisonment. The defendant's overall offense level was a seventeen for the charges. With an offense level of seventeen and a category one for criminal history, the sentencing table called for a recommended sentence of 24-30 months. Without the protection of the safety valve this man would be sent to prison for five years due to the mandatory minimum that applied.

At the sentencing hearing, the judge agreed with the opinion of the probation officer and concluded that the defendant was indeed in possession of a firearm when he really was not. The judge had no options but to impose a five year prison sentence. After the sentence was imposed, even the government argued in the defendant's behalf stating that he was not factually in possession of the firearm. The defense tried to sway the judge also, but with no success and the five year sentence stood firm.

While serving the sixty month term in a minimum security federal prison camp, the defendant filed a timely appeal and waited for his case to be heard. About a year later, an appeals court reviewed the case and ruled in favor of the defendant. The appeals court agreed that it was the co-defendant that had possession of the firearm and that the defendant should be entitled to relief via the safety valve because he now met all the requirements for eligibility. The appeals court vacated the sentence and it was scheduled for re-sentencing. The defendant was later sentenced to eighteen months imprisonment for the offense and walked out of prison a free man. Case Locator - 165 F3D 1341

United States vs. Roque - This case clearly defines how the safety valve can help a defendant receive a substantially reduced prison term. The defendant, Mr. Roque, made the decision to plead guilty in a Wisconsin District Court to one count of cocaine distribution and one count of marijuana distribution. In the plea agreement, it was agreed that the defendant's illegal conduct involved fifty-five grams of cocaine and forty-seven kilograms or marijuana.

The PSI report confirmed that the total offense level after applicable adjustments was a twenty-nine. The defendant was later granted a three level downward adjustment because of his acceptance of responsibility and an additional two levels for meeting all criteria of the safety valve. The defendant also had one criminal history point which kept his offense level under category one of the sentencing table. He was now facing 87-108 months of imprisonment.

The defendant so far had his offense level lowered by five points and also qualified for the safety valve which would allow the judge to impose a sentence under the ten year mandatory minimum sentence that the defendant was facing. Unfortunately, the defendant was still facing a possible seven to nine year prison sentence under the advisory guidelines.

At the sentencing hearing, the defendant's positive life events were discussed. At age seventeen, the defendant was part of a street gang. After a short period of time participating in gang related activities, he decided to leave the gang and try to lead a better life. The defendant started studying for his GED, held a steady job as a welder, and was involved in a steady relationship with his girlfriend who had two children of her own. The defendant admitted some past experimenting with drugs but since swore to the court that he had cleaned himself up. While on pre-trial release for nearly two years, all of his drug tests were negative and he fully complied with all conditions of his release. The defendant's family members gave the judge letters talking of the defendant's positive progress in life and these comments were also present in the defendant's PSI. The defendant's attorney took extra time pinpointing all the defendant's positive traits and accomplishments throughout his tough life. It is quite possible that the defendant's attorney and the judge knew each other well and thus was able to portray the true nature and characteristics of this defendant during some informal conversations in and around the court.

Here is what the judge had to say in a statement during the sentencing hearing, "*Considering all these factors, I've found a sentence of five years probation sufficient but not greater than necessary. This sentence allowed me to maintain the great degree of control over the defendant to ensure he stayed on the right path. Further, revocation of defendant's probation would permit me to impose any sentence that might have been originally imposed. Thus the defendant faced a significant sentence if he strayed.*" This defendant has a second chance at life!

Case Locator – 536 FSupp 2D 987

<u>United States vs. Hernandez</u> - The defendant in this particular case was stopped for a routine commercial vehicle inspection while driving. He was pulled over by an Arkansas State Highway police officer who conducted the truck safety inspection. During the inspection, three hundred pounds of marijuana was discovered in the trailer section of the eighteen-wheeler; it was hidden in a fake compartment in the rear of the trailer.

The defendant confessed to authorities stating he was responsible for transporting the marijuana and that he was compensated ten thousand dollars to transport the drugs from El Paso, Texas, to the Arkansas state line. Due to the fact that the amount of marijuana exceeded 220 pounds, the defendant was facing a mandatory minimum prison term of five years.

During the search of the truck, a shotgun was found in the truck's cab section. To be eligible for the safety valve the defendant must have committed the said offense without the use of violence or credible threats of violence, and could not have possessed a firearm or any other dangerous weapon in connection with the offense. The defendant met the other required safety valve criteria but the weapon found in his truck could ruin his chances for eligibility.

At the sentencing hearing, the government argued that the defendant did not qualify for the safety valve because of the weapon that was found in his truck. The defendant's attorney argued back the fact that the shotgun, which was discovered in the truck, was located in the front of the vehicle and not back where the drugs were hidden. It was also further made known to the court that this particular weapon was purchased long before the defendant committed the offense and that he always kept that weapon in the truck for self defense. It was also made known to the court that the defendant had purchased the shotgun only after someone attempted to break into the truck one night while he was sleeping. The judge ruled in favor of the defendant and sentenced him to eighteen months in federal prison - forty-two months less than the five year mandatory minimum that would have been required without the use of the safety valve. Case Locator - 187 F3D 806

Be kind, for everyone you meet is fighting a hard battle."

- **Plato**

7
Take a Year Off

If you have ever used drugs in your life, now may be the time to let someone know. While this may sound like a strange beginning to this chapter, it will make better sense as you read on. There is a program in the federal system, offered by the Bureau of Prisons (BOP) that focuses on inmates who have a drug or alcohol problem. Right now you may be thinking to yourself, *"Hey! No Way! Not Me!; I don't have any kind of problem."* However, any eligible person who has been sentenced to federal prison, and who subsequently completes this special five hundred hour substance abuse program successfully, is then eligible to have up to one year wiped off the remainder of their sentence. Many may now be thinking that their marijuana problem is more of a problem than once thought to be. Sure, now you are getting the picture. There are some secrets to getting priority placement into this program though, and we will discuss these throughout this chapter.

The name of the program is called the *"Residential Drug Abuse Program"* or *"RDAP."* The RDAP program is overseen by the BOP and takes approximately six to twelve months to complete. While all federal prisons are required to have some type of drug programming available for the inmates, only a select number of institutions offer the RDAP. A convenient list of federal institutions that offer the RDAP is published at the end of this chapter.

If you or someone you know is facing an inevitable sentence of federal imprisonment and is interested in the RDAP program, then there is a list of criteria that must be met before one is accepted into the program. The first requirement to get consideration into the RDAP is to have a verifiable problem with either alcohol or drugs. An inmate looking to get placement into the RDAP must have an alcohol or drug abuse problem within *the prior twelve months* from the current offense date and this drug or alcohol problem *must be verifiable*. The key word here is *"verifiable."* Guess how the BOP primarily determines if your problem is verifiable? Well, remember that very important report that we have talked about over and over called the PSI? When the probation officer prepares the PSI and interviews the defendant, there will come a time during the interview when questions about drugs and alcohol arise. The answers to these questions are clearly published in the defendant's PSI and used later by the BOP to determine if that person has a drug or alcohol problem and if he should be considered for the RDAP. Before any of this happens though, the inmate has to make the initial move after arriving at the prison and submit a formal request to the BOP stating that he wishes to be enrolled in the RDAP.

While in prison, I encountered so many inmates that were wishing they could do their PSI interview all over again. They were all being denied entry into the RDAP program because their drug or alcohol use was never mentioned or mentioned very lightly on their PSI. They all shared the same fear during the interview for the PSI; they thought it was better not to mention any kind of alcohol or drug abuse problems for fear of getting in deeper trouble. They later found out that this information would likely help them get out of prison sooner!

I remember two inmates very well, both of whom loved to talk of their *"weed smoking days"* while outside of prison. They both talked of their daily rituals from morning to evening. They both obviously smoked marijuana daily. When I asked one of them if they got the RDAP program they replied *"No, my PSI said that I only smoked a few times per week."* I then thought to myself, *"Wow isn't that enough?"* When I talked to the other man he raved how he got into the RDAP program and how his start date for the program was quickly approaching. He was being transferred to another prison camp to complete the RDAP because the program was not offered at the Estill Prison Camp where we were located. I asked him about his PSI and how he got into the program so easily. He told me that before the probation officer prepared his PSI he was already aware of the RDAP pitfalls of not clearly disclosing any and all drug and or alcohol use on the PSI. He then told me when the probation officer conducted the interview for the PSI, and the questions about drug use came about, he made his drug abuse impeccably clear on the report. He made sure the probation officer copied down his statement word for word and even asked her to read back the information. He told the probation officer that he used marijuana every day and drank alcohol quite often too. He told the officer that his smoking had become a serious dependency problem and that he was seeking some type of program to help him quit. He mentioned that he *"woke up to a joint,"* went through the days mostly high, and then went to sleep with a joint every night. The probation officer then asked him how much he smokes. He replied *"Well I smoke anywhere from five to ten joints per day and I never go a day without using marijuana. It has become a part of my life. I have to quit this addiction or else I will die."* This man got placement into the RDAP without any problems and to my knowledge will get up to a year off his sentence once the program is completed.

The amount of time that an inmate gets awarded off his sentence will primarily depend on how much time is remaining on his sentence when the RDAP has been successfully completed. Successful completion of the RDAP also entitles an inmate to at least six months placement into a halfway house. So, in total, one can knock off up to two years from their total prison sentence with the successful completion of the RDAP.

Now that you know the first trick to getting preferential consideration into the RDAP, let's discuss some of the program's other requirements. The *"Residential Drug Abuse Program"* targets inmates who volunteer for treatment for drug/alcohol abuse and who have a diagnosable and verifiable substance abuse disorder. The inmate must be available to participate in the entire RDAP course and must meet the following criteria:

1) Have a verifiable substance abuse disorder.

2) Sign an agreement acknowledging program responsibility.

3) Complete all required components of the program.

To start the whole process off, an inmate should submit a *"Inmate to Staff"* request (i.e., copout) to the prison psychologist. Once the psychologist receives the copout he will schedule an initial screening of the inmate. It is here where the psychologist will refer to the inmate's PSI to help determine if a potential drug or alcohol problem exists. The psychologist will conduct an interview with the inmate to confirm his substance abuse history and additionally confirm the inmate's personal interest for placement into the RDAP. After determining that an inmate may be eligible for the RDAP, the psychologist will then refer that inmate for a follow up screening with the institutions *"Drug Abuse Program Coordinator"* (DAPC). An inmate may also submit a copout directly to the DAPC for initial RDAP consideration instead of the psychologist. The DAPC will conduct an initial inmate screening to determine if the inmate should be referred to the RDAP. The DAPC will review the inmate's file and make sure once again there is documentation available to verify the inmate's problem with the use of drugs/alcohol. The DAPC will make sure the inmate also has adequate time remaining on his sentence to complete the RDAP; a time frame of 24-36 months is usually sufficient time to complete the entire program including the halfway house segment. The DAPC will also consult with the education department to make sure that inmate is able to participate in the program in either the English or Spanish language. The program is conducted in English at most institutions, with the exception of a few institutions which offer the program in both English and Spanish.

Once the DAPC has determined that an inmate should be placed into the RDAP, he will then have the inmate sign the appropriate documents for entry into the program, namely BP-A0749, which is *the "Agreement to Participate in the Bureau of Prisons Residential Drug Abuse Treatment Program."*

The personal interview conducted by the DAPC will usually not occur until the inmate has approximately 24 to 36 months remaining on his sentence. Once the DAPC has confirmed an inmate's need for the RDAP, and the forms are filled out, that inmate will be placed on the RDAP waiting list and enrolled in the next available class. If there is no RDAP program available at the inmate's current location then he will be transferred to another institution at the appropriate time to begin the course.

The RDAP course consists of a minimum of five hundred hours conducted throughout a time period of not less than six months. The program is conducted on work days and is substituted for one half of the inmate's work day. The RDAP also offers achievement awards and it is advisable for all inmates to work hard to obtain as many achievements as they can throughout the program. Remember, after an inmate successfully completes the RDAP course he will be considered for maximum halfway house placement of up to a year and then get up to a year wiped off the remainder of his sentence. Earning achievements through the RDAP course would likely get that particular inmate serious consideration for the most time off. Program awards are achieved by simply showing up on time, having no absences, not leaving the group, being attentive, not eating or drinking in class, being active in the group, dressing properly, not sleeping, and complying with any other education or financial programs that the inmate may have.

Now that you know the basics about getting a year off for having a verifiable drug or alcohol problem, you may be saying to yourself, "*Well that's great but I have already been sentenced and I am already in prison!*" this is a common problem for many inmates. So many people, who are convicted and then sentenced for a federal offense, wind up in federal prison with little or no knowledge of the RDAP course and its valuable incentives. Many inmates get to prison and attempt to get into the RDAP with little or no reference to their drug or alcohol use on their PSI. They then are told that they do not qualify for the RDAP, but they can enroll in the non-residential drug program if they wish. The non-residential drug program, while still helpful, offers no *"time off"* incentives for its successful completion. The only program that awards time off one's sentence is the RDAP. So what is one to do?

Luckily, there are still some alternative options that an inmate can utilize to try and get referred into the RDAP. Obviously, the easiest and best way to provide documentation that verifies a substance use disorder is on the inmate's PSI. If the problem arises where there is not any substance use listed on the inmate's PSI then that inmate can legally obtain other documentation verifying a substance or alcohol disorder. This documentation can come from a probation officer, parole officer, social services representative, or doctor verifying the inmate's substance abuse problem. If any of these sources can provide written documentation which supports the inmate's drug or alcohol abuse problems, then this can be used as valid proof of a substance abuse. Additionally, if the inmate, during any time within the twelve months prior to the current offense, engaged in any type of substance abuse treatment, then a written letter from the treatment center providing verification can also be used. While this is not the most effective way to gain entrance into the RDAP, it is a permissible method for getting consideration. Another way that an inmate can still be considered for the RDAP is if he had two or more drunk driving convictions (i.e., DUI's) within the previous five years from the current offense. Once again, this would have to be proved with documentation submitted by the inmate. The last resort, if all else fails, would be if the inmate has any type of physical proof of drug abuse, such as track marks, abscesses, etc. Only if verifying documentation or physical proof is provided, will the inmate be interviewed by the DAPC. Once an inmate is selected for the RDAP he will be responsible for completing all phases of the program.

The RDAP course contains three different phases: the unit based phase, transitional phase, and the community phase. The unit based portion of the program is the primary part of the course. This phase consists of the five hundred hour initial course which will take from six to twelve months to complete. In 2011 the BOP began a new curriculum for the unit based program that allows inmates to complete the course in six months. The length of course will ultimately depend on what location the inmate was required to take the program. The course consists of numerous classes and activities provided by drug abuse treatment specialists and the DAPC.

The transitional portion of the course is for inmates who have completed the initial unit based portion and are awaiting transfer to a halfway house to begin the community based, final portion of the program. Once the unit based program has been successfully completed the inmate will be transferred to community confinement (i.e. a halfway house). Here the individual will complete the final phase of the RDAP. This community phase is conducted while living at the halfway house and is an extension of the unit based program. It typically consists of a couple of "TDAT" meetings per week while living at the halfway house.

"Inmates who have completed the unit-based program and (when appropriate) the follow-up treatment and are transferred to community confinement must successfully complete community-based drug abuse treatment in a community based program to have successfully completed RDAP." - BOP Manual

    The location as to where an inmate will be required to attend the RDAP course will be determined by the Designation and Sentence Classification Center (DSCC) in Grand Prairie, Texas. Inmates who are incarcerated at institutions that do not offer the RDAP will be transferred to another institution of the same security level that does offer the RDAP. For example, an inmate who is serving time in a medium security institution must complete the RDAP course at a medium security institution unless the inmate's security classification has changed while he is waiting for program enrollment. Institution staff are required to monitor RDAP waiting lists to make sure inmates are transferred to begin the RDAP course while they still have sufficient time remaining on their sentence. This will ensure that the inmate will be able to complete the entire RDAP course. Inmates are generally transferred to their designated RDAP institution with approximately 24-36 months remaining on their sentence. Inmates who are already housed at an institution that offers the RDAP will generally be able to complete the program at that location notwithstanding circumstances which are out of the inmate's control such as class availability, program delays, and time remaining on one's sentence.
    Proper conduct, while waiting for, during, and after the RDAP course, should be appropriate otherwise the inmate will be promptly removed from the RDAP. Depending on the severity of the misconduct, that inmate may be able to reapply for the RDAP after a six month cooling off period, or he may be banned from ever being able to apply for the RDAP again. Additionally, inmates that have been designated as deportable aliens are ineligible to apply for the

RDAP. This also applies to inmates whose charges included any type of firearm offense or enhancement. However, there are rumors of inmates with firearm enhancements still being able to enroll in the RDAP at some of the Western U.S. federal institutions. This should be discussed with the inmate's counselor and case manager.

All inmates participating in the RDAP are required to live together in a specially designated RDAP housing unit. Inmates with physical disabilities or medical conditions can still qualify for the RDAP course provided they are able to participate in all aspects and phases of the program. Inmates that require special medical treatment or handicap accessibility may be exempt from living in the RDAP housing unit per approval of the Warden. The following is a list of federal institutions that offer the RDAP course:

Federal RDAP Institutions

State	Name	Security Level	Sex	Language
AL	FPC MONTGOMERY	MIN	M	Eng / Span
AL	FPC TALLADEGA	MIN	M	ENGLISH
AL	FCI TALLADEGA	MED	M	ENGLISH
AZ	FCI PHOENIX	MED	M	ENGLISH
CA	FPC DUBLIN	MIN	M	ENGLISH
CA	FCI DUBLIN	LOW	F	ENGLISH
CA	FCI LOMPOC	LOW	M	ENGLISH
CA	FCI TERMINAL ISLAND	LOW	M	ENGLISH

CO	FPC ENGLEWOOD	MIN	M	ENGLISH
CO	FCI ENGLEWOOD	MED	M	ENGLISH
CO	FPC FLORENCE	MIN	M	ENGLISH
CO	FCI FLORENCE	MED	M	ENGLISH
CT	FCI DANBURY	LOW	F	ENGLISH
FL	FCI COLEMAN	LOW	M	ENGLISH
FL	FCI MARIANNA	MED	M	ENGLISH
FL	FPC MIAMI	MIN	M	Eng / Span
KY	FMC LEXINGTON	ADM	M	ENGLISH
MD	FPC CUMBERLAND	MIN	M	ENGLISH
MD	FCI CUMBERLAND	MED	M	ENGLISH
MI	FCI MILAN	LOW	M	ENGLISH
MN	FCI SANDSTONE	LOW	M	ENGLISH
MN	FCI WASECA	LOW	M	ENGLISH
NJ	FCI FAIRTON	MED	M	ENGLISH
NJ	FCI FORT DIX	LOW	M	ENGLISH
NC	FCI BUTNER	MED	M	ENGLISH
OK	FCI EL RENO	MED	M	ENGLISH
OR	FPC SHERIDAN	MIN	M	ENGLISH
OR	FCI SHERIDAN	MED	M	ENGLISH
PA	FPC LEWISBURG	MIN	M	ENGLISH
PA	USP LEWISBURG	HIGH	M	ENGLISH

PA	FCI MCKEAN	MED	M	ENGLISH
SC	FPC EDGEFIELD	MIN	M	ENGLISH
SD	FPC YANKTON	MIN	M	ENGLISH
TX	FCI BASTROP	LOW	M	ENGLISH
TX	FCI BEAUMONT	LOW/MED	M	ENGLISH
TX	FPC BRYAN	MIN	F	ENGLISH
TX	FCI FT. WORTH	ADM	M	ENGLISH
TX	FPC LATUNA	MIN	M	ENGLISH
TX	FCI LATUNA	LOW	M	ENGLISH
TX	FPC LEAVENWORTH	MIN	M	ENGLISH
TX	FCI SEAGOVILLE	LOW	M	ENGLISH
TX	FPC TEXARKANA	MIN	M	ENGLISH
TX	FCI TEXARKANA	LOW	M	ENGLISH
WV	FPC ALDERSON	MIN	F	ENGLISH
WV	FPC BEKLEY	MIN	M	ENGLISH
WV	FCI BEKLEY	MED	M	ENGLISH
WV	FCI MORGANTOWN	MIN	M	ENGLISH
WI	FCI OXFORD	MED	M	ENGLISH

8
Post Sentencing Reductions

Inmates who are serving long prison terms should be aware of two sentence remedies that are available, one through the BOP, and one from who else; our president. These are called the *"Compassionate Release"* and *the "Commutation of Sentence."* Both of these provisions will vacate an inmate's sentence, but we would like to forewarn anyone seeking these remedies; they are the toughest of any sentencing reducing procedures available. Although several have been successful obtaining a *"Commutation of a Sentence"* from the president, or a *"Compassionate Release"* from the Bureau of Prisons, they are far and few in between. Regardless of the stats, it is always wise for an inmate, with valid reasons, to file these forms as soon as he has the time. If an inmate is serving a relatively short time of a few years or less and there are no valid reasons to back up a request for a *"Compassionate Release"* or *"Sentence Commutation"* then it will likely be a waste of ink filling out the forms.

Compassionate Release

First we will discuss the Compassionate Release as set forth in 18 U.S.C 3582(c)(1)(A). The Compassionate Release was created so that the inmates serving time in federal prison, who have compelling and extraordinary circumstances that could not be foreseen by the court at the time of sentencing, can request to have the remainder of their sentence vacated.

To even be eligible to start the process an inmate should have some type of compelling reason to support the need for the Compassionate Release. Things like severe health problems, family members with severe health problems, or terminally ill loved ones that need caring for are valid reasons. Inmates who have valid reasons must then fill out the appropriate forms which can be obtained from their case manager and then submitted to the warden of the institution.

A request for Compassionate Release can also be done by another person on behalf of an inmate such as having a family member, friend, attorney, or other inmate fill out the request forms. When filling out the forms, as much information as possible should be provided to substantiate the need for this type of request. At the minimum, the request should contain the details of the compelling circumstances and precise release plans that the inmate will adhere to, such as where the inmate will live, how he will support himself, where he will seek medical treatment, how the medical treatment will be paid for, etc. Once the forms are filled out, they should then be submitted to the inmate's case manager. From the case manager, the request will then travel up to the Warden. If approved by the Warden, the request will then have to be approved by the BOP's Regional Director and then the General Counsel for the Bureau of Prisons.

While this does sound like the traditional pipe dream, there have been several cases where a particular inmate was in fact granted a Compassionate Release. If the request is originally approved by the Warden then there is a good chance for it to hold weight as it moves up through the BOP hierarchy. Consequently, if a particular inmate has a poor rapport with the Warden then this will likely reflect the Warden's decision for the request. As with everything in this world, politics play an important part here also. Should it be the inmate's lucky day and the Warden decides in favor of the inmate, it will then be up to the Warden to continue the process. After a Warden approves a Compassionate Release request, he will then be required to refer the matter to the Regional Director of the BOP for further review. The Warden will be required to forward the following documents along with the recommendation for approval: a copy of the inmate's judgment order, a current inmate progress report not more than thirty days old, the inmate's medical records, a copy of the inmate's PSI, information on fines and restitution, central inmate monitoring status, probation forms, comments from the U.S. attorney's office, custody classification forms, and more. There is a huge amount of paperwork that is involved with this process and that is what makes a successful attempt even harder to achieve.

After all the necessary documents have been forwarded, it will then be up to the Regional Director to review all information and make a decision whether to approve or deny the Warden's request for the Compassionate Release. If the Regional Director determines that the request warrants further approval then he will forward the information along with his recommendation to the Office of General Counsel. The General Counsel will then seek the opinions of either the BOP Medical Director or the Assistant Director for the BOP Correctional Programs Division. If the release request is accepted by the General Counsel then the entire package is sent to the Director of Prisons for the final decision.

Now you can see why this type of request is more than just a handful. Most requests for Compassionate Release never make it past the Warden and it is the Warden's decision that is probably the most significant, in that the Warden's approval will start the ball rolling and help the request carry significant weight all the way up the ranks. If the request makes it all the way to the Director of Prisons and is subsequently approved, the U.S. Attorney's office in the district where the inmate was sentenced will be contacted and informed of the BOP's decision to make a motion to the sentencing court to vacate the remainder of the inmate's term of imprisonment.

When an inmate is denied the request for Compassionate Release, the official who disapproved the request will provide the inmate with a written notice and statement of reasons for the denial. At that time, the inmate may elect to file an appeal using the administrative remedy procedures starting with form BP-9. The only circumstance when an inmate would lose the right to appeal a denied request would be when the request for Compassionate Release was denied by the BOP General Counsel. Additionally, only inmates who were sentenced to a term of federal prison without parole prior to November 1, 1987, are ineligible for a Compassion Release.

Commutation of a Sentence

A *"Commutation of Sentence"* is a request made by an inmate, to the President of the United Sates, in hopes of having the remainder of one's sentence absolved or *"commuted."* Similar to the Compassionate Release, this petition is very difficult to get approved. A person seeking this type of executive clemency must fill out and submit the appropriate forms to the President of the United States. The actual mailing address for sending the petition is:

Pardon Attorney
Department of Justice
Washington, DC 20530

Inmates can obtain the proper forms from their case manager or from the Warden of the institution where they are being held. A petition for commutation of a sentence should be submitted when all other judicial and administrative avenues have been exhausted. If there are other ways that are applicable to an inmate, such as a Compassionate Release, then these remedies should be addressed and exhausted first. An inmate should seek the help of an expert in the field of writing and one who has some legal knowledge about submitting this type of petition. It is crucial to make sure the forms are filled out correctly, complete with details explaining the extraordinary reasons for the request for clemency.

Once the petition for commutation of sentence is completed and submitted, the Attorney General will initiate an investigation as to the matter. The investigation may involve any appropriate officials or agencies of the government, including the Federal Bureau of Investigation, DEA, ICE, etc. Additionally, if the inmate is seeking clemency for an offense that included a victim, then the victim would likely be contacted by one of the government agencies to notify them of the inmate's attempt to seek clemency. The victim may be asked to submit personal comments regarding the clemency.

After the investigation is complete, the Attorney General will then decide if the petition is favorable for approval by the President. If deemed to be favorable the Attorney General will then send the President a written recommendation stating the reasons why he should grant approval of the petition. The approval rate for getting a sentence commuted is very low, and unless that particular inmate has reasons that are way beyond normal circumstances, or has multiple letters of recommendation by high ranking officials like senators and governors, then chances are that the petition will be denied.

After the Attorney General learns of the President's approval or denial of the petition he will notify the inmate with written documentation sent to the Warden of the institution. There is no cost for an inmate to submit a petition for commuting a sentence except any personal expenses that the inmate may incur while seeking professional help as well as the cost of the stamp.

RDAP

Anyone who has been convicted of a federal crime and subsequently sentenced to a term of imprisonment, who successfully completes the Residential Drug Abuse Program (RDAP), will then be eligible for release from the prison institution as much as two years early. The RDAP program awards inmates with up to one year off a prison sentence and up to one year placement in a halfway house for successfully completing the program. Preparing for successful acceptance into the program starts way back before someone is sentenced beginning with the preparation of one's PSI. Anyone who is interested in learning more about the RDAP and the sentencing relief that it can provide should go back and read the chapter titled "Take a Year Off."

Maximizing Halfway House Placement

Halfway houses, also referred to as *"community correction centers" (CCC's), and "residential re-entry centers" (RRC's)*, have been established to accommodate eligible inmates during the final portion of their prison term. A halfway house is designed to help provide inmates with a smooth transition back into the community. These correction facilities are located throughout the United States and are usually situated in and around major cities. These community centers provide housing, job placement, structured programs, and counseling services to inmates.

The BOP policy on halfway houses is to supposedly afford each inmate, who meets the eligibility requirements, an adequate period of time in a halfway house or similar conditions. This period of time can not exceed twelve months unless special conditions require the inmate to remain for an extended period of time and the proper approvals are granted.

Some of the obvious benefits of halfway house placement are the chance to work a full time job in the community, relocate closer to family and friends, earn weekend and evening passes to spend time with family and loved ones, and participate in other community activities. Additionally, once an inmate has secured full time employment and proved to be stable in the community, he will likely be rewarded with weekend passes where he would be permitted to go home for weekends. Eventually this will lead to home confinement where the inmate will be required to be at home during non-working hours and no longer be required to live at the halfway house.

As set forth in Title 18 U.S.C. 3624(c), *"The Bureau of Prisons shall, to the extent practicable, assure that a prisoner serving a term of imprisonment spends a reasonable part, not to exceed twelve months, of the final portion of the term to be served under conditions that will afford the prisoner a reasonable opportunity to adjust to and prepare for the prisoner's re-entry into the community. The authority provided by this subsection may be used to place a prisoner in home confinement. The United States Probation Office shall, to the extent practicable, offer assistance to a prisoner during such pre-release custody."*

The primary goal for the operation of these community correction centers is *to "increase public safety while aiding the transition of an offender back into the community."* The BOP's theory on this suggests that an inmate, who has access to the abundance of resources that a halfway house provides, will be less likely to commit another crime after being released to the community. While this theory does do an okay job for some, inmates who may be classified as dangerous and a threat to the community are considered ineligible for placement into a halfway house. Inmates of this classification will likely complete their sentence in prison and then be released directly back to the community under the watch of a probation officer. Therefore, while halfway houses are a sensible means for preparing an inmate for outside life, they are not the answer for all who have been incarcerated.

Anyone who spends time in a federal prison, or any prison for that matter, will quickly find out that the most talked about subjects on the compound are sports, girls, halfway houses, and release dates. Most inmates want to get out of prison as soon as possible and a halfway house is the perfect nexus to reach that goal. Inmates are constantly consulting with other inmates about their progress with halfway house placement and projected release dates. Unfortunately, each prison institution will work slightly different; what one learns in one prison may not exactly apply in the next one. For example, a couple of significant differences that are commonly seen in the prison system is the amount of individual attention which an inmate will receive from his case manager concerning his release to a halfway house and the amount of time that will be remaining on one's sentence before an inmate actually finds out what his halfway placement date is. In this chapter we will discuss the various factors and steps involved to make the process go as smooth a possible, but in the end it will ultimately be the responsibility of the inmate to make sure his paperwork is being filed and the necessary steps are being fulfilled for a successful transfer and sufficient time allotted in a halfway house.

The first vital piece of information that every inmate should know before they get to the prison is that halfway house placement is not in anyway a reward for good conduct, nor is it the right of any inmate. I have witnessed all too many inmates bring the demanding attitude like *"I want seven months halfway house time!"* to their case managers only to wind up getting minimal placement or even no time at all in a halfway house. It is best to leave the *"I deserve it and I am entitled to it!"* attitude at the door. This will not help an inmate get extra time on a halfway house referral form ever. With that being said, good behavior from an inmate will surely not hurt one's chances for a good referral to a halfway house.

There are several factors that are supposed to be used when determining an inmate's need and length of placement into a halfway house and also a few things that an inmate can do to help with a satisfactory referral. Referrals for halfway house placement are supposed to be conducted on a case by case basis. The big word we should focus on here is *"supposed."* It is important to remember that we are dealing with government employees here who determine an inmate's halfway house fate. They are not paid by the job nor do they make any commissions on their duties. From this you should be able to make a fairly accurate assumption that one inmate's needs are not going to be addressed any more intensively compared to the next inmate in line unless maybe there exists some unusual or extraordinary circumstance that may get the case manager's attention.

The entire halfway house referral process starts with the case manager. This is the inmate's direct connection to the next higher up. Many times, an inmate's case manager becomes complacent and maybe even a bit lazy and begins to determine halfway house placement using a method similar to this, *"I gave Joe a recommendation for thirty days halfway house placement on his one year sentence so I am going to get Jim and John's referral done with the the same thirty day request considering that they also had one year sentences."* Generalizing inmates like this, while depriving and unfair, will surely lighten the workload and thought process of the case manager compared to conducting a personalized interview of each and every inmate. Therefore, it is easy to see how the halfway house *"case by case"* referral process can break down.

The prison where I resided in Estill, SC, had two of the most incompetent case managers one could imagine. The entire system was corrupt, disorganized, and it completely deprived an inmate from getting an honest and true analysis of what he may need in terms of length of time in a halfway house. The hopes of helping a prisoner make a successful transition back to the community was not the primary concern of these case managers. I got to witness this debauchery first hand. When I first arrived at the institution, I was given the A&O handbook which outlined the important rules, regulations, and operating procedures of the prison. As I read through this guide I eventually came to the part that discussed the different stages of an inmate's progress. It was here where I read about how each inmate would receive scheduled *team meetings* at various time intervals throughout his sentence and how these meetings would be conducted to assist an inmate with pre-release guidance. I will not digress too much here, but let me just say that my initial team meeting consisted of me and my case manager and no one else. He made a few grunts, told me I was ineligible for any halfway house time, and then told me we were done. There I stood with a perplexed look upon my face staring at this man who I thought was there to help me. I later found out that this was common practice at the institution. The case managers; there were two of them; would lie to the inmates assuming that they did not know any of the laws or their rights in an effort to get off doing as little paper work as possible. At first I did not believe this, but as days progressed and I talked to more and more inmates, my beliefs changed. I was in fact a recipient of one of the lies. My case manager blatantly told me that because my case originated out of Pennsylvania, and I lived in Florida, he would have to send in paperwork to have my probation department changed from Pennsylvania to Florida. He further stated that because of this I would have to get an approved release plan from the Florida probation department. He continued to state that because I would then have an approved release plan that I would no longer be eligible for any halfway house time but I would be eligible for home confinement. I already knew that halfway house placement could be given to any eligible inmate for up to twelve months and I also knew that the BOP is restricted to a ten percent window for placement of an inmate into home confinement. Regardless of what this man told me, it was all a flat out lie. The follow up meetings with this case manager went just as the initial meeting, a five minute session with no communication about my personal needs for time in a halfway house. I was the sole provider for my family, we were in the midst of losing our house, and he knew about it but never cared. With all the newfound confusion now instilled inside my head, I found it in my best interest to research this matter a little more deeply.

The one advantage to being in a prison environment is the diverse group of people you will find inside the fence. It did not take long before I got to know several attorneys, non-attorneys, and legal junkies who were successful in getting a longer halfway house placement than the average inmate. Unfortunately for the rest, the two case managers deprived most from much needed transitional time in a halfway house. As for my case manager, the general attitude towards all the inmates was, *"Sign this paper, now get out!"*, and that was it. Even worse, was the condescending demeanor of this case manager. I tried no less than three times to shake this man's hand only to have him back off the first time and say, *"No I don't do that!"* On subsequent attempts he would just pull his hand back as if I were a germ. This was surely disheartening, especially for inmates who were incarcerated for long periods of time. Imagine trying to adjust back to outside life after being imprisoned for twenty years and being afraid to shake someone's hand at a job interview. Talk about the complete opposite of *"preparing one for a successful re-integration into society,"* which is supposed to be the primary goal of our prison system. The overall conduct of these case managers cast a widespread feeling of insecurity, lack of self confidence, low self esteem, and vast condescension to all inmates on the prison compound. This type of behavior by the case managers is probably a wide spread problem in most federal prisons and especially minimum security prison camps.

Unfortunately, referrals for halfway house placement can indeed be tainted with favoritism, prejudice, and lack of

Post Sentencing Reductions - 175

individual consideration for one's needs. With that said, there will be two avenues on which an inmate can travel to try and secure the maximum amount of halfway house time allowed. The first way will be the diplomatic approach which involves some good behavior, and politics. The second will be the all out legal approach where an inmate will go over the head of his case manager and fight for his legal right for time in a halfway house.

If an inmate decides to use the diplomatic approach he should still prepare for a legal argument as a backup plan. *"Preparing"*, simply means keeping notes and tabs on each and every meeting that an inmate has with institution staff. It is wise to keep a log of all conversations from day one. An inmate should record the date of the meeting time, who attended, how long it lasted, and any comments that were made by the institution staff. These will be vital for documented proof of anything valuable that may have been said. I can guarantee to you that the case manager is not recording the events of these meetings and will forget all that was discussed by the next week. With regards to the diplomatic approach, the ultimate goal here is to try and get twelve months of halfway house placement. While this may be hard to do, an eight or nine month referral compared to a three month referral is still a substantial benefit to any inmate.

The very first thing an inmate should do when he gets to his assigned institution is to wait for the first *"team meeting.""* This usually happens shortly after one has arrived and settled in. My team meeting was conducted after a couple of weeks, some take less, some longer. The rules say that this meeting should occur within the first few weeks. This meeting should be conducted with proper etiquette such as *"yes sir," "no sir," "thank you sir,"* and nothing derogatory. During this meeting, an inmate should feel out his case manager to see how he acts and responds. Towards the end of the meeting is when an inmate should ask the case manager to commit to a precise answer. An inmate at the prison where I stayed used this introduction when called in for his first meeting, *"Sir I am completely aware that halfway house time is not a reward for good behavior but my only hope is to get back to supporting my family as soon as I can. I do plan on being a model inmate and was wondering if there is anything that you may be able to suggest or recommend that I can do or participate in that would help my chances for the longest possible halfway house referral?"* That's it! He asked the question and it served several purposes. Obviously if the inmate does not have a family then he should cite another critical reason that warrants maximum time in a halfway house. This question first alerted the case manager to the fact that the inmate knew a little about the halfway house rules. He said that he knew halfway house placement was not a reward for good behavior. Most inmates are not aware of this fact. It then showed that the inmate was going to give a display of good conduct regardless. Third, it advised the case manager that the inmate was in critical need to get back to his family to help support them. Lastly, the statement opened the door to a direct response from the case manager. It asked him for advice on how to get extra time in a halfway house. This opening statement will give a good indication for the road ahead.

The very next thing to do is find out from other inmates when they have been learning of their halfway house transfer date. This will be the day in which the inmate is officially released from prison and transferred to the halfway house. The timing of this is crucial. An inmate can also ask his case manager for an approximate date when the paperwork begins for a halfway house referral. Some institutions will have the entire process complete when an inmate still has one to two years remaining on their sentence while others are so far behind that inmates learn of their halfway house transfer date just weeks before they go.

The next step is to fulfill any educational requirements. If an inmate does not have a GED, then he is required to study for it and hopefully will pass the test. Get this done! Getting a GED while incarcerated is priceless, not to mention it can't hurt when trying to get extra halfway house time. If an inmate already has a GED then he should enroll in as many educational courses that he has time for. Obviously, this will depend on how much time an inmate has. If the sentence was only a year then there will not be much time, but if an inmate has ten years to go then time won't be a problem. Get to know the staff in the education department. Develop a good rapport with them. This good rapport will hopefully result in a favorable referral towards the end of one's sentence.

Whatever job an inmate gets assigned, it should be done satisfactory and without conflict. It is advisable to get a job where an inmate will have direct communication with his boss. Try to secure a position that involves some type of vocational duties where good job performance makes the boss's job easier. This will allow for an inmate to establish a friendly working relationship and a favorable rapport with the boss. If an inmate finds himself at a job that does not fit the above description, or if his boss is unwilling to get along with any of the inmates, then he should put in a request for another job. The inmate should find out which jobs have friendly and fair bosses and then seek a position with that individual. Once an inmate has found the right job, with the right boss, he should act as a model employee by showing up to work on time, being polite in all conversations, and offering to take on extra duties as they become available.

The final step of this diplomatic process is to uncover a valid reason that supports the need for extra halfway house placement. There should be some kind of extraordinary need that inmate can use as the foundation for the need of maximum halfway house placement. If an inmate's family is having tough financial problems and he was a primary provider then this can be used as a valid argument. Maybe a family member is ill and the inmate needs to get back to the community as soon as he can to provide support. An inmate can even claim that he needs extra time under halfway house supervision to minimize his risk of recidivism, or needs extra time for the counseling and job finding services that the halfway house offers. Whatever it is, he should find a good reason that, in the eyes of the case manager distinguishes his situation from other inmates.

Shortly then before an inmate expects his paperwork to begin he should request an unscheduled meeting with the case manager to discuss his circumstances. Here is when the inmate should express his need for maximum halfway house time and disclose the information about whatever crisis is brewing in his outside life that makes it critical for maximum time in the halfway house. Shortly before this meeting, the inmate should have asked his boss to make a phone call or pay a personal visit to the case manager and personally ask the case manager to consider him for extra halfway house time due to his personal needs. If the inmate's boss is a genuine person and sincere then he will agree to help out the inmate and put in a good word with the case manager. After all, the boss has had plenty of time to witness first hand the great attributes that this inmate possesses. A request like this will carry big weight considering it is coming from a fellow worker who the case manager has to work with week after week. In fact, of the few times that I heard about this being done by an inmate. They all seemed to get the most halfway house time. The case manager will take the request into serious consideration and likely put that inmate in for extra time. This is more or less using politics to help get more halfway house time. Unfortunately, the inmate who really needs more halfway house time almost never gets to completely discuss the reasons behind it and it takes these types of tactics to secure extra weeks and months in a community confinement setting. If an inmate asks around he will quickly find out what inmates did to get more halfway house time and the stories about how they did it. During this unscheduled meeting the inmate should also find out how much time the case manager is going to recommend for placement in the halfway house; if of course the inmate still has not been notified of this. It will be at this time that the inmate should decide if he is satisfied with this referral or if it will be in his best interest to seek additional time using the legal process. If satisfaction was not rendered, and the case manager is simply too uncooperative and unruly to negotiate, then the inmate needs to start the legal process at once.

Many inmates whom I associated with while in prison were taken advantage of by their case manager simply because they were unaware of the laws and policy guidelines that govern the operating procedures for an inmate's halfway house placement. Let's take a look at how the BOP sets forth the procedures for determining an inmate's halfway house placement. Federal law states that all eligible inmates are to be considered for halfway house placement and the length of placement should be calculated via an individual case by case basis using the following five factors as written in 18 U.S.C. 3621(b):

1) The resources of the facility contemplated;

2) The nature and circumstances of the offense;

3) The history and characteristics of the prisoner;

4) Any statement by the court which imposed the sentence;

5) Any pertinent policy statement issued by the Sentencing Commission;

Additionally, as a result of a new BOP halfway house guidance memo released on June 24, 2010, all eligible inmates should be considered for a minimum of ninety days halfway house placement whenever possible. There is a also side note under this memo that talks about considering minimum security inmates for direct placement into home confinement. Inmates confined to a federal prison camp would be classified as minimum security. In the past, an inmate would always have to report to a halfway house and spend time there before being released to home confinement. Under this new policy, the BOP can now release inmates, who qualify, directly to home confinement. There is an underlying problem with this though. Inmates who are sent direct to home confinement will be restricted to such placement no earlier than their *"ten percent date."* This means that an inmate will have to remain in prison until he has reached the *"ten percent remaining"* part of his sentence. For example, if an inmate had a sentence in which he would be required to serve twenty months, then he would not be eligible to go to home confinement until there was two months remaining on his sentence. This ten percent date has a maximum allowed value of six months also. More than six months home confinement is not allowed unless ordered by a judge. This six month restriction does not apply to halfway house time and an inmate can be sent to halfway house for up to twelve months or even longer in special circumstances. So, while the thought of going home early is surely great, the ten percent restriction on the home confinement rule makes the halfway house option more appealing for most inmates.

The June 24, 2010, *"Revised Halfway House Memo"* has been a step in the right direction for providing inmates additional halfway house placement. The memo clearly makes some positive remarks regarding halfway houses and the guidelines that control their utilization. A copy of the complete June 24, 2010, memo is published in the appendix in the back of this book. Some of the significant changes made in the memo are as follows:

- ✓ Institutional staff are no longer required to seek approval from the Regional Office for halfway house referrals greater than six months;

- ✓ CCM staff cannot deny a prisoner placement in a halfway house or postpone the date the prisoner is sent to a halfway house unless the halfway house lacks bed space or resources to accept the prisoner;

- ✓ BOP staff may now consider sending prisoners with serious medical or mental health conditions directly to home confinement rather than to a halfway house, if the halfway house cannot accommodate the prisoner and appropriate arrangements can be made for community support for a prisoner placed on home detention;

- ✓ Federal prisoners may now turn down placement in a halfway house without being subject to disciplinary action;

- ✓ Federal prisoners who have had some disciplinary problems or who have refused to participate in some prison programming (e.g., treatment, education) may still be placed in halfway houses if, in the staff's judgment, the prisoner is deemed ready to take advantage of the opportunities and expanded liberties of halfway houses;

Post Sentencing Reductions - 181

- ✓ All prisoners should be considered for at least 90 days in a halfway house, and prisoners at higher risk of recidivating should be considered for longer placements than lower-risk inmates;

- ✓ Minimum-security inmates (except RDAP program graduates) with an approved release residence may be considered for a direct transfer to home confinement on the prisoner's home confinement eligibility date (the lesser of 6 months or ten percent of the prisoner's term of imprisonment), rather than being transferred to a halfway house first. This direct transfer to home confinement can be made even if it means that the prisoner will be on home confinement for less than 90 days;

- ✓ CCM staff must ensure that procedures are in place so that eligible minimum-security inmates may be (1) placed directly on home confinement or, (2) if not directly placed on home confinement, they may be released to home confinement after staying only 14 days or less in a halfway house. Additionally, CCM staff must explain to the BOP why eligible minimum-security inmates in halfway houses are not transferred to home detention within this time-frame;

- ✓ Higher-risk inmates who have a high risk of re-offending, who have completed many prison programs, and who still need to establish a community support system will be considered for longer halfway house placements;

The fate of an inmate's halfway house placement starts with his case manager and then travels up the line to the unit manager or administrator and eventually into the Warden's hands. The legal process for extra halfway house placement will also proceed in a similar fashion. A legal argument for maximum halfway house placement should be started as soon as possible once an inmate decides on this approach. The secret to winning the halfway house legal battle is to argue one's personal needs for extra time in a halfway house and any other BOP protocol that may have been ignored or overlooked during the process. One primary factor that is supposed to factor heavily into determining the amount of halfway house time an inmate requires is the inmate's need for the exclusive halfway house services. Whether this may be counseling, job placement services, or the need for guidance to minimize an inmate's risk for recidivism, these factors should give substantial weight as determining factors.

The legal battle for longer halfway house placement should be initiated by an inmate no less than twenty-four months before his scheduled release date. This will provide adequate time to go through the various administrative steps and allow extra time for any delays during the process. If an inmate is not sure of the approximate length of halfway house time that the institution will refer him for, then this should be addressed through an informal meeting no later than one to two years from one's release date. Inmates serving shorter sentences of two years or less should start the administrative remedy process as soon as it is practical but may find themselves running out of time before the problem is resolved. Inmates who are serving a sentence of less than a year can still start the administrative process, but may just be wasting their time due to insufficient time remaining. Inmates who were sentenced to six months or less imprisonment should plan on serving out their entire sentence minus a couple of weeks for possible home confinement.

To begin the administrative remedy process, one should first remember the laws that govern halfway house decisions. Earlier we talked of the five factors that the BOP staff are instructed to utilize when determining an inmate's halfway house placement. In addition to these factors, there are also additional laws that mandate some important procedures. In 18 U.S.C. 3624, federal law requires that placement of an inmate into a community correctional facility is:

A) conducted in a manner consistent with section 3621 18 U.S.C. 3621(b) of this title;

B) determined on an individual basis;

C) of sufficient duration to provide the greatest likelihood of successful reintegration into the community;

Part-A of this law reverts back to the five factors previously mentioned in this chapter. It will be parts B and C that should be used as a foundation of one's argument for additional halfway house placement. It is likely that an inmate's halfway house needs were not determined on an individual basis as they should have been during the many meetings that were conducted between the inmate and his case manager. This fact alone would be an obvious violation of Part-B of this statute. Next is the big one; Part-C. Part-C of this law clearly sets forth the language that an inmate's halfway house placement should be long enough for his best chance at a crime free transition back into the community. Any inmate nearing the end of his sentence, who is consequently facing some type of crisis in the outside world should be able to use this argument as sufficient evidence that a particular request for "x" number of months of halfway house time (i.e., whatever the case manager is recommending) is an insufficient duration.

So what exactly would constitute a crisis that would substantiate extended placement in a halfway house? We did talk about this briefly earlier and one of the very first items that could constitute a crisis would be if the defendant's family is having financial difficulties and desperately needs the financial support of the defendant. If there is imminent danger of the defendant's family losing their place of residence, or even worse, becoming homeless as a result of financial hardship, and an earlier release of the defendant into community confinement will allow him to secure employment and possibly save his family's home, then this is clearly a crisis that can substantiate a longer placement in a community correctional facility. After all, the inmate will be allowed to have full time employment while residing at the halfway house, therefore being able to help with any family financial problems.

Other circumstances that could be considered as a crisis for the defendant would be if he had ill family members who required caretaking and financial assistance. If this inmate was way ahead of the game and already had a job lined up that involved a mandatory upcoming start date, then this may also substantiate a request for extra halfway house time. All of these are good examples of different scenarios that can validate additional placement in community confinement.

If an inmate decides there is no crisis he can use for his argument, then the simple language of 18 U.S.C. 3624(c) can be used. This subsection states that an inmate's community corrections placement should be of *"sufficient duration to provide the greatest likelihood of successful reintegration into the community."* This sentence alone can be used as the foundation of the argument. Obviously the longer an inmate's halfway house placement is, the greater his chances will be for successful reintegration back into the community.

Once an inmate has decided on the plan of attack and basis of his argument for the need of maximum placement into a halfway house, the next step will be to fill out the first form in the process. The inmate should start with an *"Inmate Request to Staff"* form (Form BP-A0148), also referred to as a BP-8 form. This form should be filled out and given to the inmate's case manager with a copy sent to the unit manager and administrator. It should be filled out neatly and accurately; typing it up is best. In the subject line of the form it will ask for the inmate to *"Briefly state your question or concern and the solution you are requesting."* The request should be candid and contrite. The inmate should state his reasons for his request for *"x"* amount of halfway house time. He should clearly list any crisis that may exist to justify the request. The inmate should also mention how the extra time is needed for the greatest likelihood for successful reintegration back into the community. The request should also contain a reference to the June 24, 2010 *"Revised Halfway House Guidance Memo"* that instructs the BOP to consider inmates for a minimum of ninety days halfway house placement. Double check the form for spelling and accuracy and then submit it to the case manager.

An inmate will then have twenty days from the response date to the BP-8 to submit the next form. If the BP-8 form went unanswered or the inmate received an unsatisfactory answer from the case manager, then form BP-9 must be filled out and submitted next. If the case manager came back with an acceptable answer, then further action may not be necessary. It would be wise to discuss the matter with the case manager more in depth to decide if the next course of action will be needed.

If a BP-9 form is to be filled out then the same format should be used. Obtain the form from the unit counselor and fill it out as instructed using the same type of request that was used for the BP-8. The BP-9 form (Form BP-229) should then be delivered to the inmate's counselor. The counselor will deliver the form to the unit manager and administrator. The BOP staff will then have twenty days to respond to the formal request with the possibility of an additional twenty day extension for a decision. The inmate will be notified if any extensions are needed.

If an inmate receives an unsatisfactory response to the BP-9, then the next step is to file form BP-10 (Form BP-230). This form will go to the regional director of the BOP. After a response is received as to the BP-9 form the inmate will have an additional twenty days to fill out and submit the BP-10 form. Once again, the inmate's counselor should be able to provide the inmate with the appropriate BP-10 form. This form must be mailed direct to the BOP regional office. The form should be addressed to the Administrative Remedy Coordinator of the BOP. The inmate's counselor should be able to provide the correct mailing address for this also. A copy of the original BP-9 form must also be included with the BP-10. Both of these forms must be mailed together or the BP-10 will be rejected. After the form is received, the BOP regional office will have thirty days to respond. They will also have the option of extending the time limit an additional thirty days. An inmate will be notified of the extension if it is required.

Should an inmate still find no relief after the submission of the BP-10, then the final step in the administrative remedy process is to file an appeal to the central office of the BOP. This national appeal must be made on a BP-11 (Form BP-231). The inmate should fill the form out as instructed and also attach copies of both the BP-9 and BP-10 forms. The address to use when mailing the BP-11 is:

**National Inmate Appeals Administrator
Office of General Counsel
320 First Street, N.W.
Washington, DC 20534**

An inmate should carefully prepare the BP-11 and make sure it is written professionally with proper grammar and punctuation. The form should contain a statement of facts, grounds for relief, and the type of relief requested. If an inmate knows any other inmates that have legal experience then they should ask them for assistance when submitting and filling out the BP-11 form. Once the BP-11 has been submitted it will take up to sixty days to get a response. The BP-11 will be the last available resource for an inmate to utilize for their halfway house argument.

Nonetheless, some individuals will never be classified as eligible for placement in a halfway house. This list of criteria that makes an inmate ineligible to receive placement into a community correctional center is listed below. Inmates in the following categories shall not ordinarily participate in CCC programs:

A) Inmates who are assigned a *"Sex Offender"* Public Safety Factor;

B) Inmates who are assigned a *"Deportable Alien"* Public Safety Factor;

C) Inmates who require inpatient medical, psychological, or psychiatric treatment;

D) Inmates who refuse to participate in the Inmate Financial Responsibility Program;

E) Inmates who refuse to participate, withdraw, are expelled, or otherwise fail to meet attendance and examination requirements in a required Drug Abuse Education Course;

F) Inmates with unresolved pending charges, or a detainer, which will likely lead to arrest, conviction, or confinement;

G) Ordinarily, inmates serving sentences of six months or less;

H) Inmates who refuse to participate in the Institution Release Preparation Program;

I) Inmates who pose a significant threat to the community. These are inmates whose current offense or behavioral history suggests a substantial or continuing threat to the community. Examples of this are inmates with repeated, serious institution rule violations, a history of repetitive violence, escape, or association with violent or terrorist organizations;

LIST OF FEDERAL HALFWAY HOUSES:

ALABAMA

BIRM. COMMUNITY SVCS.
1609 7TH STREET NORTH
BIRMINGHAM, AL 35204
PHONE: (205)324-8015

DISMAS CHARITIES
125 E. FLEMING
MONTGOMERY, AL 36105
PHONE: (502)636-2033

MOBILE COMMUNITY SRV.
4901 BATTLESHIP PKWY.
SPANISH FORT, AL 36527
PHONE: (251)626-5094

ALASKA

NORTHSTAR CENTER
P.O. BOX 449
ESTER, AK 99725
PHONE: (907)474-4955

ARIZONA

BEHAVIORAL SYSTEMS SW
950 E. DIVERSION DAM RD.
FLORENCE, AZ 85232
PHONE: (520)868-0880

BSSW-CSC
2846 EAST ROOSEVELT RD.
PHOENIX, AZ 85008
PHONE: (602)273-6293

BSS-CSC
2846 E. ROOSEVELT RD.
PHOENIX, AZ 85008
PHONE: (602)273-6293

BEHAVIORAL SYSTEMS SW
6420 SOUTH PARK AVE.
TUCSON, AZ 85706
PHONE: (520)573-3111

DISMAS CCC
3443 S. RICHEY BLVD.
TUCSON, AZ 85705
PHONE: (520)624-0075

NEW BEGINNINGS CTR.
2445 N ORACLE ROAD
TUCSON, AZ 85705
PHONE: (520)624-0075

ARKANSAS

CITY OF FAITH COMM. CTR.
1401 SOUTH GARFIELD DR.
LITTLE ROCK, AR 72204
PHONE: (501)615-1090

CALIFORNIA

TURNING POINT CCC
1101 UNION AVENUE
BAKERSFIELD, CA 93385
PHONE: (661)325-5774

CORNELL CORRECTIONS
11750 RAMONA BLVD.
EL MONTE, CA 91732
PHONE: (626)454-4593

TURNING POINT CSC
3547 S. GOLDEN STATE
FRESNO, CA 93725
PHONE: (559)442-8075

GARDEN GROVE CCC
11112 BARCLAY DRIVE
GARDEN GROVE, CA 92841
PHONE: (714)537-3607

VINEWOOD RE-ENTRY CCC
5520 HAROLD WAY
LOS ANGELES, CA 90028
PHONE: (323)464-0817

CORNELL CORR
9411 S. CENTRAL AVE.
LOS ANGELES, CA 90002
PHONE: (323)563-1126

GATEWAYS CCC
1801 LAKESHORE AVE.
LOS ANGELES, CA 90026
PHONE: (323)644-2020

CORNELL CORRECTIONS
205 MAC ARTHUR BLVD.
OAKLAND, CA 94610
PHONE: (510)839-9051

RUBIDOUX RE-ENTRY CCC
3263 RUBIDOUX BLVD.
RUBIDOUX, CA 92509
PHONE: (951)684-4840

TURNING POINT
116 EAST SAN LUIS
SALINAS, CA 93901
PHONE: (831)422-9171

CORR. ALTERNATIVES
2727 BOSTON AVENUE
SAN DIEGO, CA 92113
PHONE: (619)232-1066

CORR. ALTERNATIVES
551 S. 35TH STREET
SAN DIEGO, CA 92113
PHONE: (619)232-8600

CCI MOTHER W/INFANT
111 TAYLOR STREET
SAN FRANCISCO, CA 94102
PHONE: (415)346-9769

CCI CORR-SAN FRANCISCO
111 TAYLOR STREET
SAN FRANCISCO, CA 94102
PHONE: (415)346-9769

COLORADO

COMCOR, INC.
3950 N. NEVADA AVE.
CO. SPRINGS, CO 80907
PHONE: (719)260-8002

INDEPENDENT HOUSE
2765 S. FEDERAL BLVD.
DENVER, CO 80236
PHONE: (303)936-2035

INDEPENDANT HOUSE
1479 FILLMORE STREET
DENVER, CO 80206
PHONE: (303)321-1718

HILLTOP HOUSE CORR.
1050 AVENIDA DEL SOL
DURANGO, CO 81301
PHONE: (970)382-8406

LARIMER COUNTY CORR.
2255 MIDPOINT DRIVE
FT COLLINS, CO 80525
PHONE: (970) 498-7527

CONNECTICUT

HARTFORD HOUSE
10 IRVING STREET
HARTFORD, CT 06112
PHONE: (860)547-1313

CHASE CENTER
21 CLIFF STREET
WATERBURY, CT 06710
PHONE: (203)596-0783

WATKINSON HOUSE
136 COLLINS STREET
HARTFORD, CT 06105
PHONE: (860)547-1313

DC

DC DEPT CORR
1514 8 STREET, NW
WASHINGTON, DC 20001
PHONE: (202)232-1932

FAIRVIEW CSC
1430 G STREET, NE
WASHINGTON, DC 20002
PHONE: (202)396-8982

HOPE VILLAGE CSC
2840 LANGSTON PLACE, SE
WASHINGTON, DC 20020
PHONE: (202)678-1551

HOPE VILLAGE CCC
2840 LANGSTON PLACE, SE
WASHINGTON, DC 20020
PHONE: (202)678-1551

DELAWARE

MORRIS COMMUNITY CORR
300 WATER STREET
DOVER, DE 19904
PHONE: (302)739-4758

SUSSEX WORK RLS. CTR.
23207 DUPONT BLVD.
GEORGETOWN, DE 19947
PHONE: (302)856-5790

PLUMMER COMM CORR
38 TODDS LANE
WILMINGTON, DE 19802
PHONE: (302)577-3039

FLORIDA

DISMAS HOUSE CHARITIES
141 NW 1ST AVE.
DANIA, FL 33004
PHONE: (954)920-6558

SALVATION ARMY
2400 EDISON AVENUE
FT. MYERS, FL 33902
PHONE: (239)332-0140

JACKSONVILLE COMM CTR.
2020 DAHLIA STREET
JACKSONVILLE, FL 32254
PHONE: (904)783-7618

RIVERSIDE HOUSE
968 NW 2ND ST.
MIAMI, FL 33128
PHONE: (305)545-0926

SPECTRUM PROGRAMS
120 NW 59TH ST.
MIAMI, FL 33127
PHONE: (305)758-3634

OCALA RES. CENTER
3838 NE 41ST ST.
OCALA, FL 34479
PHONE: (352)368-2127

DISMAS OF ORLANDO
6860 EDGEWATER
COMMERCE PKWY.
ORLANDO, FL 32810
PHONE: (407)295-1989

PENSACOLA REENTRY CTR.
225 BRENT LANE
PENSACOLA, FL 32503
PHONE: (850)474-1991

TALLAHASSEE CCC
3190 SPRINGHILL ROAD
TALLAHASSEE, FL 32305
PHONE: (850)425-1181

TALLAHASSEE MINT PGM.
3190 SPRINGHILL ROAD
TALLAHASSEE, FL 32305
PHONE: (850)425-1181

HILLSBOROUGH CO. RRC
4102 W. HILLSBOROUGH AVE.
TAMPA, FL 33614
PHONE: (813)877-2257

THE SALVATION ARMY
1577 NORTH MILITARY TRL
WEST PALM BCH, FL 33409
PHONE: (561)689-1212

GEORGIA

CSC-DISMAS CHARITIES
300 WENDELL COURT
ATLANTA, GA 30336
PHONE: (404)691-1425

RRC-DISMAS HOUSE
744 SECOND STREET
MACON, GA 31201
PHONE: (478)745-8733

CCC-BANNUM, INC.
1150 ARMSTEAD AVENUE
SAVANNAH, GA 31408
PHONE: (912)963-0032

HAWAII

MAHONEY HALE CCC
909 KAAMAHU PLACE
HONOLULU, HI 96817
PHONE: (808)748-4301

IOWA

SECOND JUDICIAL DISTRICT
111 SHERMAN AVENUE
AMES, IA 50010
PHONE: (515)232-3774

6TH JUDICIAL DISTRICT IA
1051 29TH AVE., SW
CEDAR RAPIDS IA 52404
PHONE: (319)398-3668

COMM SANC CENTER
1228 SOUTH MAIN
COUNCIL BLUFFS, IA 51503
PHONE: (712)325-9306

7TH DAVENPORT CENTER
605 MAIN, BOX 2A
DAVENPORT, IA 52803
PHONE: (563)322-7986

5TH JUD DISTRICT IOWA
1917 HICKMAN ROAD
DES MONIES, IA 50314
PHONE: (515)242-6325

5TH FT. DES MOINES RES.
70 THAYER AVE.
DES MOINES, IA 50315
PHONE: (515)242-6956

DEBUQUE SEX OFFENDER
1494 ELM STREET
DUBUQUE, IA 52001
PHONE: (563)556-6196

FIRST JUDICIAL DIST. OF IA
1494 ELM STREET
DUBUQUE, IA 52001
PHONE: (563)556-6196

2ND JUDICIAL DIST. OF IA
311 1ST AVENUE SOUTH
FT. DODGE, IA 50501
PHONE: (515)955-6393

2ND JUDICIAL DIST. OF IA
P.O. BOX 1226
MASON CITY, IA 50402
PHONE: (641)424-3817

MONONA CTY WORK RLS
909 7TH STREET
ONAWA, IA 51040
PHONE: (712)423-1414

8TH JUDICIAL DIST. OF IA
245 OSAGE DRIVE
OTTUMWA, IA 52501
PHONE: (641)682-3069

FIRST JUDICIAL DIST. OF IA
314 E. 6TH STREET,
POBOX 4030
WATERLOO, IA 50703
PHONE: (319)291-2015

WATERLOO MENTAL HLTH
314 E 6TH STREET,
P.O. BOX 4030
WATERLOO, IA 50703
PHONE: (319)291-2015

WATERLOO MENTAL HLTH
314 E 6TH STREET,
P.O. BOX 4030
WATERLOO, IA 50703
PHONE: (319)291-2015

WATERLOO SEX OFFNDR
314 E 6TH T.P.O. BOX 4030
WATERLOO, IA 50703
PHONE: (319)291-2015

FIRST JUDICIAL DIST. OF IA
500 SOUTH PINE
WEST UNION, IA
PHONE: (563)422-5758

WEST UNION SEX
OFFENDER PGM
500 SOUTH PINE
WEST UNION, IA
PHONE: (563)422-5758

IDAHO

PORT OF HOPE
218 NORTH 23RD STREET
COEUR D'ALENE, ID 83814
PHONE: (208)664-3300

PORT OF HOPE
508 EAST FLORIDA
NAMPA, ID 83686
PHONE: (208)463-0118

ILLINOIS

PRAIRIE CENTER
122 W. HILL ST.
CHAMPAIGN, IL 61820
PHONE: (217)356-7576

SALVATION ARMY FCTR.
105 S. ASHLAND
CHICAGO, IL 60607
PHONE: (312)421-2406

SUBSTANCE ABUSE SVCS.
1307 W. MAIN ST.
MARION, IL 62959
PHONE: (618)997-5336

RESIDENTS IN TRANSITION
711 NORTH EAST MONROE
PEORIA, IL 61603
PHONE: (309)671-8966

TRIANGLE CENTER
120 NORTH 11TH ST.
SPRINGFIELD, IL 62703
PHONE: (217)544-9858

TRIANGLE CENTER MINT
120 NORTH 11TH STREET
SPRINGFIELD, IL 62703
PHONE: (217)544-9858

INDIANA

COMM CORR CENTER
811A E. FRANKLIN STREET
EVANSVILLE, IN 47711
PHONE: (812)423-1949

ALLEN COUNTY JAIL
12103 LIMA ROAD
FT WAYNE, IN 46818
PHONE: (260)449-7450

VOA INDIANA CSC
611 N. CAPITOL
INDIANAPOLIS, IN 46204
PHONE: (317)686-9841

PACT-BRADLEY HOUSE
132 EAST 6TH ST.
MICHIGAN CITY, IN 46360
PHONE: (219)878-8549

KANSAS

CORNELL COMPANIES INC.
4715 BREWER PLACE
LEAVENWORTH, KS 66048
PHONE: (913)351-0728

MIRROR INC.
P.O. BOX 711
NEWTON, KS 67114
PHONE: (316)283-7829

MIRROR INC.
236 SOUTH PATTIE
WICHITA, KS 67211
PHONE: (316)264-5999

KENTUCKY

ASHLAND HOUSE CCC
455 29TH STREET
ASHLAND, KY 41101
PHONE: (606)324-4572

WARREN COUNTY JAIL
920 KENTUCKY STREET
BLG. GREEN, KY 42101
PHONE: (270)843-4606

DISMAS OF LEXINGTON
909 GEORGETOWN PIKE
LEXINGTON, KY 40511
PHONE: (859)231-8448

LAUREL CO W/R CTR.
206 WEST FOURTH ST.
LONDON, KY 40741
PHONE: (606)878-9431

DISMAS CHARITIES
124 WEST OAK STREET
LOUISVILLE, KY 40203
PHONE: (502)634-3608

PIKE COUNTY WRK. RLS.
172 DIVISION ST. #103
PIKEVILLE, KY 41501
PHONE: (606)432-6291

PULASKI CTY WRK. RLS.
300 HAIL KNOB ROAD
SOMERSET, KY 42501
PHONE: (606)678-4315

LOUISIANA

ECUMENICAL HOUSE
6753 CEZANNE AVENUE
BATON ROUGE, LA 70806
PHONE: (225)924-5757

CINC, INC
1101 CANVASBACK STREET
LAKE CHARLES, LA 70615
PHONE: (337)439-5082

CITY OF FAITH PRISON
1408 JACKSON STREET
MONROE, LA 71202
PHONE: (318)322-5711

VOLUNTEERS OF AMERICA
2929 ST. ANTHONY STREET
NEW ORLEANS, LA 70122
PHONE: (504)944-5678

CITY OF FAITH PRISON IND.
752 AUSTIN PLACE
SHREVEPORT, LA 71101
PHONE: (318)424-2701

MAINE

PHAROS HOUSE
5 GRANT STREET
PORTLAND, ME 04101
PHONE: (207)774-6021

MARYLAND

VOLUNTEERS OF AMERICA
4601 EAST MONUMENT ST
BALTIMORE, MD 21205
PHONE: (410)276-5880

MONTGOMERY PRE RLS
11651 NEBEL STREET
ROCKVILLE, MD 20852
PHONE: (240)773-4200

MASSACHUSETTS

BARNSTABLE ELEC. MON.
1445 OSTERVIEW
W. BARNSTABLE, MA 02668
PHONE: (508)375-6160

MCGRATH HOUSE
699 MASSACHUSETTS AVE.
BOSTON, MA 02118
PHONE: (617)424-1390

COOLIDGE HOUSE
307 HUNTINGTON AVENUE
BOSTON, MA 02115
PHONE: (617)424-1390

BARNSTABLE CO. REL. CTR
6000 SHERIFF'S PLACE
BOURNE, MA 02532
PHONE: (508)375-6200

W. MASS. REG. CORR.
701 CENTER STREET
CHICOPEE, MA 01013
PHONE: (413)547-8000

CORR. ALTERNATIVES
165 MARSTON STREET
LAWRENCE, MA 01841
PHONE: (978)750-1900

CORR. ALTERNATIVES
165 MARSTON STREET
LAWRENCE, MA 01841
PHONE: (978)750-1900

HAMPDEN CTY. PRE-REL
325 ALABAMA STREET
LUDLOW, MA 01056
PHONE: (413)547-8000

WOMEN IN TRANSITION
197 ELM STREET
SALISBURY, MA 01952
PHONE: (978)750-1900

HAMPTON CITY ELEC. MON.
311 STATE STREET
SPRINGFIELD MA 01105
PHONE: (413) 547-8000

MICHIGAN

KALAMAZOO PROB. ENHAN.
203B BRIDGEN
BATTLE CREEK, MI 49014
PHONE: (269) 963-2085

KALAMAZOO PROB ENHAN.
497 WAUKONDA AVENUE
BENTON HBR, MI 49014
PHONE: (269) 926-1284

HEARTLINE, INC
8201 SYLVESTER
DETROIT, MI 48214
PHONE: (313)923-4200

GENESIS CCC
11105 E. JEFFERSON AVE.
DETROIT, MI 48214
PHONE: (313)822-4060

RENAISSANCE
11105 E. JEFFERSON AVE.
DETROIT, MI 48214
PHONE: (313)822-2021

MONICA HOUSE CCC
15380 MONICA
DETROIT, MI 48238
PHONE: (313)345-3600

PROACTION BEHAVIORAL
801 COLLEGE S.E.
GRAND RAPIDS, MI 49507
PHONE: (616)776-0891

BANNUM PLACE
2209 NORMAN STREET
SAGINAW, MI 48601
PHONE: (989)401-2340

KPEP
519 SOUTH PARK STREET
KALAMAZOO, MI 49007
PHONE: (269)383-0444

KPEP
1701 OLMSTEAD ROAD
KALAMAZOO, MI 49007
PHONE: (269)383-1386

GREAT LAKES RECOV. CTR.
241 WRIGHT STREET
MARQUETTE, MI 49855
PHONE: (906)228-7611

GRAND TRAVERSE CO.
320 WASHINGTON STREET
TRAVERSE CITY, MI 49684
PHONE: (231)922-4531

MINNESOTA

N.W. REG. CORR. CTR.
816 MARIN AVE, SUITE 110
CROOKSTON, MN 56716
PHONE: (218)727-3828

BETHEL WORK RLS. PGM.
23 MESABA AVE
DULUTH, MN 55806
PHONE: (218)727-3828

BENTON COUNTY JAIL
581 HWY 23 N.E.
FOLEY, MN 56329
PHONE: (320)968-8263

VOLUNTEERS OF AMERICA
2825 EAST LAKE STREET
MINNEAPOLIS, MN 55406
PHONE: (612)721-6327

RENVILLE COUNTY JAIL
104 SOUTH 4 STREET TH
OLIVIA, MN 56277
PHONE: (320) 523-1161

OLMSTEAD COUNTY JAIL
101 4 STREET, SE TH
ROCHESTER, MN 55904
PHONE: (507)328-6795

VOLUNTEERS OF AMERICA
1771 KENT STREET
ROSEVILLE, MN 55113
PHONE: (651)488-2073

SCOTT COUNTY JAIL
301 FULLER ST. SOUTH
SHAKOPEE, MN 55379
PHONE: (952)496-8930

MISSISSIPPI

HATTIESBURG CORR. CTR.
5029 HWY 42 BYPASS
HATTIESBURG, MS 39401
PHONE: (601)582-0843

BANNUM PLACE
1031 WHOLESALE ROW
JACKSON, MS 39201
PHONE: (601)949-7888

BANNUM PLACE
630 A & D CENTER
TUPELO, MS 38801
PHONE: (662)841-7888

MISSOURI

REALITY HOUSE
P.O. BOX 1507
COLUMBIA, MO 65205
PHONE: (573)449-8117

SOUTHEAST MISSOURI CTC
HWY 32 E.,
P.O. DRAWER 459
FARMINGTON, MO 63640
PHONE: (573)756-5749

COMM CORR CENTER
1514 CAMPBELL ST
KANSAS CITY, MO 64108
PHONE: (816)421-6670

CYDKAM CENTER, LLC
1081 HART STREET, BOX 68
NEELYVILLE, MO 63954
PHONE: (573)989-6514

ALPHA HOUSE
MPO #852 2300 E. DIVISION
SPRINGFIELD, MO 65801
PHONE: (417)831-3033

MH SVCS DISMASS HOUSE
5025 COTE BRILLIANTE
ST. LOUIS, MO 63113
PHONE: (314)361-2802

METRO TRNG PROGRAM
1727 LOCUST ST.
ST. LOUIS, MO 63103
PHONE: (314)241-1133

MONTANA

ALPHA HOUSE
104 NORTH 31 STREET ST
BILLINGS, MT 59101
PHONE: (406)259-9609

ALPHA HOUSE WOMEN
1001 SOUTH 27 ST. TH
BILLINGS, MT 59101
PHONE: (406)294-9609

BUTTE PRE-RELEASE CTR.
62 WEST BROADWAY
BUTTE, MT 59701
PHONE: (406)782-23116

GREAT FALLS PRE-RLS CTR
1019 15 STREET NORTH
GREAT FALLS, MT 59401
PHONE: (406)727-0944

Post Sentencing Reductions - 197

NEBRASKA

HALL COUNTY WORK RLS.
131 S. LOCUST
GRAND ISLAND, NE 68801
PHONE: (308)381-5200

WESTERN ALTERNATIVE
101 SOUTH HASTINGS AVE.
HASTINGS, NE 68901
PHONE: (402) 462-2757

NEW HAMPSHIRE

STRAFFORD HOUSE
266 COUNTY FARM ROAD
DOVER, NH 03820
PHONE: (603)742-3310

HAMPSHIRE HOUSE
1490-1492 ELM STREET
MANCHESTER, NH 03101
PHONE: (603) 518-5128

NEW JERSEY

COMPREHENSIVE SANC.
20 TOLER PLACE
NEWARK, NJ 07114
PHONE: (973)642-4299

NEVADA

CORNELL CORRECTIONS
2901 INDUSTRIAL BLVD
LAS VEGAS, NV 89109
PHONE: (702)953-1162

NEW MEXICO

DISMAS CHARITIES, CSC
2331 MENAUL BLVD, NE
ALBUQUERQUE, NM 87107
PHONE: (505)255-6213

DISMAS CHARITIES, CSC
1595 W. PICACHO
LAS CRUCES, NM 88005
PHONE: (505647-1447

NEW YORK

VOLUNTEER OF AMERICA
295 CLINTON STREET
BINGHAMTON, NY 13902
PHONE: (607)797-2258

COMMUNITY CORR. CTR.
2534 CRESTON AVENUE
BRONX, NY 10468
PHONE: (718)561-4155

BROOKLYN CCC
988 MYRTLE AVENUE
BROOKLYN, NY 11206
PHONE: (718)574-4886

BUFFALO HALFWAY HOUSE
115 GLENWOOD AVENUE
BUFFALO, NY 14209
PHONE: (716)882-0027

VOLUNTEERS OF AMERICA
175 WARD STREET
ROCHESTER, NY 14605
PHONE: (585) 454-0489

SYRACUSE PAVILION
701 ERIE BLVD. EAST
SYRACUSE, NY 13210
PHONE: (315)442-5949

N. CAROLINA

SALVATION ARMY CCC
204 HAYWOOD STREET
ASHEVILLE, NC 28802
PHONE: (828)253-4723

198 - Reduce My Prison Sentence

MCLEOD COMP. SANC. CTR
309 REMOUNT ROAD
CHARLOTTE, NC 28203
PHONE: (704)332-3180

TROY HOUSE CCC
1101 NORTH MANGUM ST.
DURHAM, NC 27701
PHONE: (919)683-8331

BANNUM PLACE
952 BRAGG BOULEVARD
FAYETTEVILLE, NC 28301
PHONE: (910)484-6442

GASTON CTY. WORK RLS.
475 NORTH MARIETTA ST.
GASTONIA, NC 28052
PHONE: (704)866-3550

DISMAS CHARITIES
307 N. CHURCH STREET
GREENSBORO, NC 27401
PHONE: (336)370-4357

CAVALCORP COMM. SANC.
312 TRYON ROAD
RALEIGH, NC 27603
PHONE: (919)773-1834

BANNUM PLACE
716 PRINCESS STREET
WILMINGTON, NC 28401
PHONE: (910)762-4235

SALVATION ARMY CCC
1255 NORTH TRADE
ST/POB 1205
WINSTON-SALEM, NC 27102
PHONE: (336)722-8271

N. DAKOTA

SWMCCC WORK RELEASE
66 WEST 12TH STREET
DICKINSON, ND 58601
PHONE: (701)456-7790

CENTRE, INC
100 6TH AVE SE
MANDAN, ND 58554
PHONE: (701)663-8228

CENTRE, INC
123 15TH STREET, N
FARGO, ND 58102
PHONE: (701)237-9340

OHIO

ORIANA HOUSE WOMEN
222 POWER STREET
AKRON, OH 44304
PHONE: (330)996-7595

ORIANA HOUSE MEN
55 E. GLENWOOD AVENUE
AKRON, OH 44309
PHONE: (330)375-6454

TALBERT HOUSE FOR MEN
2216 VINE ST
CINCINNATI, OH 45214
PHONE: (513)684-7965

TALBERT HOUSE WOMEN
1616 HARRISON AVENUE
CINCINNATI, OH 45214
PHONE: (513)557-2500

ORIANA COMP. SANCTION
1829 EAST 55 ST TH
CLEVELAND, OH 44103
PHONE: (216)881-7882

ALVIS HOUSE FOR WOMEN
868 BRYDEN RD
COLUMBUS, OH 43205
PHONE: (614)252-1788

AVIS HOUSE FOR MEN
1755 ALUM CREEK DR
COLUMBUS, OH 43207
PHONE: (614)443-4989

Post Sentencing Reductions - 199

AVIS HOUSE COPE CENTER
42 ARNOLD PLACE
DAYTON, OH 45407
PHONE: (937)278-8219

AVIS HOUSE OHIO LINK
2012 MADISON AVENUE
TOLEDO, OH 43604
PHONE: (419)241-4308

COMMUNITY CORR ASSOC
1764 MARKET STREET
YOUNGSTOWN, OH 44507
PHONE: (330)742-8664

OKLAHOMA

OKLAHOMA HALFWAY HSE.
517 SW SECOND STREET
OKLAHOMA CITY, OK 73109
PHONE: (405)232-0231

OREGON

LANE COUNTY W/R
75 W. 5TH AVENUE
EUGENE, OR 97401
PHONE: (541)682-2297

JACKSON COUNTY W/R
5505 SOUTH PACIFIC HWY
PHOENIX, OR 97535
PHONE: (541)774-6610

OREGON HALFWAY HOUSE
6000 N.E. 80 AVENUE TH
PORTLAND, OR 97535
PHONE: (503)231-7785

PORTLAND YWCA
1111 S.W. 10 AVENUE TH
PORTLAND, OR 97205
PHONE: (503)294-7424

PENNSYLVANIA

COLUMBIA CTY. WORK RLS.
721 IRON STREET
BLOOMSBURG, PA 17815
PHONE: (570)784-4815

CUMBERLAND WORK RLS
1101 CLAREMONT ROAD
CARLISLE, PA 17013
PHONE: (717) 245-8787

BUCKS CTY WORK RLS
1730 S. EASTON ROAD
DOYLESTOWN, PA 18901
PHONE: (215)345-3700

CAPITOL PAVILION CTR.
2012 NORTH FOURTH ST.
HARRISBURG, PA 17102
PHONE: (717)236-0132

CLINTON CITY WORK RLS.
SHOEMAKER ROAD
(POBOX 419)
MCELHATTAN, PA 17102
PHONE: (570) 769-7680

LUZERNE COMM. CORR.
600 E. LUZERNE STREET
PHILADELPHIA, PA 19124
PHONE: (215)634-8960

THE KINTOCK GROUP (CSC)
301 EAST ERIE AVENUE
PHILADELPHIA, PA 19119
PHONE: (215)291-7600

RENEWAL, INC FEMALE
702 2 AVENUE ND
PITTSBURGH, PA 15222
PHONE: (412)697-1616

RENEWAL, INC
339 BLVD. OF THE ALLIES
PITTSBURGH, PA 15222
PHONE: (412)697-1616

200 - Reduce My Prison Sentence

CATHOLIC SOCIAL SRVS.
409-411 OLIVE STREET
SCRANTON, PA 18509
PHONE: (570)342-1295

LACKAWANNA WORK RLS.
614 SPRUCE ST
SCRANTON, PA 18503
PHONE: (570) 963-6509

PUERTO RICO

VOLUNTEER OF AMERICA
1606 FERNANDEZ JUNCOS AVE
SAN JUAN, RQ 00909
PHONE: (787)771-0470

S. CAROLINA

CSC ALSTON WILKES SOC.
1218 BULL STREET
COLUMBIA, SC 29201
PHONE: (803)765-1394

RRC-ALSTON WILKES SOC.
441 W. CHEVES STREET
FLORENCE, SC 29501
PHONE: (843)292-0388

RRC-BANNUM INC.
1605 EASLEY BRIDGE RD.
GREENVILLE, SC 29611
PHONE: (864)269-3150

RRC-ALSTON WILKES SOC.
3290-A MEETING STREET
N. CHARLESTON, SC 29405
PHONE: (843)744-4917

S. DAKOTA

STEPPING STONES REHAB.
901 SOUTH MILER
MITCHELL, SD 57301
PHONE: (605)995-8180

PENNINGTON SHERIFF'S DEPT
725 N. LACROSSE
RAPID CITY, SD 57701
PHONE: (605)394-6128

COMM. ALTERNATIVES
5025 HWY 79 SOUTH
BOX 2273
RAPID CITY, SD 57709
PHONE: (605)341-4240

BEHAVIOR MGT. SYS.
703 ADAMS STREET
RAPID CITY, SD 57701
PHONE: (605)394-6185

GLORY HOUSE
4000 S. WEST AVE,
PO 88145
SIOUX FALLS, SD 57109
PHONE: (605)332-3273

WINNER CITY JAIL
217 E. THIRD STREET
WINNER, SD 57580
PHONE: (605)842-3324

TENNESSEE

SALVATION ARMY CTR.
800 MCCALLIE AVENUE
CHATTANOOGA, TN 37403
PHONE: (423)756-1023

MIDWAY REHAB CENTER
1515 E. MAGNOLIA AVENUE
KNOXVILLE, TN 37921
PHONE: (865)522-0301

DIERSON CHARITIES
1629 WINCHESTER ROAD
MEMPHIS, TN 38116
PHONE: (901)395-0947

DIERSEN - NASHVILLE
808 LEA AVENUE
NASHVILLE, TN 37203
PHONE: (615)254-0006

TEXAS

MCCABE CENTER CSC
1915 E. MARTIN LUTH KING
AUSTIN, TX 78702
PHONE: (512)322-0925

BANNUM INC
1310 PENNSYLVANIA
BEAUMONT, TX 77701
PHONE: (409)835-7575

REALITY HOUSE
405 E. WASHINGTON
BROWNSVILLE, TX 78520
PHONE: (956)541-2771

DISMAS CORPUS CHRISTI
1023 MESTINA STREET
CORPUS CHRISTI, TX 78401
PHONE: (361)881-9888

SANCTIONS CENTER, RIO
1306 E. GIBBS STREET
DEL RIO, TX 7884
PHONE: (830)775-1580

MID-VALLEY HOUSE
402 WEST CHAPIN STREET
EDINBURG, TX 78539
PHONE: (956)383-0663

DISMAS CHARITIES, CSC
7011 ALAMEDA AVENUE
EL PASO, TX 79915
PHONE: (915)781-1122

VOLUNTEERS OF AMERICA
2710 AVENUE "J"
FORT WORTH, TX 76105
PHONE: (817)429-1087

VOLUNTEERS OF AMERICA
2710 AVENUE "J"
FORT WORTH, TX 76105
PHONE: (817)429-1087

LIEDEL SANCTION CENTER
1819 COMMERCE STREET
HOUSTON, TX 77002
PHONE: (713)224-0984

VOLUNTEERS OF AMERICA
800 W. WINTERGREEN RD.
HUTCHINS, TX 75141
PHONE: (972)225-5472

DISMAS CHARITIES
6752 GILBERT ROAD
LAREDO, TX 78041
PHONE: (956)727-0552

CCC DISMAS CHARITIES
709 E. 49TH STREET
LUBBOCK, TX 79404
PHONE: (806)747-5055

DISMAS CHARITIES, CSC
24 INDUSTRIAL LOOP
MIDLAND, TX 79701
PHONE: (432)686-9188

CROSSPOINT CSC
605 AUGUSTA STREET
SAN ANTONIO, TX 78215
PHONE: (210)271-0521

COUNTY REHAB. CTR.
12137 CR 46
TYLER, TX 75704
PHONE: (903)593-3131

SALVATION ARMY CSC
500 FOURTH ST
WACO, TX 76706
PHONE: (254)756-7276

UTAH

CORNELL CORR. INC.
1585 WEST 2100 SOUTH
SALT LAKE CITY, UT 84119
PHONE: (801)973-3800

VIRGINIA

LEBANON COMM. CORR
168 ROGERS STREET, PO BOX 879
LEBANON, VA 24266
PHONE: (276)889-1530

REHABILITATION SERVICES
7718 WARWICK BLVD
NEWPORT NEWS, VA 23607
PHONE: (757)244-0027

REHABILITATION SERVICES
300 WEST 20 STREET TH
NORFOLK, VA 22603
PHONE: (432)686-9188

NORTHWESTERN REG. ADC
141 FORT COLLIER ROAD
WINCHESTER, VA 22603
PHONE: (540)665-6380

WASHINGTON

BELLINGHAM RRC
1641 BAKER CREEK PLACE
BELLINGHAM, WA 98226
PHONE: (360) 671-0597

FRANKLIN CTY. WORK RLS.
1016 N. 4TH STREET
PASCO, WA 99301
PHONE: (509)545-3549

PIONEER FELLOWSHIP
220 11TH AVE.
SEATTLE, WA 98122
PHONE: (206)667-9674

SPOKANE RRC
3614 EAST FERRY AVENUE
SPOKANE, WA 99201
PHONE: (509)535-3572

GEIGER WORK RLS. CTR.
S. 3507 SPOTTED RD.
SPOKANE, WA 99224
PHONE: (509)477-1501

TACOMA RRC
922 SO "J"
TACOMA, WA 98405
PHONE: (253)274-0248

TACOMA PROGRESS HSE.
1119 S. ALTHEIMER ST
TACOMA, WA 98405
PHONE: (253)627-0246

W. VIRGINIA

BANNUM PLACE
260 MONTICELLO ROAD
CLARKSBURG, WV 26301
PHONE: (304)624-7634

MINT/MOTHERS & INFANTS
H 64 BOX 126
HILLSBORO, WV 24946
PHONE: (304)653-4882

DISMAS CHARLESTON
113 EDGAR STREET
ST. ALBANS, WV 25177
PHONE: (304)722-5801

BANNUM PLACE
1070 MARKET STREET
WHEELING, WV 26003
PHONE: (304)233-1081

WISCONSIN

FAHRMAN CENTER
3136 CRAIG ROAD
EAU CLAIRE, WI 54701
PHONE: (715)835-9110

ATTIC CORR. SERVICES
2670 UNIVERSITY AVENUE
GREEN BAY, WI 54311
PHONE: (920) 469-2569

ALTERNATIVE PROGRAM
203 W SUNNY LN RD
JANESVILLE, WI 53546
PHONE: (608)741-4510

ARC HOUSE
2009 E DAYTON ST
MADISON, WI 53704
PHONE: (608)241-7616

SCHWERT HOUSE
3501 KIPLING DRIVE
MADISON, WI 53704
PHONE: (608)249-6226

PARSONS HOUSE
2930 #25 ST
MILWAUKEE, WI 53206
PHONE: (414)445-3301

WYOMING

VOLUNTEERS OF AMERICA
P.O. BOX 1346
GILLETTE, WY 82717
PHONE: (307)682-8505

COMMUNITY ALTERNATIVES
10007 LANDMARK LANE
MILLS, WY 82644
PHONE: (307)268-4840

The Rule 35

A *"Rule 35"* is a post sentencing motion to reduce one's sentence. The Rule 35 is similar to that of a 5K1 motion because it involves a motion that is filed by the government, which asks the court to reduce a defendant's sentence due to substantial assistance that was provided by that defendant. This motion is filed after a defendant has provided assistance in the investigation of prosecution of another person and is a post sentencing motion. There is also a second part of the Rule 35 that allows the court to correct a clerical or technical error within fourteen days after a sentencing hearing.

A Rule 35 motion can not be made when a defendant was previously granted a 5K1 motion; it is either one or the other. Both the 5K1 and the Rule 35 ask the court to reduced one's sentence and therefore can not be used in conjunction with each other. There are a few small differences between the two motions though. First, the 5K1 motion is filed by the government before a defendant is sentenced. The 5K1 motion asks the court to reduce the defendant's sentence as a result of the substantial assistance that the defendant provided to the government regarding the investigation or prosecution of another individual. The one difference between the 5K1 and the Rule 35 is the rules concerning a mandatory minimum sentence. When a defendant, who is facing a sentencing involving a mandatory minimum, is afforded the benefit of a 5K1, the judge will only be able to sentence that defendant below the recommended guideline range (i.e. offense level range). If there is also a mandatory minimum that applies, then the judge will not be capable of imposing a sentence under the mandatory minimum unless the government also files an additional motion under 18 U.S.C. 3553(e) or if the defendant is eligible for the safety valve sentencing relief provision. But, if a defendant has a post sentence Rule 35 motion filed, and subsequently receives a reduction of his sentence under that motion, the judge will then be able to reduce the sentence without regard to any mandatory minimum that one prevailed. Other than these two slight differences, both the 5K1 and Rule 35 motions are very

Post Sentencing Reductions - 205

similar in nature. The guidelines regarding a Rule 35 motion are listed below:

Upon the government's motion made within one year of sentencing, the court may reduce a sentence if the following conditions are met:

A) the defendant, after sentencing, provided substantial assistance in investigating or prosecuting another person; and:

B) reducing the sentence accords with the Sentencing Commission's guidelines and policy statements.

The law was also amended back in 1991 to allow the government to file a Rule 35 motion extending beyond the one year time limit from the sentencing date. This part of the Rule 35 law states, *"Upon the government's motion made more than one year after sentencing, the court may reduce a sentence if the defendant's substantial assistance involves:*

A) information not known to the defendant until one year or more after sentencing;

B) information provided by the defendant to the government within one year or more after sentencing, but which did not become useful to the government until more than one year after sentencing: or

C) information the usefulness of which could not reasonably have been anticipated by the defendant until more than one year after sentencing and which was promptly provided to the government after its usefulness was reasonably apparent to the defendant."

The Rule 35 now enables a defendant to benefit from providing assistance to the government extending beyond the original one year deadline from defendant's sentencing date. There have been many occasions where a defendant was reluctant at first to provide substantial assistance to the government, then was sentenced to a lengthy term of imprisonment, and ultimately decided to offer assistance to the government in hopes of a reduced sentence under the Rule 35.

The Appeal

Defendants who are found guilty via a trial or who plead guilty in federal court are entitled to an appeal unless a waiver of appeal is signed. An appeal challenges the conviction on one or more grounds and can help a defendant with sentencing relief if done successfully. Sometimes though, defendants give up their right to appeal pursuant to the terms of a plea agreement. When this happens (i.e., a waiver of appeal is signed), the appeal process can be much more difficult and it would have to be proved that either the government breached the plea agreement or the defendant signed the plea agreement involuntarily or unknowingly. Other grounds in which a defendant would be able to file an appeal after signing a waiver of appeal would be if the defendant had ineffective counsel or if the sentence imposed was above the recommended guidelines.

The rules of each court do vary so it is best to discuss the possibilities of an appeal with an experienced appellate advisor or qualified attorney. Defendants who wish to appeal their case but lack ability to pay for the appeal, and are subsequently confirmed to be indigent, can have a Federal Public Defender appointed for representation.

Of all the cases appealed in federal courts, approximately ten percent result in reversal or remand. The remaining cases have their sentences upheld with no changes. Of the ten percent of the cases that are reversed or remanded, about one-half of those are ruled in favor of the defendant. Those rulings will usually result in some form of sentencing relief for the defendant. The other five percent of cases that are ruled in the government's favor often open the door for a stiffer sentence for the defendant.

An appeal can be filed by either the defendant or the government. The appeal is filed by the defendant's attorney using a document called a *"notice of appeal."* This document must be filed with the District Court's clerk after sentencing. The appeal can be filed immediately after the sentencing and up to ten days after the District Court has filed the judgment conviction forms. Some of the most common grounds used for an appeal are, as follows:

- problems with the evidence;
- problems with the judge's instructions or rulings;
- issues with jury selection or jury instructions;
- prosecution misconduct, etc.;

During the appeal process, only the information that has been submitted to the District Court can be used. Any new information, such as new evidence or testimony, is not allowed to be admitted into the appeal case.

There will be three judges assigned to the appeals case. The judge that originally imposed the sentence in District Court is never allowed to be one of the appeals judges. Each party (i.e., defense and prosecution) will submit written argument for the appeal citing facts, laws, and details of the case. On occasion, the Appeals court will ask for oral arguments also. Once the defendant and the government have submitted their arguments, the judges will review and then rule on the case. The results will either merit a re-sentencing, reversal, or the sentence will be upheld. If the defendant loses the appeal he will then have fourteen days to file a petition for a rehearing. If the defendant loses the rehearing, or if the rehearing goes unanswered or denied, then the defendant will be eligible to file a petition to the Supreme Court. This petition is called a *"writ of certiorari"* and must be filed within ninety days after the last appeals judgment was filed with the court. From start to finish, the appeals process takes approximately one year to have a case ruled on.

Another method for a defendant to seek relief is via a *"2255 motion,"* pursuant to 18 U.S.C. 2255, which is a motion to vacate, set aside, or correct a sentence. The legal name for this petition is *"writ of habeas corpus."* There are substantial differences between the 2255 motion and a direct appeal though.

To begin with, a defendant can only file a 2255 motion if he is in custody. The requirement for being in custody can be satisfied if the defendant is imprisoned, serving a term of probation or supervised release, on parole, on pre-trial release, or free on bond. With the 2255 motion, unlike a direct appeal, a defendant can introduce new facts, testimony, and evidence to support the basis of the motion. As stated by law, the 2255 motion allows a prisoner to seek relief *"on the ground that the sentence was imposed in violation of the Constitution of laws of the United States, or that the court was without jurisdiction to impose such a sentence, or that the sentence was in excess of the maximum authorized by law, or is otherwise subject to collateral attack."*

There will be limits though as to what arguments an individual can bring forward in a 2255 motion and these will depend on what Circuit Court the motion is filed with. The majority of 2255 motions filed are to argue the fact that a prisoner's counsel was ineffective.

The time limit for filing a 2255 motion is generally one year from the date when the judgment of conviction becomes final. There are several circumstances that extend beyond the scope of this book that will permit an extension to the filing deadline. The rules do vary from circuit to circuit, so it is best to discuss the possibilities of a 2255 motion with an experienced attorney.

A third method which is available to seek relief from a conviction is the 2241 petition. This petition, also known as a *"writ of habeas corpus"*, is available to prisoners who wish to challenge the legality of their custody. The most common uses of the 2241 petition are for prisoners to file suit challenging the conditions of the institution where they are being held or to challenge the length of their sentence. Unless there is not adequate time remaining on one's sentence, all inmates are otherwise required to utilize and exhaust all available administrative remedies before filing a 2241 petition. The petition should be filed in the District Court for the institution where the inmate is being held. Once the petition is filed with the court, it can take up to sixty days for a response. Once again, it is best to seek the advice of someone who is experienced with filing the 2241 petition before it is mailed out.

9
Year and a Day

Have you ever read through the newspaper, saw an article about someone who was sentenced to federal prison, and then skimmed over the article and read something like, "John Doe was sentenced to federal prison for one year and a day."?

Well there is a little bonus to that extra day that some are not aware of; even some attorneys believe it or not. If someone is facing federal charges then they should make sure they get an attorney who practices federal law, not state, not state and federal, strictly federal law. We have talked about this before and here is another great reason for it.

It was April 28, 2010, and I was sitting in the hotel room in Pittsburgh, PA, getting ready to go to my plea hearing. My attorney was downstairs having some coffee and reading over the newspaper. We met shortly before leaving for the courthouse. My stomach was jittery and I passed on any breakfast that morning. I did decide to glance at the newspaper though and check out the front page. It was there that I saw an article of some stock guru who was convicted of securities fraud. Inside the article was information concerning the plea deal and subsequent sentencing of this man. About half way through the article I read about the sentence the judge imposed which was *"one year and a day."* I then queried my attorney about this only to get a reply, *"Hmmm I am not sure, that's a good question."* I am thinking to myself, *"What? Are you kidding me?"* Anyway, that evening I did my own research and found out the significance of that extra day. I also found out that this attorney who accompanied me to Pennsylvania practiced primarily in state, not federal law. I immediately sought the assistance of another attorney in the firm who practiced federal law.

This extra day in one's sentence only has significance in federal, not state imposed sentences. So what is the significance of the extra day? In the federal system there is a reward that inmates earn for good behavior. It is called

Good Time Credit or *"GTC."* GTC is awarded at the end of one's sentence. The total amount of GTC that an inmate receives is forty seven days per calendar year. Soon this will be raised to fifty-four days and maybe even higher if some new laws get passed. There is talk about the attempt to raise GTC to as much as 120 days per year but only time will tell. The BOP is currently only awarding forty-seven days of GTC per year and this is incorrect. The total amount of GTC as of January 2012 should be fifteen percent of one's served sentence. If we do the math we will see that fifteen percent of one calendar year is approximately fifty-four days and not forty-seven days. Inmates are being deprived of seven days GTC for each year served but this issue has been in Congress for many months now and hopefully will be corrected soon. Nonetheless, the GTC that an inmate earns is deducted from his total sentence.

The problem with this good time though is the minimum sentence that must be imposed for it to be triggered. The law states that GTC is only available for inmates serving over one year of imprisonment. Therefore, no matter who they are or what they did, if a judge sentences someone to eleven months and thirty-one days in federal prison (i.e., twelve months) then that person must serve the entire sentence with no possibility of an early release due to good behavior. Inmates can still benefit from an early release due to placement in community confinement but they will not enjoy any benefit from awarded good time days. Of course this type of sentence should not preclude an inmate from conducting himself accordingly as the BOP can still impose sanctions for misconduct such as loss of phone, commissary, visiting, and halfway house privileges and more.

When a judge imposes a sentence that is more than one calendar year, the GTC becomes applicable for the inmate's total length of sentence. For example, someone sentenced to thirty-six moths imprisonment would serve only about thirty-one months with the GTC, providing this inmate has no conduct violations which result in the abolishment of his good time. Additionally, anyone who is being sentenced in federal court, who is expecting a sentence of imprisonment of approximately one year, should make sure his attorney is fully aware of the GTC laws and ready to make a swift request to the court to have an extra day added to the sentence in the event that the judge does hand down a one year term. Anyone who is sentenced to a term of 10 ½ - 12 months imprisonment will be able to benefit from having their sentence increased to a year and a day.

Some judges will not oppose the year and a day request provided there is some kind of reason to back it up. The extra day sentence will entitle an inmate to roughly six weeks off of his total sentence per each calendar year. Once the laws change, this value will increase to as much as twelve weeks per calendar year. An inmate with a year and a day sentence can reasonably expect to walk out of prison and off to a halfway house in about eight to nine months on average. A good way for an attorney to substantiate the request for the year and a day would be to alert the judge that the defendant intends on being a model inmate while incarcerated and would like the opportunity to have his good behavior rewarded with the possibility of good time credits as seen fit by the BOP.

"Life's challenges are not supposed to paralyze you, they're supposed to help you discover who you are."
- Bernice Johnson Reagan

10
Putting it all Together

If you look up *"attorney"* in a dictionary, the definition you will find is will be something like this; *"a legal agent qualified to act for suitors and defendants in legal proceedings."* With that being said, I do not want to mislead all who read this book by casting a dim light on attorneys. There are in fact a select number of fine attorneys in the system and some perform *"above and beyond"* the aforementioned definition, but for the most part one should not expect the *"dream team"* caliber of defense as you may have witnessed in the O.J. and Casey Anthony cases. Yes, an attorney will represent you and defend you, but when it comes time for a court sentencing, a defendant must be clever and independently capable of mustering up as much mitigating ammo as possible for his attorney. Without this ammo, it will be likely that the sentencing hearing concludes like most other typical cases; a stiff and unfair prison sentence. A defendant must find ways to make his case appear *"outside the heartland"* of other typical and similar cases. This is the time to gather up extraordinary and unusual circumstances relevant to one's case and life. Extraordinary and unusual circumstances will yield extraordinary and unusual sentences.

Do not expect the typical criminal defense attorney to flat out tell a defendant about each and every possible mitigating defense tactics that can be used to reduce his sentence either. He just will not do it. Why you ask? Let's compare the vast amount of possible mitigating arguments and defense tactics that an attorney can use at a sentencing hearing to that of a pizza topping. When you go to your favorite pizza place and order up to one of those monstrous thick crust pies there are usually dozens of tasty topping to choose from. Each delicious topping you select does two things: it increases the cost of the pizza and the workload of the chef who is making it. Now let's apply this to one's court case. Lets say that an attorney goes to his client and spends hours upon hours covering every possible mitigating fact that he may be able to argue in the defendant's behalf during the sentencing hearing. His client then selects each and every factor that may apply and possibly help him get a lighter sentence. We will say that this particular defendant has family and health issues that require substantial time to gather facts on and prepare a presentation for the court showing their mitigating value. The attorney needs substantial time to gather written statements from his client's doctors, health specialists, and other important people. These mitigating factors, if proven to be extraordinary in nature, may be able to substantiate the request for a reduced sentence under section 5K2 of the sentencing guidelines. These are also the *"pizza toppings."* The attorney then performs this same time consuming task for all his other clients. They all select their relevant mitigating factors for the attorney to prepare extensive arguments for. Well guess what? The attorney now has dozens and dozens of extra pizza toppings to manage. Some of his clients have many defensive arguments to present to the judge. His workload just increased four fold and his compensation for all this extra work will not increase, regardless if he is a private attorney or a public defender. The attorney will not be compensated any more for his extra hard work and effort. Do you think this attorney is going to go out of his way for each and every one of these cases? Probably not! This is why you must do your part to protect yourself in any criminal case. Keep the information and communication lines open and flowing always.

Once again, your attorney will represent you and defend you but do not expect the superstar defensive tactics and strategies unless you help take charge of your own legal battle. One must also not forget that this attorney probably has several other clients that he is representing at the same time. Each case he takes on requires an additional allotment of professional time. If this attorney spent all his time solely trying to get every one of his clients the lowest possible sentence, all while exercising every possible sentencing relief option, then he would likely run out of time and never succeed in the fast paced legal world. This is why you are reading this book!

It is therefore critical for any defendant to have at least a basic understanding of the facts and laws that surround his case. Using these principles, I found multiple factors in my case that I put in front of my attorney and requested that they be put into action. I was the sole financial provider of my family, had no criminal history, and my offense clearly fit under the description of aberrant behavior. All of these factors played a role in the outcome of my sentence. I prepared several pages myself describing each and every mitigating circumstance in my life as you should also. For instance, if someone served time in the U.S. military then this can be used to help persuade a lower sentence, but only if there are unusual circumstances involved. In a case like this the military service needs to be cast into the spotlight. It must be distinguished from all others or else it will be written off as just another individual serving in the Armed Forces; while that is honorable, it is not really extraordinary, and therefore not deserving of a reduced sentence. The defendant needs to write about why his service was extraordinary in itself. Maybe that person received special awards, saved a life, spent years away from family members due to service duties, got injured while on the front line, or used the military to turn away from a past filled with drugs or gangs. Hopefully as you're reading this you can see what will make a judge sway towards a more lenient sentence and what will make him just move on to the next case. Submitting pages of supporting information to an attorney, and not merely a paragraph or two, is a great way to keep the logs on the fire.

A defendant should also make sure his attorney prepares and submits a sentencing memorandum which clearly details all relevant mitigating factors applicable to the defendant. The sentencing memorandum should also have in it, a request for a reduction in the defendant's sentence and thoroughly back up the reasons for the request clearly detailing each mitigating factor. The judge will read this sentencing memorandum along with the defendant's PSI before he imposes sentence at the sentencing hearing.

A judge may or may not allow character witnesses to speak at the sentencing hearing. Regardless, supportive letters from family and friends, the more the better, should be filed with the sentencing memorandum. I spent dozens of hours contacting family and friends asking each of them personally to write a character witness letter about me. A defendant should make sure that his attorney will be bringing each and every mitigating argument forth at the sentencing hearing and saving the best for last. Having supportive friends and family members at the sentencing, while difficult for some to do, will never hurt one's chances for a lighter sentence.

When a judge does calculate the appropriate sentence for a defendant, he is required by law to impose a sentence sufficient but not greater than necessary. The law also states that the judge **MUST** consider seven factors when determining a particular sentence. These factors are as follows:

1) The nature and circumstances of the offense and the history and characteristics of the defendant;

2) The need for the sentence imposed to reflect the seriousness of the offense, to promote respect for the law, and to provide just punishment for the offense. The sentence shall afford adequate deterrence to criminal conduct, protect the public from further crimes of the defendant and provide the defendant with needed educational or vocational training, medical care, or other correctional treatment in the most effective manner;

3) The kinds of sentences available;

4) The kinds of sentence and the sentencing range established for applicable category of the offense committed by the applicable category of defendant as set forth in the guideline;

5) Any pertinent policy statement issued by the Sentencing Commission pursuant to section 994(a) (2) of title 28, United States Code;

6) The need to avoid unwarranted sentence disparities among defendants with similar records who have been found guilty of similar conduct;

7) The need to provide restitution to any victims of the offense;

People reading this book may have heard of the expression *"Booker"* or *"Post-Booker."* In this landmark case, United States vs. Booker, the Supreme Court ruled that the once mandatory sentencing guidelines were no longer mandatory. When a defendant was sentenced in court before the Booker ruling, the judge was required to impose a sentence within the guideline range. There was no discretion afforded to the judge and a sentence within the offense level guideline range was mandatory. A good example of this was the case of United States vs. Martha Stewart. In this case Stewart was found guilty via a jury trial. The resulting offense level as determined by the probation department was a twelve. The recommended sentence for an offense level twelve in category one of the sentencing table was 10-16 months imprisonment. In the *"Post-Booker"* era, the judge would have had discretion to sentence Stewart to home detention or probation for the offense level. However, since the offense occurred prior to the Booker ruling, the judge in Stewart's case was required to impose at least a split sentence (i.e., five months imprisonment and five months home confinement). In fact, the judge actually expressed his regrets to Stewart when imposing the sentence of five months imprisonment and five months of home confinement. It was clear that the judge wanted to hand down a lighter sentence but was not allowed to make that decision.

With *"Post-Booker"* law, the guidelines are now completely advisory and no longer mandatory in nature. The judge at sentencing now has more freedom to impose sentences that reflect the true nature and circumstances that surround the offense and also the offender. The fact alone that the once mandatory guidelines are now advisory, gives new hope to defendants who can present formidable mitigating factors to the judge.

By the time sentencing day has arrived, a properly prepared defendant should have previously double checked his PSI report for accuracy and worked diligently with his attorney to help prepare a fruitful pre-sentence memorandum. The memorandum should have been filed with the court shortly before the sentencing date. The memorandum contained abundant information about the defendant's personal life, education, religious background, plans for the future, mitigating factors, good works, etc. This wise defendant has also persuaded his attorney to help him prepare a detailed probationary schedule containing an approved treatment program (if applicable) and a job training or work schedule. For example, a defendant who was in need of a substance abuse program, who then thoroughly prepared a post sentencing treatment and rehabilitation plan to present to the judge at sentencing, will likely have a better chance at leniency than the same defendant who submits no proposed plan of action. A defendant's chances for a non-prison sentence will improve with a creative and carefully planned out post sentence plan of action. Even better, would be a defendant who was already enrolled in a treatment program, before his sentencing. This type of pro-active behavior clearly demonstrates the defendant's commitment to rehabilitate himself. If these efforts are also mentioned in the defendant's PSI report, then they will serve as another plus when sentencing day arrives.

Creating a dialogue of mitigating factors should have also been atop the defendant's list of priorities. A well prepared defendant has spent many hours contributing facts and stories to his attorney regarding all possible mitigating arguments that can be used. Many of those mitigating examples that may apply to one's case have probably been exemplified in this book. The defendant has worked with his attorney via frequent meetings and consultations keeping him aware that his case is not going to be placed on the back burner. A defendant who talks to his attorney once every few weeks for a quick five minute conversation will likely not get the quality of legal representation that he deserves and requires. Frequent contact is critical! This diligent defendant has asked that his attorney file a motion to the court for a downward departure before the sentencing date. This may be done in conjunction with the sentencing memorandum or filed in a separate motion. This motion will detail the defendants mitigating arguments which should support the motion for the reduced sentence. In addition to this, the defendant has asked his attorney to include a proposed *"statement of reasons"* that will give valid reasons for a reduced sentence that the sentencing judge may be able to adopt into his decision. The judge is required by law to provide his own written statement in the event that he imposes a sentence below the advisory guideline and this formal statement submitted by the defendant's attorney may be timesaving and helpful to the judge.

This well prepared defendant has gathered as many character witness letters as possible from family members, friends, employers, employees, counselors, teachers, treatment specialists, doctors, etc. These letters were given to the defendant's attorney well before the sentencing date and were attached as part of the sentencing memorandum. If the defendant has a speech that he wishes to deliver at the sentencing hearing, then this speech has been memorized and rehearsed to perfection. The speech clearly shows the defendant's acceptance for his actions and a sense of true remorse for the judge to see. The defendant and his attorney have thoroughly discussed the different sentences that could result at the hearing and the mitigating factors that will be presented to the court.

If a term of imprisonment is ordered, the defendant had confirmed that his attorney is prepared to swiftly ask the judge to recommend designation to an institution close to the defendant's home. This is important when it comes time for the security classification and designation stage, done by the sentencing computation center in Texas.

If the defendant is seeking placement into the RDAP, then this attorney will also ask the judge to include a referral for RDAP placement on the judgment form. Although the BOP does not have to adhere to a judge's request for RDAP enrollment of an inmate, a formal suggestion by a judge can only help improve one's chances for RDAP acceptance.

If the defendant's offense level dictates, then the defendant has also confirmed that his attorney will try to argue for probation, home confinement, or a split sentence when the judge imposes sentence. Reasons to support the request for a self surrender should have also been discussed. If the judge does allow the defendant to self surrender then the defendant and his attorney are prepared to ask the judge for no less than twelve weeks before the self surrender date. Sometimes the judge will allow an eight week period of time before the surrender date and this will often allow enough time for the defendant to be appointed to a suitable institution and forgo the stressful *"diesel therapy"* saga. Top this off with proper attire and punctuality and this defendant is ready for his sentencing day.

11
Prison Blues

If you or anyone you know ever has to go to prison, remember you are never alone during these troublesome times. During my short term of incarceration I decided to keep a diary to help get through the tough times. I recommend this hobby for anyone serving a term of incarceration. Not only is it therapeutic, but it will serve as a documented chapter in one's life that can always be referred back to; it will keep a person's motivation and attitude alive and well.

During my short stay in the Estill Federal Prison camp there was not one day that went by without my family and happy life on my mind. The best kept secret to surviving any prison sentence is staying busy. One must find a way to use the prison system to their advantage. Whether it is getting in great physical shape, getting closer to God, writing a book, getting a GED, or learning to play a musical instrument, it is vital to find a variety of things to do and goals to accomplish; it does wonders. Get a plan together and stick to it. You will emerge from prison twice the person you were before you went in!

I was so intrigued by one of the inmates who I became friends with while in prison. His name was Mike and he always had a positive attitude. Poor guy was doing two years for growing marijuana plants. Mike and I worked together at the prison power plant Monday through Friday. Every day Mike would talk about his cooking plans for dinner. I always chuckled at his recipes because the only thing we had to cook with in prison was hot water so I had no idea how he was making tasty food until one day when I sampled one of his creations. There were no stoves, no microwaves, no sources of heat except hot water, but this resourceful man whipped up some of the tastiest dishes that one could imagine in this type of environment. Mike spent hours per day slicing up onions and peppers for his meals along with other time consuming prep work. He learned to cook all his hot meals using nothing but plastic bags and hot water. The task of heating food consisted of a plastic bag filled with the food items and then dropping the bag into a thermos of hot water. Just to melt cheese took about an hour of constantly changing the water in the thermos. He made the finest tasting tuna wraps and nachos and cheese that I ever tasted. Some of his other notable dishes were chicken and rice, macaroni and cheese, and a killer fried rice bowl. This was Mike's hobby and he kept busy doing it. From what I learned Mike was excited about pursuing a career in culinary arts once he was released. This is a perfect example of someone who received an unfortunate prison sentence and then used it to his advantage. Spending all those hours preparing his home cooked dinners while in prison was all he needed to unleash his passion for cooking and pursue a career in the culinary field. I wish him and his family the best!

My survival secret while in prison was reading, writing, and getting in great shape. As a result of these hobbies, I became a writer and have been enjoying writing ever since. Communication with family and friends is also one of the most important keys to prison success. Talking to family and friends on a regular basis not only gives a sense of closeness, but it keeps you connected to the ones that are likely the most important in your life. They can lift you up during a bad day and bring a smile to your face just when you thought it was impossible. The prison in Estill, South Carolina, where I stayed had an inmate email program (i.e., TRULINCS - "The Trust Fund Limited Inmate Computer System") and phone service (i.e., ITS – "Inmate Telephone System"). I talked to my family everyday whether it was via email, phone, or handwritten letters.

Having plans for a weekend visit from family or friends is even better and rivals any phone call or email. I can recall two particular inmates who got visits every weekend. They were both in the middle of long, ten year sentences with just under five years remaining. One was a former senator from Georgia and the other was a boxer. Every time I saw these two individuals they looked happy and often would cast a smile at me when I would walk by. I credited much of those upbeat emotions due to those weekly visits by friends and loved ones. It definitely helps ease tough times when you get to see and hug someone close to you.

My cellmates or *"cellies"* were all friendly and helpful throughout my stay in federal prison. There were four other inmates which I had to share living quarters with and that took a little getting used. Due to the fact I was assigned to a prison camp, the lowest security institution in the federal correctional system, I actually lived in a cube and not a cell. There were no bars or doors that locked us in. The setting was more like the hallway of an elementary school with little cubes on each side. The entire hallway was open with the exception of the five foot high walls that defined the perimeter of each cube. Each cube held either four or five inmates. The cubes were approximately fifteen feet wide by ten feet deep. They were not spacious by an means. My cube housed five guys total, including me of course. They were all black males in their thirties or forties, very good men too! I was shocked at the sentences they were serving. The inmate across from me on the top bunk was the friendliest. His name was Ernest. He was serving a twenty-something year sentence for drugs. He was originally ordered to serve life in federal prison until the new crack law was made retroactive. This reduced his sentence to twenty-five years and he only had a couple of more to do. I occasionally overheard him talking of his exciting plans when he is finally released. He seemed like a smart man with a good head on his shoulders. He studied and read all the time in our cube and I was very impressed with his uncanny ability to pass the time with such grace and ease. The guy below him was named Tim, who was a very quiet man and mostly kept to himself. We did not talk much except for an occasional hello to cach othcr in the hall. Andrew slept under me. He spent his free time watching sports, playing cards, and doing some reading. Dave occupied the middle bed. Dave and I probably talked the most. He was serving more than ten years for drugs and had a few years left just like Ernest. Dave and Tim had between five and ten years remaining in their sentence and Andrew had about eight.

The cube was setup with two double bunk beds and one single bed. I will talk about the beds a little later in this chapter; they are worth mentioning, and also worth forgetting! I knew it was extremely important to get along with my cellies or else my time would be more difficult to do.

I also knew I would not have a problem with this because of my good attitude, polite manners, and friendly disposition. If there was friction with one of the guys then I would either resolve it in a calm, polite manner, or simply avoid that individual to the best of my ability. The inmates in the cube next to me had different plans. They flat out did not like each other. There was constant arguing and complaining going on. I can only assume this made time go by much slower and thank God that I was not assigned to that cube. The final straw was drawn when one of them told the other that *"If he didn't eat so many beans then he would not fart so much!"* The other replied, *"I will fart until Jesus comes! I used to fart against the wall, but now I will turn towards you each time I have to fart!"* It was actually a very comical battle between the two and caused a chuckle or two from my mouth. In the end, no punches were thrown and the *"non farter"* decided to put in a request to move to a different cube. He was granted that request the following week and peace once again reigned over the housing unit.

During my entire stay I can only recall one actual fight that ensued. The brawl, if that is what you want to call it, took place in the TV room between a sixty something year old man and another guy. The old man hit the other inmate with his chair because he changed the TV station and would not change it back. It was broken up quickly by the other inmates and luckily none of the correctional officers found out about it. I tried to avoid the TV rooms as much as I could due to the high tension that lurked in the musty air. Watching TV was also not high on my priority list of things to do. I would try to find a seat occasionally to watch a Boston Celtics or New England Patriots game but that was the extent of my TV needs.

There were two large and two small TV rooms in my housing unit. The large rooms had five televisions and the small rooms had two televisions. One of the small TV rooms was designated as the Spanish TV room for inmates wishing to watch the Spanish speaking shows. None of the televisions had sound, well they didn't have sound in the traditional sense. An inmate would have to purchase a radio from the commissary to listen to any of the televisions. Each television was preset to an assigned FM radio frequency. To listen to that TV, you would have to tune your radio into the correct station and then put your headphones on. The cost of batteries clearly became an issue for some inmates.

For me it was the library that made my time pass the fastest. There was a general library and also a law library at the prison. As mentioned before, it was so important to find a hobby or an interest in something while in prison. The library was small but had a fair amount of books, encyclopedias, and movies for the inmates. There were a few small TV's in the library for the inmates to use for movies and educational videos. It was the vast amount of legal books and publications inside the law library that consumed most of my time while incarcerated. Much of the helpful information I learned from the various books, inmates and attorneys who were serving time with me, is published in this book.

If there is one thing that will make anyone do a double-take when going to prison for their first time, it will be their first glimpse of the bed which they will be required to sleep atop every night. Believe me, when I first saw that little bed I thought I would not sleep one night in that place. The cheaply made rubber-like mattress is only about three feet wide by six feet long and has *"prison"* written all over it, not literally of course. I am happy to report though, after about the fourth or fifth day I was sleeping throughout most of the night. During the beginning portion of my sentence, I found that all the exercise and walking I was doing wore me out enough so that I was exhausted by 9:00 pm. and ready to shut my eyes. I even got used to the snoring by the second or third week. It is just amazing how the human body learns to adapt to dynamic situations and offer up assistance during times of duress and discomfort.

There were about eighty inmates in the wing of the housing unit where I lived. There were two wings per housing unit and about 160 inmates housed in each unit. A total of two housing units sat on the property. During my stay, the inmate population roughly averaged three hundred inmates at any one given time. There also was a medium security prison next door which held about 1500 inmates. Unfortunately, the prison camp frequently suffered enduring lockdowns and shakedowns due to the frequent trouble that often arose next door at the medium security institution.

There were only eight showers to share between the eighty or so inmates in each wing so taking a shower occasionally took some planning. Overall, the best time to grab a free shower was later in the evening or right before the 4pm count. The showers all locked from the inside and had plenty of hot water available.

The one thing that will definitely remind someone that he is in prison is the multiple counts that are conducted each day and night. Although each prison has slightly different ways of doing things, they all have frequent daily and nightly inmate counts. A *"count"* is the appropriate name given to the time when all inmates must report to their assigned cells or cubes so that the correctional officers can walk through and compile an accurate census of inmates. The counts were obviously important to account for all inmates and provide an accurate way to detect missing or escaped inmates. The two basic types of counts conducted were the *"stand up"* count and *"regular"* count.

The stand up count is, as its name suggests, a count of inmates who must be in their assigned cells or cubes and standing up. The regular count is the same as the stand up count except an inmate does not have to be standing during this count. Additionally, there were several different occasions when counts were announced aside from the regularly scheduled counts such as during foggy days or in an emergency situation. All inmates were required to be quiet during the counts and no one was allowed out of their cubes until the count was completed and cleared. On a couple of occasions one of the inmates struck up an argument with one of the officers and it usually ended up with the inmate escorted off to the Special Housing Unit or *"SHU."* There was no benefit to trying to argue, reason, or bargain with a correctional officer. Even if an inmate was right it was senseless to try to resolve it during count time. Estill Prison Camp had five counts each day. They counted us at 9:30pm, 12:00am, 3:00am, 5:00am, and 4:00pm. On weekends and holidays there was an extra count conducted at 10:00am. The 9:30pm and 10:00am counts were stand-up counts. Depending on the guards on duty, night time counts could be performed with a flashlight being stuck in your face or the bunk bed being shook to see if there was a live body under the sheets and not a bundle of pillows and blankets.

The worst for me was the sound of those oversized jingling keys. Oh yes, that does happen in real life prisons and not only on television as some people believe. I was awestruck at the immense size of those things! They must have added five pounds of weight to the officers carrying them. Maybe this also explained the cumbersome pace of the typical correctional officer. You always knew a guard was nearing when that eerie jingle filled the air.

The number of guards on duty at any one time depended on the security level of the prison. At a minimum security institution there was usually only one officer on duty for the entire compound. During counts though, there would be two guards that walked through the halls during the count. Like any prison there was the list of good guards and bad ones. The bad often outnumbered the good by about three to one. Because I was as always friendly and polite to everyone, and never broke any of the rules, I was never bothered much at all by any of the guards. I can recall three specific guards that none of the inmates particularly cared for. They subsequently got assigned interesting nicknames. The first correctional officer (CO) was a short black male that was known as *"little shorty"* by the inmates. The second CO, who was disliked the most, was a female guard who many thought resembled a chicken. Whenever she would come walking down the compound I would hear other inmates say, *"Look out, here comes cluck cluck."* She was forever branded with that secret nickname. The third least liked CO was a man who towered over everyone. He stood a full six and a half feet tall and inherited the appropriate name *"Green Mile."* I personally liked this guard because even though he was very strict and serious about his job, he had a level of compassion and fairness that was given to the inmates who behaved properly. He was not a bad guy, but don't get caught doing something illegal by him or else! Luckily I never had any problems with him or any of the CO's throughout my entire stay. The fact of the matter was that if you did your time quietly, legally, and kept to yourself, there was no reason for any of the CO's to pester or harass you.

228 - Reduce My Prison Sentence

Before I came to prison I was very unsettled not knowing what the prison environment would be like. Now I can confidently say that a group of inmates inside a prison is really no different than a group of people in the stands at a New York Giants football game. Even though I was at a minimum security institution, the conversations that I had with others who stayed at higher security prisons told me that the environment was similar at those places also. At the higher security prisons there was more gang activity but if you weren't involved with a gang and simply minded your own business, you would not be bothered. If you exhibited an attitude that involved trouble and disrespect then you would get the same treatment in return. Prison is all about respect, respect, respect.

Inside any prison there are all races, ages, colors, and religions, of men and women alike, the men and women segregated of course. Every prison will have its share of troublemakers, loud mouths, and snitches but for the most part the inmates behave themselves accordingly and by the rules. I was actually surprised at how polite and mild tempered most of the inmates acted. My time was made easier by minding my own business and making the important decision to not partake in any prohibited activities like smoking, gambling, stealing, etc. I always had a good intuition for judging people and met a few other inmates who I became friends with. I also knew which inmates to steer clear of. There were only a couple and it was obvious which guys had a bad attitude.

Illegal activities are alive and well in prison. Whether it was alcohol, cigarettes, or gambling to suit your needs, it was accessible in prison. I can recall one time when the entire group of inmate landscape workers were thrown in the SHU. The SHU or *"hole"* is the name given to the Special Housing Unit. This group of individuals got the privilege to work outside the prison mowing grass and trimming hedges. The temptation of this *"outside of the fence"* job got the best of them. One of the workers had a friend on the outside that agreed to hide a stash of hard liquor in one of the bushes, Jack Daniels to be exact. The following week when they were outside doing their grass cutting duties, one of the inmates grabbed the liquor and managed to smuggle it inside. Getting the alcohol inside was not a difficult task and only involved walking through a steel gate and past one of the guards who very rarely searched anyone. So now that this group of inmates had alcohol, guess what? Yes, time to have a party! A few of them got together and obviously emptied the bottle of *"Jack"* through the course of the evening. With a stomach full of whiskey and a good buzz, an inmate decided to shoot off one of the fire extinguishers in the housing unit. Sulfur spray filled the hallway and housing unit. Luckily it was the other housing unit where this happened. The guards eventually found out, whether it was a result of the sulfur smell or via a snitch, and the entire group of inmates got sent to the SHU for several weeks. They also got written up with a violation, also known as a *"shot,"* which can affect everything from good time, phone and email privileges, commissary privileges, and more. Serious shots can lead to additional charges and transfer to a higher security institution depending on the seriousness of it.

With regards to less serious illegal activities, well of course there is always a poker game to be found at any prison where there is a general population. The inmates would gather in the card room and have a poker game usually every night. The game of choice was none other than Texas Hold'em. All forms of gambling was done with postage stamps. Stamps were the only form of currency allowed at the prison. Everything bought or sold inside the prison was based on books of stamps. On a few occasions I stopped by the card room and watched the game in progress for an hour or two. There were never any stamps present at the table and I am not sure how the actual gambling was done, but everything revolved around points. I can only assume that a certain number of points were equivalent to one stamp.

Cell phones were also possessed by a certain caliber of people while in prison. Congress enacted a new law in 2010 which made possession of a cell phone punishable by up to one year in prison. This law also included anyone who provided an inmate a cell phone. I can recall about three or four times when phones were confiscated and inmates punished. I remember the first incident well. It occurred in mid December, 2010, soon after the noon meal. This one inmate, Jimmy, was the one who got caught. Jimmy had smuggled a cell phone and charger into the prison. He worked in the kitchen on the serving line and always seemed like a nice guy. I am not sure who snitched on him but it was apparent that someone did because on this cool winter day, shortly after lunch, two guards swiftly went in and escorted Jimmy back to the administration building. On the way there Jimmy lunged back from the guards in an effort to ditch the cell phone. He tried to throw the phone on top of the building next to him without the guards noticing. The guards witnessed his actions and pounced on him like a bear on a barrel of fresh salmon. There was a brief struggle before Jimmy was put in cuffs and led away. He will probably have some extra time added to his sentence. The craziest thing was that this guy was only a few months away from being released after serving a two year sentence. Needless to say, Jimmy spent the Christmas holiday locked up in the SHU. He will likely be transferred to a higher security prison as a result of his conduct also. Having a cell phone clearly does not pass the risk versus reward test. Having one is not worth the risk whatsoever.

If there was gossip to hear about then the cafeteria was the place where you would learn the who's who about anyone. It was odd eating in a room full of guys who all wore the same colored shirt and pants. This was something that you get used to after a few weeks. After hearing all the horror stories about the poor quality of food served in prison I was expecting a bowl of slop to be served on my tray every day. To my surprise the food in this particular institution was not half bad. The meals were full of beans, rice, and ultra high on carbohydrates, but I did not eat in the dining hall more than once per day. The prison served up three meals per day and all the meals were prepared by inmates who worked in the kitchen. During the meals there would always be at least one guard present. During the lunch meal was when the Warden and other higher up prison officials would come by to observe. The food was served via a serving line where about four inmates served up the meal. Inmates had the choice of the standard meal or the heart healthy meal which was not much different than the normal meal. The fried chicken, for instance, would be substituted with baked chicken for the heart healthy version and the French fries would be replaced with a baked potato. There was no mixing and matching different foods and you were only allowed to go through the serving line once. There were times though, when a particular guard would allow the inmates to get back in line for a second serving of food. This was the obvious humane choice because any food that was leftover went directly into the trash that day. Some of the guards had a power fetish and denying an inmate extra food was just one way to satisfy the fetish.

The key to okay meals in prison depended on what inmates did the cooking. If the prison had a good group of inmates that knew a thing or two about cooking then we would usually see at least average quality meals served up. There were plenty of days that consisted of bland meals, but for the most part the food was not bad. There were no knives in the dining hall, only spoons and forks, therefore cutting up a chicken breast was a task. As far as beverages, soda was non-existent in the cafeteria. There was a self serve juice machine that pumped out water, ice tea, grape juice, and orange flavored juice. These were flavored juices and not real juice. Real juice was prohibited because the inmates could make *"hooch"* from it. Hooch is the name given to the process where orange juice is fermented into an alcoholic beverage.

The cooks did a decent job with desserts too. They made tasty peanut butter cake that was served every Monday. Other desserts they baked were peanut butter cookies, bread pudding, sugar cookies, and a vanilla flavored cake. The task at hand for many inmates was to successfully hide a stash of food in an empty potato chip bag and sneak it out of the dining hall. Only certain guards who worked would search inmates as they exited the dining hall. If an inmate got caught it usually concluded with a warning and confiscation of the food.

All inmates, unless excused for medical reasons, were required to have a job while serving time. Shortly after arriving to federal prison an inmate will go through A&O, better known as Admissions and Orientation. This period of time, typically a few weeks long, ends with an A&O meeting where all the new inmates gather together and hear a short speech from several prison officials and department heads. We heard quick speeches from the head of security, safety, unit counselor, education, recreation, and one of the correctional officers. The purpose of the meeting is to give information about the institution and the various rules. At the conclusion of this very boring meeting is when the unit counselor will decide on a job for each inmate. At the A&O meeting an inmate will be required to fill out a form and list any and all job qualifications. Since I was mechanically inclined and good with my hands I was appointed to work in the prison power plant, also called the powerhouse. Other inmates got appointed to kitchen, landscaping, warehouse, maintenance, and other jobs around the compound. Regardless of what job an inmate received, they were all very easy and consisted of no more than a couple of hours of actual work each day. My pay scale obviously did not commensurate with my experience level but twelve cents per hour was not too shabby for a newbie - I am kidding. My paycheck totaled just shy of twenty dollars per month and was enough to pay my email and phone expenses for a week. It was better than nothing. I would be amazed at how the inmates would argue about deserving a raise for their job and how they were going to keep asking their boss for one.

My job was to monitor the boilers, hot water heaters, back-up generators, and air conditioning units. I would take readings once per hour and if all was running okay then I could sit in the tool room and read or write or play cards until it was time for the next reading. The readings only took ten minutes to record on paper. While the job was easy, it did not come without days of me sitting, looking into outer space thinking about my family. I missed them so much every single day. Being separated from family is surely the hardest part of going to any prison.

For leisure and recreation there was a fair amount of resources available at this prison camp. Inmates could play bocce, horseshoes, foosball, ping-pong, softball, basketball, soccer, or jog the track. There were no free weights but this institution did have a few exercise machines for inmates to use. There were four or five guitars that inmates could sign out and play also. There were one or two highly talented musicians that would often play guitar on the bleachers. One of them was finishing up a long sentence of ten years and his guitar playing skills were amazing. He learned to play while in prison and will surely get noticed on the outside when he picks up a guitar. There was also a summer softball and basketball league that kept inmates busy. But regardless of the recreational activities available, boredom was always lurking around the next corner. One can only play so many games of horseshoes and ping pong before enough is enough. Luckily, my new found desire to become a writer filled the voids during boring spells throughout my sentence. The prison also had a leather shop where inmates could sign up to take classes on leather crafting. The leather shop room was small and could only accommodate a handful of inmates. Those that took the class went on to make truly fabulous pocketbooks, wallets, and purses. I was impressed at the hidden talents that many of the inmates possessed.

If you want to know what typical daily life is like in a federal prison, well, I do not want to discourage anyone who may be making the trip soon, but I would choose a job cleaning sewage tanks over it any day. No, but really, daily life while incarcerated has that ho-hum feeling of repetition. A typical weekday for me would consist of waking up to toilets flushing, inmates passing gas, showers running, and inmates scuffling around getting ready for either their early morning jobs or for the dining hall to open for breakfast. This all happens before 6am too! The kitchen workers had to report to work by 5am to get the breakfast meal ready. As a result, I usually was awake in my bunk around 5-6 in the morning. I would usually role off my mattress and then climb down my cold steel framed bunk bed ladder at 6am or somewhere close to that time. I would throw on my navy green uniform and head to the bathroom to wash up and brush my teeth. I did not dare attempt to take a shower in the morning. They were almost always full in the morning hours. At about 7:30am the guard on duty would yell over the loudspeaker, *"Attention on the compound, attention in the housing quarters, work call, work call, the grey gate is open, work call, work call!"* The grey gate is the ugly steel gate that many of the workers, including me, had to pass through to get to the adjacent building where the powerhouse, warehouse, maintenance, and landscaping offices were. So off through the grey gate I would scurry, and work from 7:30 to 10:30. At 10:30am the guard would once again open the grey gate to let all the workers back through for the lunch meal. I would grab a place in line and wait until they called: *"Attention on the compound, mainline is open, mainline is open."* This means *"lunch is served"* to you and me. It was approximately a thirty minute wait to get the lunch meal. After lunch it was back to work at noon time. Once again, the loudspeakers would come alive. These speakers were positioned all around the camp, indoors and outdoors. At noon time it was more of *"Attention on the compound, attention in the housing quarters, work call, work call, this is pm work call, work call, work call."* You probably know the routine by now. Yes, back through that same ugly grey steel gate and to the powerhouse I would go again. I would continue my job duties at the powerhouse until 2:30pm when the grey gate would be opened one last time to let the inmates back in. From then until the 4pm count I was free to do whatever I wanted. I use the term *"free"* very loosely here too. This is when I could be found in either the leisure library or law library writing, typing, or doing research. At 4pm it was the time for the afternoon stand up count. That would usually only take ten minutes or so to complete. After the count was complete the loudspeaker would once again come to life and announce the dinner meal. I would usually skip the dinner meal and resort to a tuna or mackerel wrap that I bought from the commissary. I have no idea how I did not get completely sick of fish while incarcerated but I ate it almost every night. I would usually head back to the library after the 4:00 count and do some more writing, typing, and research. This would be broken up by a frequent game of *"spades"* with some of the other regular card players.

All the inmates needed to be back inside to their respective housing units no later than 8:30pm each night. My plan when back inside would be to call my family, check my email, and then chat with a couple of friends. After that I would head back to my cube and continue to read or write until 9-10pm which was when I would hop back up into that poor extra slim and sleek bed, grab my *"Mighty Night Light"* reading light and read until my eyes became too heavy to hold open.

Now that you have an idea what a typical daily itinerary consisted of in a federal prison camp, imagine doing this day after day after day. As tough as it may sound, it really was a matter of attitude and thinking about good times ahead. These thoughts, combined with my perseverance to complete my first book made the days cruise mostly. If anyone reading has to make the dreaded trip to a federal prison, find a hobby as soon as you can, challenge your mind, and keep busy. The one advantage that one will have is that inside prison an individual will have ample time to complete goals and achieve things that never would have been possible in the outside world. Take these hidden opportunities and grab them by the ears. Stay close to your family and loved ones, don't break any prison rules, find a couple of good friends, and watch yourself emerge from prison twice the man or woman you were before you went in.

12
Prison Diary

For the few weeks prior to, and then after my self-surrender to the Estill Federal Prison Camp on November 1, 2010, the day after Halloween, I decided that keeping a weekly log of my daily life while incarcerated was important to me. Below is an exact duplicate of my weekly entries describing my emotions, feelings, and thoughts of what daily prison life is like. The following entries have been published exactly how they were written and no corrections to spelling or grammar have been made. These entries can help convey the true feelings and emotions that one may typically experience when being sentenced to a short term of imprisonment in a federal institution.

November 1st, 2010 - The last two days of my life have truly been the most challenging. Yesterday I woke up in my own bed with my beautiful wife and little ten year old girl. It was Sunday, October 31st, Halloween morning, and one day before I had to surrender at Estill Federal Prison Camp in South Carolina. I hugged my little girl while she cried and explained to her that this nightmare will be over soon. We then went and made a *"Flat Daddy"* out of paper. Anyone who knows what a *"Flat Stanley"* is can surely relate to the *"Flat Daddy."* It is a simple paper figure with cut out arms and legs and a picture of my face pasted on. This flat daddy would replace me for several months. This is how I would be with my family for the next several months.

My mom and dad have been such a godsend and have been staying with us for the last few days to help ease the pain of this trivial time. My little girl went for a bike ride with my mom at about 11am on Sunday and my wife was at the farmer's market selling our herbal tea. Here was my cue to exit while everyone was gone and occupied. I hopped in our truck and started the engine and drove off. This would be the last time I would see my family and friends for a long time. Ahead of me lay the long and lonely five hour drive to Estill, South Carolina where I would spend the night in a motel and then self surrender the next morning. As I drove through our neighborhood I passed the playground up the street where I take my family often. As I passed the playground I looked over and there was my little girl riding on the swings with my mom. My heart just dropped, my body got hot, and some tears accompanied me for the first part of my journey. *"Why is this happening to me?,"* I said somberly to myself.

I got to Estill, South Carolina, at about 3pm and checked into the only motel in the town. The town consisted of a few stores at a crossroads and that was it. I then went to call my family but realized there was no cell phone signal. I drove down the road to see if there would be a signal but nothing. This town is in the middle of nowhere, no cell phone signals, no cabs, no public transportation, one motel, and only two places to eat. By now I am realizing this truly is one of the worst days of my life. I went back to my motel room and paced for a while. I ordered some crab rangoons and noodles as my last meal before I surrendered to federal prison the next morning. I then drove by the prison to see how far it was from the motel. It was about five miles from the motel. I knew with the luck I was having that I would end up walking myself to prison so I set my alarm for about 6am. I barely slept at all that night thinking about my family. It was a horrible night.

The next morning I took a shower around 7am and got dressed. I had to run the shower for about ten minutes to get rid of the black water spewing from the rusted nozzle. After that I paced around the room quite a bit more and then decided it was time to go. I went outside and put all my belongings, except my driver's license, into my truck, and locked it. I put the keys in the gas tank so the tow truck guy could retrieve them when he came to pick up the truck to tow it back to Florida. I opted not to have my family drive with me to spare them the hard time of dropping someone of to prison. I then went to the front office to drop off the key and asked the man at the counter about any possible bus or cab service. He said there was none and then asked me where I was going. I told him that I was going to the prison to visit my brother and my truck would not start. I did not want to tell him I was going there to self surrender so as not to scare him in hopes of maybe getting a ride from him. Who knows what people may think when they are told that the person they are talking to is on their way to prison. This nice man then offered to drive me to the prison and I thanked him greatly. He dropped me off at the front and I gave him ten bucks for his courteous deed. I then told him my truck would be there for a day or so until the tow truck comes for it. He smiled and drove away.

So here I am standing in front of this huge prison, nothing on me except $400 and my driver's license. I have to say I was a little worried about what may lie ahead for me. The most daunting thing was the triple razor wire fence that surrounded the medium security prison in front of me. It took every ounce of power to walk the last fifty feet to the front door. I took one last deep breath and opened the door and went inside. Inside the lady at the front desk said, *"Can I help you?"* I replied, *"Hello I am here to self surrender."* It was about 9am and I got a little hot and sweaty after saying those words but kept my composure. The nice lady suddenly got stern and told me to have a seat. About ten minutes later a man approached and called my name. He said, *"Sharp come with me."* I smiled gingerly and proceeded to follow this giant man down a corridor. We stopped at the R&D room (Receiving and Discharge) and he asked me several questions probably to verify I was who I said I was. He asked me my mother's maiden name, length of my sentence, date of birth, etc. He then asked me if I had anything with me. I gave him all I had, which was my address book, driver's license, and the $400 in my back pocket. He then gave me a receipt and said that the money would be deposited into my account and would take a few days to get there. I then sat down again for a short wait. After about fifteen minutes this giant but gentle guard came and said once again, *"Sharp C'mon!"* I followed again completely masked behind his towering stature and this time we went through a couple of electric doors, the kind you see on television in real prisons. I could not believe I was at a real prison but I was. As I exited the last door I then realized I was inside the prison complex and on the outdoor grounds of the medium prison. Now I know that this was the way that inmates got to the camp next door. I was speechless and a bit dumb founded at the lack of noise and absence of inmates. I then turned to the guard and asked, *"Is it always this quiet?"* The main prison held about 1500 inmates, some who are doing life, and there was no one around. He then removed the last amount of civilization I had inside me when he replied in a somewhat humorous tone, *"No it's never this quiet. The whole prison is on lockdown again for another stabbing."* Well that was enough for me. Where's the exit? I'm outta' here. My heart beat a little faster as I entered the next building. I knew I was not going anywhere so it was time to toughen up and face the music.

The guard then led me into a small room that had blankets, clothes, and other supplies. He threw me a trash bag and told me to put all my clothes inside the trash bag. He then handed me a white oversized jump suit to put on. It looked like the kind of jump suit the ice cream man would wear. I would also later find out the significance of this white jump suit. After I was dressed I was brought into the next room where I was photographed and finger printed. I was then put into a holding cell until the medical team could come and check me. A medical check is standard for all new inmates. About an hour later two medical people came and gave me a tuberculosis shot and checked my blood pressure, pulse, and temperature. They then asked me some basic health questions and were done. The whole medical evaluation lasted about ten minutes. Back into the holding cell I went until the psychologist came next. This period of wait was about two hours and finally the psychologist came and asked me some questions like, *"Are you suffering from any depression?,"* *"Are you suffering from any anxiety?,"* etc. I knew I had anxiety but this was normal under the circumstances. If filled out a health questionnaire and then that was it. Then it was back in the holding cell again. Now I was told that they were waiting for someone to come and get me to bring me over to the camp. This compound was separate from the medium facility. The lady then told me to remember E440 upper. This was my cube and bed assignment. I instantly memorized it.

Finally, after about a six hour stay in R&D, another guard came to get me and bring me to the prison camp. As I entered the prison compound through the front doors I looked around and quickly noticed everyone was wearing green pants with a green shirt. I also realized that everyone was looking at me. I then asked the guard, *"Where do I get the green clothes?"* He laughed and said *"All new inmates wear white for the first day."* Oh great, just great! I looked like a cross between an elf and an ice cream man and I knew I would stand out like a sore thumb with my new white duds. The guard then dropped me off at one of the housing units and simply walked away. I assumed this was my unit so I proceeded to walk inside. I opened the door to and headed inside grasping my blankets, sheets, and toiletries tightly. Once I got inside it was either a left or a right turn and just as I turned right an older gentleman helped me find my bunk and respective cube. Of course it was a left turn after all. Now I know hoe a newbie feels when they get here. The helpful inmate led me to my cube and pointed out my bed. I said thank you and then he smiled and walked away. At about the same time a few other inmates from adjacent cubes came up and said hello. They offered up assistance if I needed any and then we chatted a bit. The most asked questions are, "What are you here for?," and "How long you going to be with us?"

The housing unit looked like a replica of the inside of my elementary school. The walls were all white painted concrete blocks with oversized windows across the perimeter wall. There were no drapes or shades therefore the sun's rays burned through at will. I then took a good look at my bed and said, "no way!" There is no way that my body was going to fit on that bunk without falling five feet to the cold hard floor. I then seemed awestruck that there were five of these little beds in this tiny little cube. This was my new home for the next several months.

I will say that I was relieved that I was not required to be confined in a cell and soon after learned that none of the minimum security prison camps has cells, only cubes. The cubes were small, only about fifteen feet wide by ten feet deep. One of my cellies was in the cube when I got there and we talked briefly. He showed me my locker and then told me to ask him if I had any questions. I was very surprised by the amount of assistance that was offered up by the inmates. I dropped my blankets and sheets atop my 36" x 60" mattress and then loaded my few toiletries into my locker that sat mounted to the wall at the head of my bed. I was not surprised to see one broken razor, one half eaten bar of soap, one toothbrush, and one packet of tooth paste as my total inventory to unload into my four foot by two foot locker.

A few minutes later a bunch of inmates came rushing down the hallway and into their assigned cubes. I then heard a man's voice yell, "Count time, count time, stand up count!" I soon learned that it was time for the daily 4pm stand up count. All the inmates were required to be in their assigned cubes standing up for the count. I also learned that there were multiple counts every day and night. The count times were 9:30pm, 12am, 3am, 5am, and for weekends and holidays there was an extra stand up count as 10am.

In total there were two housing units at the prison camp. Each housing unit contained two sections and each section had two wings. Each wing housed about forty inmates and about eighty inmates per each section. There were about 160 inmates in each housing unit which made the total capacity of the camp about 320 inmates. During my stay the population fluctuated from 300-310 inmates. Each section had a total of seven showers, three urinals, and three toilets to be shared between eight inmates.

After the count some more inmates came up to me and said hi. One of them gave me a t-shirt to wear and another gave me a pair of shower shoes to wear. No one went barefoot ever. It was just a completely unsanitary thing to do. At about 7pm I climbed into my top bunk and tried to get a little rest. I had not eaten all day and was still wearing my white jumpsuit. Getting rest was impossible so I just decided to lie in my bunk and pass the time.

That night consisted of no rest and I was counting the minutes until sunrise so I could exchange my white clothes for the standard green uniform. At about 6am my name was called over the loudspeaker to go over to the laundry room. I asked another inmate where the laundry was and headed over there in an instant. It was a short walk across the compound and into a little room where a few inmates worked washing clothes, blankets, and linens. I told them my name and they set me up with four pairs of pants and shirts. I also got a few pairs each of boxers, socks, one brown winter hat, one green fabric belt, one jacket, and one pair of black steel toed work boots. I changed in the next room and then handed one of the inmates my white jumpsuit.

After finally looking like everyone else on the compound I decided to take a walk around the prison grounds. The first thing I noticed to my surprise was the intimidating razor wire fence that surrounded the entire complex. "What was this?," I thought to myself. I thought none of the camps had fences around them. Well this one had a good one. I later learned that this prison camp never had a fence around it until a few years prior when the Warden had one put up because of the problems with contraband being smuggled in. Seeing the fence conveys the feeling of what a dog may feel while being caged up in a kennel. As I walked to the rear of the compound I noticed there was a baseball field. I was curious how the ball was retrieved if someone hit one out of the park. There was an entirely new meaning of hitting it "over the fence" in this place. There was a jogging track that circled the ball field, a bocce court, horseshoe pit, volleyball court, an outdoor basketball court, and an indoor basketball court. In the gym there was a small room with a few guitars that could be signed out by the inmates. There was also a ping pong and foosball table inside the gym. There were no free weights but a few old pieced of exercise equipment stood on the far side of the gym.

After I was done exploring the grounds I headed back inside to my cube and waited for the 4pm stand up count. After the count I waited for the dinner meal to be announced and then headed over to the dining hall to wait in line for chow. In the dining hall rice and beans were served up with bread pudding for dessert. All the utensils were plastic and there were no knives. After I finished eating I walked around a bit and then headed back inside to wait for the 9:30pm count. I tried once again to sleep but it was close to impossible to get more than fifteen minutes of rest at a time.

November 3, 2010 – Day three has been the worst and I wish I could forget it. At about 1pm today I was walking around the compound again and my emotions simply got the best of me. My beautiful family and everyone close to me was on my mind. In my pocket sat my little address book that the guard let me keep when I self surrendered. Inside this address book I taped one of my favorite pictures of my two best friends, my wife and little girl. It was a picture from a camping trip a couple of months prior in Debary, Florida. I sat down on one of the picnic tables and took out the address book, opened it, and touched the picture with my finger. As hard as I tried to suck up my tears they came flowing down my face. I knew that showing emotion in any prison environment was not a good idea so I did my best to hide my face. As I looked up I saw an inmate walking towards me. The library was behind me so I figured he was headed there and would walk by. Then I heard a voice say, "C'mon help me move this table into the sun where it is warmer." I got up and wiped my eyes quickly and then helped this man move the picnic table. After we moved the table he told me to have a seat. I sat down and then this man said, "It will get better. The first few weeks are hard but it will get better." I sucked up my emotions and listened to this man who was there to help me. He then asked me if I had a family and I handed him my address book and pointed to the picture of them. His name was Doc; his real name Dan but everyone called him Doc. He asked me how much time I had and I told him nine months. He then said, "Steve your family will be stronger because of this and all will be okay." I then learned that Doc was a chiropractor who had been at the prison camp for about three years already. We talked for another thirty minutes or so and then I shook his hand and thanked him for his words of solace.

It was now time to get in touch with my family. My phone still was not activated because I was still waiting for the $400 cash to be cleared in my account. I was told that it should be cleared by Wednesday after 4pm. I went inside and dialed 118 to hear my account balance. I was so relieved to finally hear $400 and not $0. I deposited $20 into my phone ITS account and dialed up my family. When they answered, an automated voice started talking and saying that the phone call was from an inmate at a federal prison. I thought to myself, "Oh brother!" Then the call went through and I was connected to my wife and little girl. They were relieved to hear from me and my mind was put at ease knowing they were okay. After the phone call I walked around some more and then went to bed.

Sleeping in prison is nothing like anything you ever experienced. Imagine sleeping in a room with fifty other guys and in a bed three feet wide with disturbing guard counts all through the night. I guess I will get used to it but for now the sound of those jingling skeleton keys attached to the waist of each guard wakes me up. Each guard has many keys and some of the keys are like ten inches long. Even more disturbing was the guard saying: *"Count Time! Count Time!"* before the start of each count. The slew of snoring was even more intriguing. The last couple of nights I swear that I was in a room with a backfiring diesel engine. I even heard one guy talking in his sleep last night. Last night consisted of little sleep if any.

November 4, 2010 - I woke up early Thursday morning about 6am and brushed my teeth and got dressed. Now that I had some money in my account I was able to go the commissary and buy some much needed items. Each inmate had one shopping day per week and today was my day. I filled out the form and walked over to the part of the building that said *"Commissary"* and dropped off my order form. Once your order form is dropped through the little slot in the door it can take up to an hour or two before your name is called. You then sign a receipt and your items are slid down a little slide. You then quickly put your stuff in your laundry bag and carry them back to your locker. I finally had shampoo, real soap, a real razor, a radio, and some real socks. At about 8am I heard over the loudspeaker, *"Attention at the camp, Fog Count, Fog Count."* When it is foggy, the inmates are required to go back to their assigned cube for a special fog count to make sure no one slipped away.

It is now 10am and I am waiting for the fog count to finish as I write this. Next to me one of my cellies is telling another cellie about all the fights he witnessed while in other prisons throughout his ten year bid. Getting into a fight is not high on my list of things to do. I have no desire to spend time in the hole either. This place is known as the "SHU" which stands for "Special "Housing "Unit." If an inmate breaks any of the rules then this is where he will be sent. The SHU is like a typical cell in a county jail; nothing in it but steel bed and a toilet. Inside of the SHU an inmate is allowed only a bible and a couple other limited items. Doing time in the SHU is hard time to the fullest. There is also an administrative part of the SHU where inmates are put when they may have an infectious disease or something contagious or are under investigation for one reason or another. Inmates in the administrative section are allowed more items then inmates in the disciplinary section. Either way I will avoid both of these. I bought vitamins today to help stay healthy.

Well the fog count ended at 10:45 and we are once again allowed out of our unit. If I have learned one thing about prison during the last week it would be respect and manners. I always conduct myself with manners and respect and it surely pays off. Prison is all about respecting others and in turn getting respect back. Today I got to witness an inmate who lacked this valuable attribute. At lunch I sat across from one particular inmate. I began to eat my meal which consisted of chicken, rice, and some veggies. As I looked up I saw something I did not want to see. This guy was eating his chicken, well it was more like devouring it like a dog would. He was chomping away and spitting out the bones into his tray as he ate. It was disgusting and obviously this guy was absent when the manners part of life was taught. I decided to finish my lunch early and leave the cafeteria. I almost said something but then remembered where I was and hushed up. No need to have conflict in here.

After lunch I met up with a friend who I met a couple days earlier. His name was Joe and he got here the same day as me. He was here on a probation violation. We got along well. He was in a prison a few years ago due to organized crime and keeps me entertained with his crazy stories. He is a nice guy and a good friend.

Oh yeah, I forgot to mention that I have been sleeping without a pillow each night. It seems they forgot to give me one with my blankets and it has been a task to get one. Every time I go to the counselor who can get me one, she is not there. In the laundry room they can't just give me one either. It has to be signed off by the officer who runs the laundry room and he is not there much either. I hear that the officers are absent so much because of the lockdown over at the medium prison next door. When that prison goes on lockdown the officers who are here at the camp are required to go perform duties over there.

I guess I will watch tv for thirty minutes and see what news is brewing. There are two television rooms with like four televisions in each room. There is also a Spanish tv room with two televisions and another small tv room with two tv's. Outside there is a spot where you can sit with two televisions also. Television is abundant here but I rarely watch any. The funny thing is you need a radio to listen to any tv. Each tv has an assigned fm radio frequency for it so you have to tune your radio to the proper frequency to listen to it.

November 5, 2010 - Last night I finally took a hot shower after getting my shampoo and soap. It was my first shower since Monday. I had no soap or anything for the last few days. It felt so good to take a hot shower and I felt clean once again.

Yesterday I watched a little tv outside. It was funny because there was a show playing that was about undercover drugs busts. The DEA was getting ready to bust a big heroin ring and it was very interesting. I watched it for about forty minutes and towards the end of the show the drug kingpin gave an on camera interview with his face hidden. He was talking about how he would sell heroin to his brother because at least he would know that his brother was getting safe drugs. By now I was tuned into the show with my headphones playing the tv show in my ears. I was angry that this idiot really would help kill his brother by selling him heroin. As I was watched the drug dealer's interview, I muttered, *"Sure sell your brother some heroin; just another stupid drug dealer!"* At about this time, I realized where I was. Jesus! I am in prison! Prison is full of drug dealers everywhere! There was a guy sitting to the left of me and a guy to the right. Most likely one of them if not both of them were here for drug dealing. *"Shit!!"* I said to myself. *"Steve you are in prison shut up, shut up." "Stay Calm, Stay Calm!"* I will not make that mistake again and was thankful everyone sitting there had their headphones blaring loud enough not to hear what I said. That was a close one!

November 7, 2010 - Today is Sunday and it is about 4pm and we all are waiting for the official stand up count. I have been here a week now and I have learned quickly four unwritten rules for getting a good name in here and being left alone. Now I say this loosely because if someone ever tries to push me around I will not allow it. I will push back and you have to in here or people will try to take advantage of you. My own personal rules in here include minding my own business, not gossiping, acting with manners, and giving respect to others. This has worked superb so far and we will see how the future plays out.

I am so relieved to finally have my email and phone working. Each inmate is assigned a pin that he uses to access the phone and email services. I just emailed my two best friends and now will go eat dinner after the count. Today I learned what a *"cop out"* and *"call out sheet"* is. The *"cop out"* is a form also known as an *"inmate to staff"* request form that is filled out when an inmate requests something such as the need to see a doctor, sign up for an education course, or really anything. The *"call out"* sheet is a sheet that is posted on the wall every day inside the housing units. This form lets an inmate know if they have a scheduled appointment for the next day. It is usually posted before 4pm every day and lists appointments for the next day.

The food here has been okay with the exception of the occasional hair in it. Dinner is a favorite of mine because for some reason at dinner time all the cats come around. The inmates must obviously give the cats the most food at dinner time. There are about ten cats that live here on the compound. They must sleep in the sewer drains. Most of them are very friendly and will play with you. The rules say not to touch any animals but everyone pets the cats and some pick them up. I figure this rule is not enforced as I have even seen the guards handling the cats. I now engage in some friendly pet bonding whenever I have time. I miss my family greatly! I keep telling them I will be home soon!

November 14, 2010 - It has been about a week since I wrote last. I have been trying to keep busy writing a book on prison and also ways to reduce a prison sentence. Within the last week I have read over three hundred pages about many interesting federal cases involving much reduced sentences. I will continue to study these for the rest of my time here and hopefully be able to write an informative book for others. There are so many inmates in here that simply do not know about the law and their attorneys simply don't spend any time explaining it.

Tomorrow is week three for me believe it or not. I have finally gotten a little used to the regimen of life in here. I still hate all the counts conducted every day though. You really have to pay attention to what time it is because if you miss a count you are in deep trouble. For the most part all the inmates look after each other and let someone know when the count is near like if they are in the library watching a movie or reading.

It is almost 4pm here on Sunday and I am in my cube awaiting the standing count. This is the one count where we all have to be standing in our cube to be counted by the guards. It is bothersome and gives the true impression of being locked up. There is no lenience for these counts either. One inmate in the other wing took up an argument with one of the guards during count time. He was taken directly to the hole to think about it, no passing go, no collecting $200, just straight to the hole. This is the last place anyone wants to go. If someone thought this was boring multiply it by one 1000 in the hole. When you get to the hole you are locked in a cell twenty-three hours per day with nothing to do, No Thanks! I am finally sleeping a little better and finally got my pillow. The feathers in the pillow stab me in the face. They are very cheaply made pillows. Wait, the entire bed including the blankets and mattress are cheaply made. I will slowly get used to this.

November 16, 2010 - It is 9pm Tuesday night and next week I will finally conclude the completion of my first month here in OZ, or hell, whatever you want to call it. This place just sucks. I constantly think about my wife and little girl and that keeps me driving forward. I am not weak by any means but today has been a very hard and trivial day. I am going to read a little and then fall asleep and dream about being at my favorite fishing spot with my two best friends. My mom and dad have been amazing. I miss them too. I have gotten so much closer to my mom and dad because of this event. My mom and dad are keeping my blogs going strong. I write articles about my knowledge of nutrition whenever I have time.

November 18, 2010 - Today I had my Admissions & Orientation meeting, otherwise known as A&O. This is when you sit in a room with the other new inmates and hear a short speech from all the department heads such as education, kitchen, safety, etc. We only heard from about half the people that were supposed to speak. At the end we filled out a question sheet and listed our job experience history so that our counselor could appoint us a job. We also had to sign a sheet that said all the reps came and talked when only about one half actually came. Goes to show you there is corruption everywhere. It is almost 9:30pm and count time again. I am going to play cards with Joe after count and hear more of his crazy mob stories. We play spades and gin. It helps pass the time.

November 20, 2010 - Almost 4pm and time for the daily stand up count. Two of my cellies are arguing about which basketball team is better. It is a constant show between both of them. One of them is a huge Boston Celtics fan and the other a die hard Miami Heat fan. If I get involved in the argument then of course it is the Celtics! They go at it all the time, but it is all in good fun. My other cellie is next to me here laying down reading a book. I cannot wait to see what the title is but that sucker is thick. My other cellie is missing and should be here soon. He watches about twenty hours of television per day so he is probably in the tv room.

There is always a guy that mans the door to our housing unit to let everyone know when the guards are coming for the count. Once he sees them coming he flicks the lights. Once the lights flicker it becomes a shortened version of the "Running with the Bulls." Everyone hurries out of the tv rooms, card rooms, bathrooms, or any room just to get to their assigned cube before the guards come from the front door of our housing unit.

I am still waiting for my job assignment. Today one of the guards told me and Joe to go help some other inmates rake leaves. It took about an hour and we were done. I am going to write a blog article, read, and then go to sleep. I can't wait to talk to my family. I have been reading in the law library every day about other cases. The disparity between various lengths of sentences in similar cases is amazing and I am compiling information each day. I hope to have a book available within a couple of years.

December 1, 2010 - Well tomorrow is Thursday and Monday will bring the start of week six here in Oz. This place reminds me of the Wizard of Oz. It combines fantasy with little bits of reality. It has been about a week since I last wrote. I have been keeping very busy with my blogs, newsletters, and my book is about ten pages complete.

My emotions have been heavy and deep lately. I don't think my family realizes how important it is to constantly express love for someone who is in here. It is so common to experience feelings of hopelessness, even for someone with a short time here like me. Prisons are full of negative people. They are everywhere. Inmates complain about the food, the government, the life in here. They complain about the noise, the hot water, the beds, the temperature, and everything else one can imagine. Some people just need a reality slap. There really are a lot of people who embellish and dramatize everything. I really try to avoid these people but there are plenty of them. My family has been running my small nutrition business and lately the only email I receive from them are questions and problems about my nutrition business. Additionally, the phone calls lately have mostly been about the day's dilemmas and problems with my business and never *"I love you and miss you so much."* I know they are doing so much with my work so I really don't want to burden them with my love life problems but it gets very hard in here. When someone gets down as I am right now, these types of feelings only makes time drag on. Each day feels like one hundred days and that is bad. I need to know much they miss me. It is just hard to put into words what this feels like.

Well with all that off my shoulders the other news I got this week was my job assignment. I was assigned a job at the powerhouse. This is the prison power plant that delivers all the heat, hot water, air conditioning, and back up electricity to the prison across the street and the prison camp where I am. I work from Monday through Friday and the work is easy. I take reading from various meters each hour and perform other small tasks. It is 3:30pm right now and I am going to take a long shower and then eat and play cards. After that it will be 8:30pm and time for yard recall. This is when everyone has to get inside for the night. Thanksgiving came and went. I had a tough time but I am a tough person. I miss my family lots!

December 6, 2010 - Well it is week six and only about thirty or so weeks left. Oh my, that sounds like a long time. I am having a very hard day today. I miss my family greatly and don't feel much like writing. It is about 1:30pm as I sit here in the powerhouse tool room waiting for my next job assignment. Please God give me my life back soon.

December 12, 2010 - Today is Sunday, my 7th week here and it is about 9:10am. I just finished talking a long hot shower. It felt good! It is raining outside and a bit chilly but not too bad. Last night I played Spades with my usual card partners. After cards I read my favorite book, "The History of America" and I am into the era of the settlement of Jamestown, and the founding of the thirteen American colonies. I was amazed when I found out that America was named after a gentleman named Amerigo Vespucci and that the Pacific Ocean was named by Magellan, an explorer back in the 1500's. He saw this ocean after traveling though the straits of Magellan and named it because the Latin meaning of Pacific is *"peaceful";* a great history book.

My book is also coming along well! I am going to title it "Reduce your Prison Sentence." It will be full of information that lays out the various techniques and methods in which someone can help minimize a prison sentence. There are many hidden secrets in the federal judicial system which few know about. Don't expect your lawyer to come forward and tell you about all these. It only means more work for him.

I have also been dealing myself Blackjack hands to try and find a way to beat the system; yeah right. I have dealt myself about 1200 hands so far and have made about $6000 profit; on paper of course. We will see how I do after 5000 hands dealt. This passes time while I am at work in the powerhouse. Have I mentioned that I am quite bored today? Staying busy is the biggest key to survival in here. I miss my family so much but I know this nightmare will end soon. Gonna head to the library and then get back to reading and writing after the 10am count.

December 17, 2010 - Well it is another lonely Friday night here in Oz. I just came back from early dinner. There is a short line called at 3pm where inmates can grab an early dinner. We had beef and bean burritos. They were okay. I am now in my cube waiting for the guards to come through our unit for the 4pm stand up count.

This morning one guy got thrown in the hole for having peppers and onions in his locker. I guess he stole them from the kitchen while working there. Another guy got written up for having sugar in cup. They sell sugar in the store but it is sold in single serving bags. Since this guy had sugar in a jar it could be assumed that he stole it from the cafeteria and therefore he got written up. When someone gets written up it is called *"getting a shot."* There are different levels of severity and discipline when someone gets a *"shot."* This is probably on the low end of severity scale. The most serious things are fighting, refusing to take a drug test, etc.

I have been staying busy working at the powerhouse Monday through Friday as well as reading and writing. I am up to the *"Boston Tea Party"* part in my history book. The revolutionary war is about to begin. It is a very good book! I wish I could kiss my family right now. I wish I could hug them for weeks but I cannot. I will soon! I keep telling myself this! Next week is my 8th week here and it is starting to move a little faster. When I say a little; I mean A LITTLE! Next week is also the last full week of the year! Thank god! The guards are walking through our hall right now for the 4pm count. I am writing this as one of the guards is walking by my cube. The other is coming now. I am going to eat and then play cards until yard recall at 8:30pm. That is one of my favorite times of the night. This is when I call my family. I am still trying to get my mom and dad's email and phone approved. I have been communicating to them via letters. I hope to talk to them soon! My mom and dad have been a godsend. Good night!

December 21, 2010 - This is finally the last full week of the year! Today I worked again at the powerhouse from 7:30 to 2:30 and learned that I got a Christmas bonus. I got my first paycheck for $19. This was my pay for a month working at my job. Wow!! My bonus was $9. I will not even make shrewd comments or elaborate on this. I will just leave this whole subject alone. At least it will pay for a weeks worth of emails and phone. I am counting the days!

December 22, 2010 - Today is Wednesday and its almost another week down. Today has been a crazy, crazy day! The prison store, otherwise known as the commissary, is closed next week for the year end inventory so today is the last day for inmates to buy food and supplies such as shampoo, lotion, cough drops, etc. I waited in line for three hours today before they called my name and I got my soda and crackers. That is all that I purchase at the store with the exception of some personal care items that I have to buy as well as any clothes I need. I have only bought socks and underwear so far and have been wearing the institutional supplied green uniform every day. They do sell sweat pants and such but I do not want to waste the money. The commissary store is nothing like a convenience store on the outside. It is a little room you walk into about 8 x 6. You drop your order form through a little slot in the door and then wait for them to call your name. All the food and goods are in the back room so you never get to really shop. When they call your name your stuff is slid down a little metal slide where you then quickly put in your laundry bag and carry it all back to your locker.

While in line waiting for my name to be called an inmate got escorted away from one of the housing unit. I must have missed the whole event but I guess this guy had a cell phone and someone decided to rat on him. This guy was getting ready to leave here in a few months too! They came and escorted him out. While being escorted he tried to ditch the phone by throwing it on the roof of the building. The guards caught him and a brief fight ensued. Now he is facing at least another year in prison and he will now have to spend his time in a higher security level prison because of his conduct. Why the hell would someone even contemplate having a phone in here especially when you are getting ready to leave? He was here already for about three years. This surely defines stupidity. To my family, I love you and I am coming home soon!

December 23, 2010 - Merry Christmas my ass! My family and loved ones is all I can think of right now. This shit is hard enough without having to stick holidays in the midst of it. Christmas in prison is not easy for anyone. Today also bring more crazy prison news. One of the attorneys serving time here was escorted away today. This time they used handcuffs to lead him away. He was already warned once last year too about conducting business while incarcerated. It is prohibited to run any type of business while confined. I am hearing that he will most likely be transferred to a higher security prison. This guy was also a few months away from leaving. He may even have his good time taken away if his original sentence was more than a year which I think it was. I tell everyone it is just not worth it to mess around in here. There are plenty of snitches that thrive on seeing another inmate taken down and caught for something illegal.

Next week ends the year and starts month three here! I went and visited my case manager this past Monday to check in with him and see how things are going. He has my release plan ready to send to the Florida probation office. That is step number one to get out of here. They are trying to deny me halfway house time by lying to me and saying that I do not qualify for it. I am dedicated to fight back and bring this whole issue forward. I will bring it all the way to Washington DC if I am denied halfway house time. My case manager is telling me that he can not give me halfway house time and that I can only go to home confinement with about three weeks left on my sentence. The problem is that if I am sent direct to home confinement then I will not be able to leave here until the beginning of July. I have to get back to work as soon as possible and I can only do this if I am afforded halfway house time. This will allow me an extra couple of months to get back to work. Hopefully the case manager will see the dire need for me to get some halfway house time.

December 25, 2010 - As I sit here on Christmas day at 8am drinking a Diet Pepsi, I mutter to myself, *"How do these guys do it?"* For example, there is a guy in the cube next to me, his name is Chris and he is clearly a family man. He has pictures of his family posted on his pegboard. He is a fisherman from Fort Lauderdale and is here for getting caught transporting cocaine. I think he may have been trafficking it on his boat but I am not sure of the details. The judge gave him ten years in here. Yes ten years! He is a regular guy who did a bad thing. Now he will be in prison until like 2018 with some good time credit. I am having a tough time on this one Christmas but this poor guy has nine more Christmas holidays to spend in here. I can't imagine what is going through his mind. He got here about a month before I did and gave me a pair of shower shoes to wear my first night here. I know I would not be able to handle that length of sentence. I am hoping to be out of here in another four to five months god willing and this is hard enough. I just cannot imagine the thoughts that fill his head. God bless him! I pray he gets some sentencing relief to get out of here sooner.

I just spoke to my two best friends. They both have a cold and are suffering from the blues. My mom and dad arrived from Naples, Florida, on Thursday and they both will be spending a week at our house. That helps so much with the hurt. My mom and dad deserve an award. They really became saviors through all this. I am not saying they were bad before but we had our problems. All of us had faults. It feels so good to have them close.

I can't wait for this day to end. It is about 7pm now and I watched the Celtics lose to the Magic today. That just topped off an already crappy holiday. I am going to make a tuna sandwich and then go read. We had a very nice holiday dinner believe it or not. They served each of us a Cornish hen with rice, collared greens, gravy, mushroom soup, dinner rolls, sweet potatoes, and lemon pie. I ate everything but the pie. I want to stay trim and healthy for my family. I miss them so much! Good night!

December 26, 2010 - Sunday morning 10am and its raining with some snow mixed in. I actually slept until 9:30 today. That was a record for me. I usually am awake at 6am or earlier sometimes. Anyway today will hopefully go by quick. We just had the 10am count and the guards left with two trash bags full of stuff. I think one bad had a bunch of hens in it. Yes hens like the Cornish hens that we ate yesterday. No they were not alive. The inmates love to smuggle part of the lunch out of the cafeteria to eat or a sell at a later date. The guards know this and search lockers to find the smuggled food. They must have found a few hens from the Christmas dinner in some of the inmate's lockers and confiscated them. I am on my way to eat and then read and write. This life is for the birds!

On a funnier note, one thing very intriguing about this place is the nicknames that people get. For instance I have my list of favorites that I will share. For starters, there is a quiet old man who is confined to a wheelchair that watches television in the hallway every day. His nickname is *"Old Skool."* You will also not believe this. Now this is ironic; as I am typing this *"Old Skool"* just rolled into me with his wheel chair trying to get on the computer next to me. Anyway, next is the group who I refer to as the state inmates. They are a bunch of black guys that refer to themselves according to the states or cities where they live. I always here one guy yelling, "New York, New York, c'mon man its chow time, lets go! 'Chill out Chicago, I'm coming, chill man chill, lets go get that chicken.'" Next is my favorite nickname of all. There is a guy in here doing about twenty years. He was convicted on money laundering which is taking money obtained illegally and then running it through a legitimate business to try to hide its origin. His nickname is appropriately assigned as no other than *"Dirty Money."* Other than that there is a one guy who got caught hiding drugs in a hollowed out bat. Yes of course they all call him *"Bat.";* just something to laugh at and help pass the time. I hope my family is having a better time than me. I miss them dearly and pray every night. This day is will be over soon.

December 27, 2010 - No need for a reality check in this place. All throughout the housing unit there are speakers installed in the ceiling similar to what you would see in a typical school. Well at 5am this morning one of the guards yelled over the loudspeaker, *"Attention at the camp, attention at the camp, no one is allowed outside the housing unit until I* *have verbally announced COUNT CLEAR! This means no one! If I see people walking around again then you will have a new address and it will be The SHU, that's right the SHU, S-H-U, the special housing unit! Have a nice morning."* Funny we never had the problem before. Every morning after the 5am count there was never a verbal announcement over the loudspeaker saying *"Count Clear."* I just learned that there is a shift change between the correctional officers every three months so now we have to deal with this new lady CO who is not particularly nice. Regardless of this nuisance no one in here will ever get to me. You can only punish the weak.

December 28, 2010 - The new year is almost here finally! I am sitting here in the powerhouse. I am in the tool room inside the powerhouse. I just finished taking readings and checking the hot water heaters. I had to reset one of them that tripped offline. No biggie, just the reset of a little black button. I am sitting here thinking to myself, *"Am I weak?," "Am I maybe weaker than I thought?"* No way Jose!!! I am having the hardest time the last few days missing my family but I will survive. If Martha Stewart can do this so can I! I only have about five months left here so I will try my best to make the best of it. I think I am just going through some extra sadness due to the holiday. I know one thing for sure, I will NEVER, I mean NEVER, I mean NEVER EVER buy an article of green clothing EVER for as long as I live. This is a promise!

January 1, 2011 - Well New Year's Day here in OZ .... what a drag. Last night at midnight I got to watch a group of Latin guys in the tv room sing along with the famous tune *"New York, New York"* but it sounded more like, *"Thoz' little town bluez, there leaving tomorrow, its up to you New Yoke, Newwwww Yoke."* The Spanish tv room is right next to my cube so I can hear and see everything in there. There was also a celebration dance in the cube across from me. They all did a little New Years celebration dance at midnight. Going to go now and work on my book and read. Happy New Year's Day my behind!

January 6, 2011 - Today has been busy, busy. It is about 8pm here and I have been busy typing. I finally got a printer ribbon and wheel so I can use the prison typewriter and have been typing my fingers off. I am tired and ready to turn in. I know so many faces and names now. It is month three and this month is going by fast. The probation officer came by our house yesterday to approve it for my release. I have been saying my prayers every night and hope to hug my two best friends soon.

January 8, 2011 - It is 4pm and time for the stand up count. I am in the computer room typing this so I only have a minute or so. Today was a chilly day at the powerhouse. It was only about thirty degrees when I got there at 7:30am. Work was ordinary as usual. I took readings, did some writing, and played cards with two other inmates, Mike and Naz, well they are more like friends now. Mike is leaving in August and Naz is here until about 2014 on a drug charge. Mike is here for growing marijuana and got eighteen months and Naz got 120 moths. They are both good people and I enjoy their company. I watched Naz make some homemade fried rice and noodles today with basic ingredients. He used a pack of Ramen Noodles, butter, Goya seasoning, white rice, salt, pepper, soy sauce, and a turkey log. All these are available from the commissary. He did a fine job and it smelled like something you would get at a Chinese restaurant. Mike is making tuna wraps tonight for him and his cellies. They don't eat at the dining hall much at all and tonight they are serving eggs for dinner. Yuck! I am also skipping dinner and will probably make some mackerel and crackers later. I know so many people here so it makes the time pass quicker having some friends. I have to go. The guards are coming and I have to get back to my cube. Its count time!

January 10, 2011 - Today was a crazy day. This morning at about 6am I was awoken by one of the guards shouting over the *loudspeaker "Inmate Sharp, Inmate York, report to the admin building asap!"* This continued until I got dressed and headed over there. *"York"* is the last name of another guy who works with me at the powerhouse and of course I am *"Sharp."* It seems they needed someone to sand the walkway and entrance to the main prison they conveniently called upon us two. The weather was bad, the temperature about thirty-two degrees and we were in the midst of a bad ice storm. Freezing rain fell all day and it was strange seeing icicles hanging off the buildings considering I was only about a four hour drive from Daytona Beach, MY HOME!!!! It is almost 9pm now and I hope I can get some rest tonight. I have not been sleeping well at all. I miss my family bad and my heart hurts.

I worked on my book some more today and have about thirty pages to complete. It is coming along well but progressing at a snail's pace. Everyone tells me that good writing takes a long time so I use those words of wisdom. Tomorrow is commissary day and I already have about forty dollars worth of stuff picked out like soda, crackers, typewriter ribbon, book of stamps, allergy pills, tuna fish, and mackerel. I am running out of money but my family has been giving me fifty dollars per week which has helped out greatly. I am going to try and rest my head on my pillow and fall asleep. It is always noisy in here but I am used to chatter and racket now.

January 16, 2011 - Well another Sunday morning here in Estill, SC. It is quite cold this morning and I just woke up about thirty minutes ago. It is almost time for the 10am weekend count. I can't believe I slept past 9am today. It was fairly quiet this morning in my housing unit so I was able to get a little more rest. Since this is a holiday weekend, Martin Luther King day, there will be popcorn served up to all the inmates in the gymnasium today. The line is always very long in the gym for getting a bag of popcorn. I have yet to stand in line for popcorn. It will remind me too much of hanging out at the fair with my family. It hurts! I am coming up on my fourth month here in Oz. I am so looking forward to month six and seven. I have gotten used to this green uniform that I wear every day and the razor wire fence that surrounds me does not bother me a bit any more either.

I know about one quarter of the inmates now and have developed a nice routine to pass the days. Today after the count I will eat and then off to the library for some reading, studying, and typing. I will skip dinner and have some crackers from my locker. Most likely after the 4pm count I will play card until 8:30 and then head back to my cube for yard recall. I will then read and write until 10pm and then hopefully be tired enough to fall asleep.

January 20, 2011 - It is Thursday, 9am here. I am supposed to be at my job in the powerhouse but this morning there was the infamous *"Fog Count"* so all the inmates were required to stay inside their housing unit until everyone was accounted for. I guess it all has to do with the reduced visibility and the ease for someone to escape during foggy conditions.

Yesterday was my commissary day. I filled out my order slip for the store which included soda, crackers, one printer ribbon, and a package of Pringles. It took me about three hours to get my goods. The line was long in the morning and then we had another fog count yesterday so the commissary closed. Then after the noon meal the commissary opened again but my list was put on the bottom of the pile. It took half the day to get the few items that I ordered. Welcome to prison!

The CO's just came through to count us and the count should be clear any minute. I will be off through the grey gate and over to the powerhouse building to work until 10:30am, then off to the noon meal, then back to work at noon, then back at 2:30, then over to the library to do some writing until 3:30, then back to my cube for the 3:30 yard recall and subsequent 4pm stand up count. After the 4pm count I will head back to the library until the 8:30 yard recall. I will then read a little until I fall asleep at about 10-11pm. I have been staying up a little later lately. I am trying to go to sleep later so I don't wake up at 3am and then lay awake for hours. I miss my family greatly! I am hoping they will be up to visit in a few weeks. Next month is month number four for me. I can't believe it! I am hoping I get more than thirty days halfway house time. We will see.

January 23, 2011 - Well another Sunday knocked down. It is 10pm, Sunday evening here in Shitville. We just had the 9:30pm nightly count. Today was another boring day but I kept busy writing all day. I woke up today at 8am, took a shower, and then got to my cube for the 10am count. We then had omelets for lunch. I then spent the entire day at the library. Now I am going to go read and fall asleep. I talked to my two best friends about two hours ago. I miss them but I know that I will see them soon. I try not to think about the time I have left too much because it makes it go by slower. February is almost here. Bye!

January 27, 2011 - It is 10pm on Thursday evening. The guards just came through for the count and I have not been able to sleep for the last several nights. I have been only sleeping a couple of hours each night. Probably too much Diet Pepsi.

Anyway, another inmate was brought to the SHU the other day. Word has it that this guy was using the cell phone that another inmate owned and got caught with before Christmas. I guess they have been checking phone numbers used on that cell phone and going after inmates that used it. Not a good thing for them. Another guy got written up yesterday with two shots too. A shot is the name for a disciplinary write up. An inmate can lose good time, get thrown in the hole, lose commissary and phone privileges and a lot more as the consequences for getting a shot.

There are four different categories of severity for a shot ranging from a 400 series shot which is the least serious to a 100 series shot that can get an inmate transferred to a higher security prison and more. This particular inmate got caught with a pack of cigarettes in the kitchen and then his locker was then searched and twenty books of stamps were found. An inmate is allowed no more than three books of stamps at any one time.

Other than that I talked to my family a little while ago. My friend Joe has been having a hard time. His wife, who he just married, who is a stripper, is divorcing him. He had to go to the psychologist the other day.

There was almost a fight in the law library today but it got stopped by me and another inmate who got in the middle of the two. Just tensions flying high some days in here but for the most part everything is usually peaceful. Well that is it! Oh yeah, one more thing, my back is killing me from this damn bed!

January 31, 2011 - It is now 4:30pm and we are still waiting for the guards to come for the 4pm count. Last night I exited the restroom and while walking back to my cube I was distracted by the cool looking shadow that was cast on the white concrete walls as I waked by each cube. It was dark so the private lights in each cube caused my shadow to appear huge on the wall. Behind me was a gracious looking object resembling that of a kite waving behind me. I quickly realized that this object that appeared to float behind me was not me. It was about four feet of toilet paper waving in the gentle wind from the speed of my walk down to the my cube. I swiftly snatched it off and disposed of it. A quick trip to the bathroom to make sure I got all of the evidence and then back to bed it was for me. Oh brother!

I am just happy that the weekend is over. Today was a boring day at the powerhouse. We cleaned a bit and then I read and wrote. Month four is here! I am chugging forward full steam! I miss my family greatly. I don't want to talk about it right now, it hurts. Bye.

February 3, 2011 - Wow it actually is February! I can't believe it. Today is Thursday and I woke up about 6am today. Thursday is the day when all the inmates can exchange their blankets, sheets, and pillow case for fresh ones. I must admit I only change mine about once per month. The detergent they use to wash the blankets can be rough on one's skin. Other than that today was an ordinary day. Worked at the powerhouse all day and now it is night time and I am going to lie down and eventually fall asleep.

February 11, 2011 – Another boring Friday here. Nothing much going on at the camp this week. I have been working every day compiling my book together. Writing a book is probably one of the hardest things I have attempted. It is the final drafts that take the longest to finish. Then there is proof reading, then proof reading again, then editing, then proof reading, you probably get the idea. Them when this is all done a professional must do an edit and put on finishing touches. It is about 8pm here and it is a little chilly outside and overcast. Anyway, I will read and write for another few hours and then off to sleep.

February 20, 2011 – The weekend is here again and it is boring as heck. I just hate the weekends in here. The problem with the weekends is the lack of a schedule. During the week I have my work regimen which takes up a good part of the day. It helps pass the time so much better when you stay busy. On the weekend there is only so much reading, writing, studying, and typing that one can do before he need a break. The problem is that when you take a break there is nothing to do! It is 9am here and I am going to workout until the 10am stand up count and then off to the library for the day.

February 30, 2011 – It is Wednesday and half way through another week. It is 6pm here and I am feeling like crap. I slept like crap last night and that is probably why. I wish I could get a good night's rest on these beds but it is impossible. I am going to go lay my head down. I miss my family and am a little blue today.

March 12, 2011 - I am shocked to see all the devastation from the quake and tsunami in Japan. I pray for all of those innocent people. It is Saturday just before the 10am stand up count. The loudspeaker has been very active this morning calling inmates up to the administration building for visitation. A lot of inmates are getting visitors today and it is a nice sunny day out. I will head to the library after count and continue to do some reading, writing, and research. I think that is all I do for me in here. I am currently reading another book on American History and also a book on economics.

I slept like crap last night. The problem I keep having is waking up because my arm keeps falling asleep. There is nowhere to put your arms. You have to sleep either on your back and place your arms on your stomach or directly beside you, or if you sleep on your stomach your arms have to be either under your body or under your head or directly by your side. No room here to stretch out, and if you even think about rolling over you will plop right out of the bed and hit the cold floor. I am on the top bunk so that is not a good idea. The snoring in my hall has been tolerable lately. I hope to get some rest tonight. Bye!

March 17, 2011 – Wow! What a crazy last couple of days. On Tuesday another inmate was caught with a cellular phone and escorted to the SHU. Then yesterday the whole compound underwent a shakedown. This time there were like fifteen officers who searched every inmate and every inmate's locker. They found yet another guy with a phone. The incident yesterday ended with an altercation between the inmate and a correctional officer. This inmate will likely get an additional five years or something close added onto his sentence for the fight.

I just ate lunch and it is almost noon time and time to go back through my favorite gray gate and over to the powerhouse to finish off my work day. At the powerhouse things are okay and the cat that lives there is now pregnant. One of the correctional officers there, who many think is nuts, thinks that someone is trying to poison him. Yesterday he asked us all to come into the break room and then proceeded to show us how the water coming out of the coffee machine was a purple brownish color. He claims this has happened to him like five times and wants the jokester to confess. We all looked at each other with the confused look. I don't think anyone knows what he is talking about. I smelled the dirty water coming out of the coffee machine and it did smell like something similar to an antifreeze smell but as far as playing a joke like that, well that is not a joke if someone did do it. We all think he put something in the coffee machine himself. He is the type of person that would do something like that. Anyway I am headed back to work and then off to the library after work. Bye!

March 21, 2011 - Sleep has been difficult lately. I have been waking up at about 1am and then unable to fall back asleep until like 5-6am only to have to wake up at 7am. This bed is for the birds! My arms fall asleep because there is nowhere to put them except under your body or directly beside you. I wish the rest of my body could sleep as well as my arms.

This is the last full week of March and for that I am grateful. The softball league is underway here but I passed on the chance to play as I do not want to get hurt in here especially with the lack of care that exists. There is no such thing as pain medicine in here with the exception of ibuprofen. You have to tough it out for the most part.

It is about 11am here and I am skipping lunch. I ate a bowl of oatmeal about fifteen minutes ago and that will suffice for now. I am trying to avoid the dining hall as much as possible. It is impossible to maintain any type of healthy diet eating in there.

March 29, 2011 - Well it is another Tuesday night here in Estill, SC. Today was busy for me. At the powerhouse we are removing one of the water heaters and doing some other preventive maintenance on the back up generator for the prison. There is a main prison here, medium security, in addition to the prison camp so the water heaters and boilers are BIG! I am sure I have mentioned the other prison many times.

I am waiting for the 9:30pm stand up count as I write this. I just got off the phone with my two best friends. I miss them terribly and it hurts but the end is in sight. April starts Friday and only about twelve more weeks from there! I am in the middle of a card game also right now. We will finish after count. Just a friendly game of poker; no money involved in this one.

I was just talking to the guys in the cube next to me and the subject of *"serial flushers"* came up. There are some guys here who go to the bathroom and flush the toilet no less then fifty times. We call them serial flushers. It is very hard to take a shower with a serial flusher on the *"can"* because each flush causes a spike in the shower water temperature. It is like Flush!...Ouch!.....Flush!....Ouch!....

Tomorrow is everyone's favorite food day; it's hamburger day! I stopped eating the hamburgers about one month ago. The rumor that floats around is that the burger patties are from McDonalds. I don't buy it. They do have a soy burger heart healthy option also and I think I may try that option tomorrow. I am out almost out of food because the commissary is closed this week (sigh). I have about two packs of mackerel, one tuna, one bag of rice, and one half bag of refried beans left until next Monday. I miss my life! I have blended in nicely with the daily ho-hum of prison life. Bye and good night!

April 2, 2011 - I can not believe it is actually April. March seemed to last forever but it is now gone. Just April and May and then I will be reunited with my family hopefully in June. It brings a tingling feeling to my body. I miss them so much.

Today is another Saturday here in Oz. I have been doing a lot of writing for my new web site and just started doing some actually organizing to all my writing for my book. It rained all week here so it is refreshing to actually see the sun. I knew it would be sunny today because the sun rises right in my eyes and there is nothing I can do about it. There are no blinds to close in this place. Last night one of the guards came in my cube and woke up one of my cellies in the middle of the night to take a urine test. Just a random pick but the guard woke everyone up with his flashlight and deep voice.

April 6, 2011 - I have seen it all now. I truly believe that this place is probably one of the most disorganized federally run organizations around. It seems that the BOP is running out of money and they are discussing the possibility of being unable to pay their employees. This means all BOP employees including the guards. Rumor is going around that they may have to issue vouchers to the BOP employees until the problem is worked out. This all goes back to the budget and the fact that the Bureau of Prison budget plan was never approved. Anyway we will see how it all plays out.

Other than that an inmate who has been here for about a month, who subsequently works with me at the powerhouse, got called into the office yesterday and was told that he should go clean out his locker because he was getting an immediate release from prison. He shook my hand and said it was Jesus that made this possible. He was not sure what the actual reasons for the release. He looked so happy when I saw him before lunch time. He called his family and cleaned his locker out. After lunch I saw him again and he was at the powerhouse for the afternoon work shift. He did not look as happy as he did previously and then proceeded to tell me that they called him back in the office told let him know that there was a clerical error on his paperwork and that they made a mistake. He was not getting released from prison after all and would have to spend the next year and a half here. If that isn't enough then another friend of mine, Rocky, who has been incarcerated since 2001 was scheduled to be released today. He has been in prison for nine years. The BOP had NINE YEARS to get his paperwork correct. Well guess what? Yep, there was another error with his halfway house paperwork and he will have to wait another two weeks for his release.

Other than that it has been quiet here for the last week or so. It is now 9:30pm and I am waiting for the guards to come for the stand up count. After that I will read a little and then fall asleep. I was sick with a cold for the last few days but I am finally feeling better. Bye!

April 13, 2011 - What a crazy Wednesday it has been. Today started off for me with an early shower at about 5am. I could not sleep and was tossing and turning all night on my band aid of a bed so I decided to call it quits and wake up for the day. I headed off to the powerhouse for my 7:30 work call and then ate the heart healthy veggie burger for lunch. After work ended at 2:30 I was called into the secretary's office. She then asked me how I was getting back to Florida and to the halfway house. Imagine that, I am getting close now! I told her that I would need a bus ticket to get to the halfway house. I am trying to spare my family the long five hour ride so I am opting to take the bus to Orlando to the halfway house.

After that it was an afternoon of reading and playing cards and then just before the 9:30pm count one of the guys in the cube next to me played a joke on his other friend, who just happened to be confined to a wheel chair for the rest of his life. This man was talking to the other guys in the cube next to me and got out of his wheel chair to stand and stretch while talking. Well at about the same time the other guy quietly wheeled away his wheel chair and hid it in the bathroom. He then said, *"They're coming!"* which is the signal to all the inmates when the guards are coming down for the count. This poor guy turned around and had no wheel chair. Luckily they were good friends and they both laughed about it. He wheeled himself back to his cube and then we all got counted. Then during the count the guards took away two of the inmates in the hall next to us. It seems they both had a cellular phone which they shared together and someone informed the guards of this. They were taken away in plastic zip tie handcuffs and will likely spend the next several months in the SHU until they get transferred to a higher security prison. And let's not forget about the extra year and extra charge that will be added on to their sentences. Some people will never learn. I miss my family and can't wait to hug them for weeks!!

April 14, 2011 - Another lonely Friday night here. It is about 10:30pm. I have been playing cards for most of the night and now I am going to go lie down and read myself to sleep. My mom and dad sent me six books on nutrition and wellness. I am eager to read them. I talked to my family a few hours ago. My little girl is sleeping over her friend's house and my dear wife is reading a book. I miss them dearly. I can't believe that this thing is getting close to being over! Next month is almost here! Good night! The weekends are the worst for me because they drag on. Anyone who is going to prison will learn what I mean but keeping a positive attitude and staying busy will help anyone get through.

April 20, 2011 - Well it's another Wednesday and another hamburger day here in Estill. I have decided to forgo the beef hamburger and start eating the healthier veggie burger. I don't know why I was choosing the beef burger all along as I know how bad it is health wise. It is about 10am here and I am not at work because there was a fog count. I have been working diligently in the library and continuing my nutrition studying. I am counting the days when I am out of here.

One of the inmates here, Scott, who is a very successful real estate investor, has an interest in my nutrition business and may want to invest in it. And another inmate here, Eric, who is a video producer, wants to partner up for another supplement concept which I am formulating. Eric is here because he was a straw buyer for a corrupt mortgage company. He got coerced into saying yes and got a year in prison for it. Scott is here for some type of bank fraud thing. He explained it to me but it was very confusing. I am excited to launch my web site to help others who have to go to federal prison.

April 26, 2011 - Today is Tuesday and it's the last Tuesday of April. The last week has been a little hard for me even though I am leaving soon. It just went by so slow. This week is going by a bit faster. Last week my laundry came back brown from the laundry department. They were having problems with the city water and it was brown with rust for some reason or another and ruined many bags of clothes including mine. I got replacement clothes this week. Phewwwww!

Other than that the secretary called me in again this week to talk to me about my travel plans to the halfway house in Orlando. I will be taking the bus so the BOP is arranging my bus fare and schedule. I miss my family so much that it makes me blue whenever I am not busy.

I was talking to another inmate yesterday who I play cards with and asked him if he was also leaving this year. I was shocked when he said he has been in federal prison since 1998 and has almost eight years left still! I am so close to leaving this fantasy land of misfits and can't wait for the day. It is almost time for the 4pm stand up count. I just ate some oatmeal and will be having a tuna wrap for dinner. Bring on the month of May please!

May 1, 2011 - Wow! May is finally here! I can't believe it is actually here. I remember looking at the calendar that hangs on the wall in the powerhouse and looking at all the months I had to get through until May arrived. I am very grateful May is here.

Yesterday was something to write about. On Saturday I was invited to an Inepi ceremony. This is a religious event that involves an ancient Indian ceremonial. They also call it the *"sweat lodge."* The prison camp has a special section where this ceremony takes place. It is a fenced off part of the prison where the members all gather. Inside, there is a hand made Inepi hut similar to what the Indians used hundreds of years ago. The hut was hand made by the inmates using willow trees and is very authentic looking. I walked over to the ceremony about noon time and had no idea what to expect. I knew the ceremony involved darkness and heat but that was all I knew about it. I was in for an interesting surprise, many times more surprising than being in sauna.

Most of the *"lodge members"* were friends of mine so we chatted a bit before the ceremony began. I then was invited into the Inepi hut and given some education and instruction as to the purpose of the Inepi ceremony and the various rules to abide by. The hut can hold approximately ten people or maybe slightly more.

Basically, the ceremony involves lots of high heat and sweating. There are rocks that are heated using a wood fire that is lit on the outside. The fire heats the special rocks that are called the *"Grandfathers."* Once the rocks are ready, all the participants enter the hut one by one. I was second to enter. It is mandatory that you crawl around the inside of the hut in a clockwise direction until you get to your spot where you will be sitting. Once you crawl through the little door it is proper tradition to announce yourself by saying *"A-Ho."* Once inside, I crawled around and sat directly to the right of the Pipe Carrier. His name was Church; his Inepi name "Wayah", and he was the leader of the ceremony (i.e., the Pipe Carrier). Oh yes, did I forget to mention the fire pit. This is the large hole inside the hut that holds the *"Grandfathers."*

Once everyone is inside one of the members gets the *"Grandfathers"* from the wood fire blazing outside. This person uses a set of real deer antlers to cradle these red hot rocks and brings them into the fire pit. There are five rocks used for each round, one for each direction (e.g., North, South, East, West) and one for the *"Creator."* Once the rocks are in place in the fire pit, the door is closed. The hut is covered with dozens of blankets that make the inside completely dark and sealed very tightly. Once the door is shut we were all required to be quiet. Then the *"Pipe Carrier"* begins the ceremony. Oh yes, there is also a five gallon pail of water in there also. I was happy to see this thinking that it was for us to drink when we got thirsty but soon realized I was only half right on that assumption.

The Pipe Carrier began his opening prayer and as this is happening I hear *"Wshshsssshhhhh" "Psszzzzzzshhh."* Oh dear! The Pipe Carrier is pouring scoops of water over the *"Grandfathers"*. Picture a small space that is sealed very tight. In this space it is already very hot. Now we all know what happens when water falls on your barbecue lid right? Yep, that's right - STEAM! Well each scoop of water poured over the red hot rocks produced a whole crap load of steam. Steam is hot, at least the temperature of boiling water which is 212 degrees!

The Pipe Carrier then finishes his introduction prayer which lasts a few minutes. Then he calls for a song. A very upbeat song ensues but I have no idea what it is about because it is in some type of Indian language. I am sweating like crazy by this time and the temperature is rising rapidly. Next, it is prayer time. Each person holds the pipe and says a prayer. He can elect to say *"Silent Prayer"* or say his prayer vocally for all to hear. Now for the interesting part of the ceremony; for every prayer that is said, either silent or aloud, there is another *"Wshshshshshshs"* and *"Psshsshshshs."* Another scoop of water on the *"Grandfathers"* for each prayer! The pipe then comes to me and I quickly say *"Silent Prayer"* and hand the pipe to the next person. The pipe ends up back with the Pipe Carrier who closes out with his own prayer. By this time the temperature has risen to probably 150+ inside the hut and breathing is difficult. The Piper Carrier then ends the ceremony with five more scoops of water, one for each Grandparent. We then all say *"A-Ho"* and the door is opened. It is certainly not for the weak.

But guess what? We are not done yet! *"Oh my!,"* I think to myself. They tell me that I can only leave if I AM DONE WITH THE CEREMONY OR CAN'T TAKE THE HEAT. Am I going to wimp out?? I pump myself up with confidence and decide to march on. I then found out that there are a total of four rounds of this. I prepare myself mentally for the second round. I figure if I made it through the first round then the second should be a piece of cake right? Yeah right. We all stay in the hut and cool off from the fresh air blowing in through the two foot wide door. Then after about five or ten minutes the Pipe Carrier calls for more *"Grandfathers,"* more darn *"Grandfathers"*! So five more hefty, red hot, *"Grandfathers"* are added to the fire pit in the middle of the hut. It is now getting hot even with the door open. Once the *"Grandfathers"* are in place, all ten of them now, five from the first round and five from this round, the door is shut once again.

Just as the Pipe Carrier is beginning the opening prayer I hear him say, *"Brothers and sisters, this is the STRESS*

ROUND, let us all be STRONG." So here I am sitting in a pool of sweat listening to the two words that I did not want to hear - STRESS and STRONG. I think to myself, *"Oh dear, oh my, I am going to die!"* Then I gathered my composure and calmed myself down. I mean really now these guys have been doing this week after week. How bad can it really be? Let me tell you, it was hot, stressful, hard, and then hot some more. Think of Arizona in August times two! The Pipe Carrier finished his opening prayer and drenched the *"Grandfathers"* with twice the amount of water and the steam started filling the air fast. The temps climbed rapidly inside the already boiling hut. Then the stick got passed around for the individual prayers. When the stick got to me I was already putting my head down towards the ground to get some cooler air. The guy next to me is tapping me with the pipe after he finishes with his prayer and is unaware that my face is buried on the floor trying to get a breath of cooler air. After about four taps on my leg with the stick I finally grabbed it, said my prayer, and then passed it on. By the end of this round it was so hot in the hut that you could not sit up or the steam would get you!

At the end of the ceremony I had made it through the four rounds. Everyone else went the four rounds except for two guys who quit after the stress round. By the fourth round I was already well seasoned enough to know what to expect. I kept a wet towel with me also which helped with the scorching heat. All in all it was a great experience and interesting to see how different cultures pray. I recommend it to anyone who has the opportunity to experience it.

May 7, 2011 - Well I have knocked another week down here! It is Saturday morning about 9am and the weather is pleasant today. I just wrote my family an email and will be calling them when I am done writing this. Since it is a holiday weekend there is a slew of recreation tournaments that the inmates can partake in. There is a basketball free throw tourney, and other tournaments for things like horseshoes, foosball, frisbee toss, bocce ball, and several card games tournaments also. I will probably play in the foosball and horseshoe tournaments.

My pal Mike who works in the powerhouse with me was supposed to be leaving here the day after me but his case manager said that now his date was pushed back to September. I just learned this today and feel bad for him. It seems that they are giving inmates less and less halfway house time lately.

Anyway once the 10am count is clear they will call for the noon meal. They have an open faced turkey sandwich today which I will have and then hang outside for the day. I miss my family more than anyone can imagine. Yesterday the guards locked down the whole camp because someone from the outside attempted to throw a bag over the fence. The bag got caught on the razor wire and then the guards found it. I think there were some bodybuilding supplements in the bag that one of the inmate's friends must have tried to throw over the fence. Other than that it has been peaceful here. I got invited to the Inepi ceremony for today but I think I am going to skip the sweat for today. Bye!

May 9, 2011 - Monday brought with it an invitation to play a friendly game of half court basketball among friends. I accepted and now it is about 7pm as I sit here with a twisted ankle from going for a loose ball.

I am going to head to the tv room now to watch game four of Boston Celtics versus Miami Heat and then try and rest this ankle. I just took a shower and it hurts. The end is near and I am starting to get excited about having my life back. I miss my family dearly! I ate a veggie burger for lunch today and it was not half bad. It was considerably better than the meatball sub that was served up.

May 14, 2011 – Wow! Another Saturday knocked down! I get butterflies when I think about hanging out at a place like the restaurant *"Down The Hatch"* by the ocean with my two best friends. There will be lots of hugging going on! Anyway last week was very busy for me. I got my bus itinerary finally. I will be leaving from Savannah, GA, on June 7, and travel by bus to the halfway house in Orlando, FL.

I wrote a few good articles last week on health and nutrition related for my blog. Other than that, two people got in trouble last week and were sent to the SHU again. One guy, who is the *"town driver"* got in trouble. The town driver is the inmate who drives other inmates to and from appointments outside the prison grounds such as hospital appointments and also transports inmates to the bus station. This town driver got caught going to Burger King while he was en-route to the hospital with another inmate for an appointment. Then the guards conducted a search of the leather shop and found cigarettes in one of the lockers. Both inmates were hauled off to the SHU probably for a couple of weeks or more.

They just announced over the PA that the dining hall is open for the noon meal. I am on my way to have a sloppy joe. I have not eaten any red meat in months so I will see what the heart healthy option is before I choose to eat the SJ.

It is cloudy today with a chance of rain. I played cards last night until about 11pm and the read myself to sleep. I am so ready to be done with this crap. Bye!

May 16, 2011 – It's Monday night here in Oz. It is 11:38pm and I can't rest so I am writing an entry here. I twisted my ankle playing basketball a few days ago and I have a headache right now so I can't sleep. A good friend of mine, Robert, is sitting next to me typing on the computer next to me. There are four computers in this little computer room for email purposes. It is actually very quiet in my hallway right now. We did have a bad snorer in our hall but he has since moved to another hall and it is surprisingly quiet. I guess all the snorers are in a deep sleep now. I am going to try and get some rest here for a second time. I would read myself to sleep but my AA batteries that power my night light have no juice left. I'm going to buy some new ones at the commissary on Wednesday so I will be without a night light for a couple more days. There is no cord type lights allowed so this is all I can use to read in bed. Oh well, the joys of being incarcerated. Bye!

May 19, 2011 - It is Thursday about 7pm here in Oz. Time is a tickin' and I only have two more hamburgers left! Most people in here judge their time left by hamburgers. They always serve a hamburger for lunch on Wednesday therefore one hamburger equals one week therefore I got two hamburgers left! Of course I always opt for the veggie burger now. It isn't half bad either and is homemade by the inmate chefs from oatmeal and other stuff. Unfortunately they ran out of veggies burgers by the time I got up to the serving line yesterday so I got a regular hamburger and gave it to a friend and then went back to my cube and made a tuna wrap.

I am going to play cards and then read for a while. I try not to think too much about leaving here or the time just slows to a crawl. Staying busy is the whole key to success!

The cat that lives in the powerhouse had four baby kittens about a month ago and yesterday the Warden came by the powerhouse and ordered someone to come get the cats and the kittens. They trapped all the cats and let the mama go outside the compound. The kittens went somewhere else, hopefully to a good home, I pray! Bye!

May 24, 2011 - Well it is May 24th and tomorrow is hamburger day again! I only have one hamburger day left after tomorrow! Tonight I am feeling much more relaxed here. I am watching game four of the NBA semi-finals Miami Heat versus Chicago Bulls. All my friends here are Heat fans but I want the Bulls to win. It stinks that the Celtics lost but I can live with it knowing that I am leaving here soon.

It is 10pm here and we just finished the 9:30 stand up count. The hallway is a bit noisy with the game going on so I will finish watching it and then read myself to sleep. Nothing else is new here except my family has mailed me my *"going away"* clothes! I can change into normal clothes on the morning before I go to the bus station. One of the inmates who works as the town driver will be driving me to the Savannah bus station. I am counting the days. I miss my two best friends and my family so much. Today was very hot but I still got in a forty-five minute workout. I walked the track for about twenty minutes and then thirty minutes or so of sit-ups in the gym. Tomorrow I will do push-ups, curls, and walk the track, and for Thursday I will do ab-rolls and sit-ups again. I am almost down to 160 pounds! I have never weighed that little except when I was like fifteen years old! Surviving this place is all about attitude and keeping busy and staying close to loved ones! That's it! Good night!

May 25, 2011 - Just finished with the 9:30pm stand up count. I woke up today about 7am and slept exceptionally well compared to most nights here. I ate the veggie burger on wheat bread again today and again it wasn't half bad. I think I am just a bit more relaxed knowing that I am leaving here soon and will be able to hug and kiss my family, wear my own clothes, and do something simple like hang out by the ocean with my two best friends very soon. Usually I wake up with any noise, especially at 3am and 5am during the counts. Usually the guards come in and will turn on one of the lights in the hallway and then say *"Count."* This is enough to wake me up. Lately though I have been sleeping through these disruptions and even sleeping through the snoring and multiple toilet flushes each night. I would say that my body has simply adapted to this new lifestyle. I have also noticed that I am sleeping better ever since I cut out the fried foods and sweets that they serve in the dining hall. The first few months I was eating the fried stuff, the cakes, the sweets, etc. About three months ago I began to change over to the heart healthier options in the dining hall. I also only eat in the dining hall once per day and then eat my commissary groceries for my dinner. This usually entails a tuna, salmon, or chicken wrap and a few crackers.

I worked out today for about thirty minutes and then went out to the softball field and helped out fielding balls. I batted also and did pretty good. I talked to my family twice today and wrote them an email. I know I am rambling a bit but next week is my LAST FULL WEEK HERE! Gonna' go read myself to sleep.

May 27, 2011 - It is about 9am here and last night consisted of a huge riot over at the medium security prison next door. The riot made the news this morning and it seems like 50-100 inmates were involved in it. About ten were brought to the hospital and a few of them were wounded seriously rumor has it. There were police cars all around the main prison last night. It was quite a fiasco here. It looks like both the prison next door and the camp will be on lockdown for several days. That means we will be stuck indoors all day and night except for meals. I am going to take a shower and then lie down. I am 100% sick of being here and can't wait to leave this place. I am itching to feel life again and hug my family!

May 29, 2011 - Just woke up to the loudspeaker at 7am notifying everyone that the grounds are closed. This is a huge caveat about being at a satellite camp. A satellite prison camp is different from that of a regular camp in that the satellite camp is located next to another prison of higher security and whenever there is trouble at the main prison and the prison is locked down, the camp also feels the effects. A non-satellite prison camp such as Pensacola FPC is a stand alone facility therefore does not feel the effects of a problem like this. So at 7am this morning the loudspeaker whaled, *"Attention on the compound. The yard is closed. Return to your assigned units. The yard is closed."* The yard was open for a few hours yesterday until they closed it so it will likely be closed all day today. This means we are all stuck inside the housing units again (sigh). It is about 7:30am right now and I am off to read again. I can't wait until next weekend is here. My last weekend! I am counting the minutes now and time is dragging.

May 31, 2011 - About 7pm here and today was a very busy day for me. For starters, due to the trouble that happened at the prison next door, the laundry service has been shut down since last week. Therefore I was forced to bring all my dirty clothes over to the powerhouse today and wash them in the utility sink. I hand washed them all, then rung them out and hung all of them around the huge burner that supplies the prison with heat and hot water. The heat dried them in a few hours!

I also decided to get a hair cut today. It was my first hair cut since Halloween evening, the night when I cut it myself in the local motel here in Estill, SC. My hair was out of control and unmanageable. My family wanted to see me in long hair but it really just was too messy looking and I want to look nice for them when I see them next week. Other than that I got together all my books that I will be mailing back and boxed them up. The box weighs thirty-five pounds! I have lots of books!

A friend of mine came back from the SHU today and had a smile on his face. We talked briefly and he is glad to be out of the hole. He went there about two weeks ago due to some contraband that was found in the Inepi yard.

278 - Reduce My Prison Sentence

Other than that I am down to 163 pounds and last night I went to the bathroom at about 4am and looked in the mirror. I actually can see the results of my workouts coming through. It is nice to see actual progress when you work hard at something and I look so much better than when I came here. My family will be happy!

I am ready to close this chapter in my life and get on with living. I slept crappy last night as usual. The Miami Heat and Dallas Mavericks play the first game of the NBA finals tonight and that is what is being talked about the most. Most people are Miami fans here.

My mom and dad made it back to Cape Cod where they will spend the summer and I talked to my family on the phone a few hours ago. I will call them again in about an hour. I miss everyone dearly and will be hugging them for days, months, and years! Six days and a wake up left! Tomorrow is my last hamburger day. Thank god!

June 3, 2011 - Wow! June is here and it is already the 3rd. I only have 3 full days left! I am very happy to be finally leaving this place. It is 7am here and I slept okay last night. I have mailed all my books back so I have little to read for the next few days. I will have to try and find a couple of books from the library but they have a very limited selection and the good non-fiction books I have mostly read already. I am off to work and then will probably play cards tonight and then fall asleep around 10-11pm. I will be smiling the whole bus ride back to Orlando, Florida!

June 4, 2011 - It is about 8am Saturday here. It has been exceptionally quieter than usual here because the tv's are out in our unit. They went out yesterday and have not come back online yet. There was a bad thunderstorm the other day and this is probably the culprit. Due to this the inmates are all sleeping later and there is less commotion and chatter going on in my hall. It is nice. I hope they get them fixed soon though or there will be some unhappy folks in here. For some inmates, tv is their only salvation. Luckily I only watch maybe an hour or two per week at the most. Only two more days and I am outta' here. I can't wait to taste life again. I am going to call my family and then read for the day.

June 8, 2011 – I am happily writing this from a picnic table outside in the back parking lot of the halfway house here in sunny Orlando, FL. I can't believe I am finally here! Yesterday started off with a rocky start but then turned sweet as pie after I saw the two faces that I longed for so much during the last 210 days.

Yesterday at about 5:30am one of the correction officers at the prison camp woke me up with her deep raspy voice with a, *"Sharp, Sharp, Sharp, be at the admin building no later than 5:50."* Since I did not rest much anyway and was eager to finally be leaving, it took me no more than ten minutes to brush my teeth and get dressed. I then hurried off for the short walk to the front door of the administration building where the guard would let me through. On the way to the administration building I could not resist one last gaze at the razor wire fence and dull colored buildings that defined this place I was forced to call home for the last seven months. I was more than ready to leave this place I call Oz. I hurled my laundry sack full of dirty clothes and green uniforms to the front door of the laundry department, which was just a few doors down from the admin. building, and sat patiently until the guard opened the door to allow me through the front door. After a short few minute wait and some last minute handshakes with friends, the female guard opened the door and I walked on through over to the main prison. It would be here in the Receiving & Discharge (R&D) department that I would sign my release papers and officially be released from the camp! After signing the necessary documents the best part came. One of the correctional officers emerged from the back room with a priority mail package. The package's contents contained my own clothes that were sent to me by my family about two weeks prior. I sped into the changing room and ripped off my drab green prison camp uniform for the last time. The institution shirt, pants, belt, and all, went splat into the trash bag that sat next to me. I jumped into a pair of real blue jeans and a real t-shirt, slipped on a new pair of Harley Davidson boots and headed out the door. I was feeling like me again and it felt good. I took with me only a few things like bath items, a couple pairs of socks, some herbal tea, and a couple of books. The remainder of my personal goods

I gave away to other inmates who were on a very limited weekly budget.

There was one other camp inmate also being processed who was also leaving on the bus. He was being transferred to another camp so he could complete the residential drug program (RDAP). Only certain institutions offer the highly sought after RDAP program and it is the only BOP offered program that gives a reward of up to one year off one's sentence for completion of the course.

Once our paperwork was completed and we answered a slew of questions to confirm that we were who our papers said we were we headed out the door to the R&D room and up to the front of the FCI. We both then met with the cashier who provided us with our bus vouchers, cab fare and some food and gratuity cash. I received about $90 for my trip to Orlando and felt that would suffice. We then headed out the front door to the medium security prison, which coincidently was on lockdown for a riot five days earlier, and into the waiting van.

The town driver, who's name was KC and a friend of mine, would be driving us both to the Savannah bus station. We got underway at about 8am and headed on out to the West on a very desolate two lane road. It was so nice seeing all the same landscape going the other way from my dreaded trip seven months prior. Even the traffic lights and telephone poles were pleasant to look at. The simple thought of being free from that caged fence made me very happy. It felt like I have not seen these outside views for six years not six months.

Then the problems began. It was about 9:05am when we pulled in to the station and my bus was scheduled for a 9:10am departure to Orlando. I flung myself out of the front seat of the government Ford van with a very quick good bye and thank you to KC and hustled into the bus station. At about the same time a bus pulled away from the station. A lady then noticed me hustling and asked me where I was headed. I told her Orlando on the 9:10 and then she said it just left. The bus left three minutes early – imagine that. I was left standing there on the curb side of the bus station with that very familiar peculiar look on my face. *"Now I'm screwed!,"* I thought to myself knowing that I would never make it to the halfway house by my scheduled time. I was not going back to that prison camp at any costs, no way. I proceeded to the ticket counter and asked the lady when the next bus to Orlando headed out. She told me 1:35pm and that was good enough for me. She exchanged my bus voucher for a ticket on the later bus. Now I had to inform the halfway house that my itinerary had changed from previously planned. I should be able to handle that with a quick phone call no problem right?

Well inside the bus station stood a row of payphones along the front wall. Now all I needed was some change to operate the phone. Little did I know that getting change would be a task more difficult than striking gold in a hill side. As I approached the lady at the ticket counter and started to ask here for change for a dollar, she pointed at the big red sign that was taped to the cash register, *"We do not make change!"* I turned to walk away and was happy to see a little game room inside the bus station on the far side. As I got closer I noticed that big orange light that was illuminated on the front of the change machine that read *"Out of Change When Lit."* I thought to myself, *"Oh brother! Here we go again!"* and then headed out the front door to find change. I knew there must be a gas station somewhere close and sure enough there was one about six blocks up the road. I walked over to the gas station and proceeded inside. No sooner when the dollar bill in my hand was moved toward the cashier and just as I began to speak, did the non English speaking man start shaking his head back and forth and shouting *"No Change!, No Change!"* I walked away and then returned to the counter about a minute later with a bottle of water and a Slim Jim in hand, cleverly priced out at $1.10 and handed it to the cashier. He had no option but to give me change now and gave me change for the two dollars that I gave him. I was now armed with coins for my phone call!

I left the gas station and headed out to another pay phone in the front parking lot. Just as I twisted the cap off my bottled spring water I felt a firm *"Swaaap!"* on the back side of my right shoulder and upwards to the right side of my face. *"What the heck was that?"* I said to myself and then turned to my right to take a look. As my head swiveled around for a look I caught a glimpse of it. And it was performing a hammerhead maneuver to reposition for another strike. My eyes widened and I grabbed my grey tote bag, lifted it over my head, and swung it violently to deter my oncoming foe – a cat bird! This was cat bird with war on its mind and I was its target. It was obviously having a bad day and using me to make him feel better. As it came back for its third air assault I let out a vocal burst which entailed a couple of profanities and then threw my bag in the air. It swooped away and retired to the high tension wire overhead. A couple of tweets later we both agreed to a cease fire and the battle ended.

Finally able to catch a breath I walked the last fifty steps to the payphone and dropped in a quarter. I quickly dialed the number to the halfway house and the automated lady asked for another fifty cents to complete the call. I dropped in two more quarters and the phone began to ring. After about ten rings a man answered the phone and spoke in Japanese. I had no idea what he was saying but he was not happy and was calling me a *"SieJeeeLuuuHaa"* or something close. I kept asking him if this was the Dismas Charities halfway house and by the third time I asked I heard a loud click and then the line went dead. I stood there again with that precarious look on my face and stared at the sky. What the hell is going on here? I must confess I was on alert for that bird still too. I mean really, are you serious? Is this a joke someone is playing on me? Back into the store and then back out with another fresh Slim Jim in hand and seventy more cents to give the phone. I was hoping that it was just a misdialed number that I made and prayed that that same man would not answer the phone again. If he is in charge then I am in deep trouble. I dropped in another seventy-five cents and proceeded to dial the number again, but this time much more slowly and with an annunciated confirmation of each number as I pressed it. *"Presto!"* A lady answered the phone from the halfway house. I explained to her my situation and then gave her my new bus schedule. She told me no problem and to call her once I got to Orlando. Well that was easier than I thought and I was now relieved knowing that I would not have to head back to the prison camp. I then called my two best friends and told them how much I missed them and how excited I was to finally be wearing my own clothes.

So now I have four hours to kill and by glancing around it seems there is nothing here to do. What I did notice though during my walk back from the gas station was a big red sign that read *"Hampton Inn."* I thought, *"Sit in the bus station for four hours or in the confines of the amenity rich hotel up the road?"* Within the next fifteen minutes I had my feet up on a plush leather recliner that was positioned about four feet back from a huge flat screen high definition Sony 42" television. A computer desk stood about ten feet away with complimentary internet access, a fresh copy of USA Today waited on the table next to me, and fresh hot coffee was free in the next room. There was also a continental breakfast but I decided to pass on all the extra amenities and simply take advantage of the relaxing seat and clear tv picture that made my wait for the bus one to remember.

Anyone who has been to prison for an extended stay can surely relate to my emphatic description of this simple event; it was truly extraordinary in my mind. After all, I spent the previous seven months sitting on nothing better than a hard blue plastic chair and watching television with a set of headphones on for sound and in a room filled with loud and expressive inmates who felt they should comment on every tv show that they watched.

I reluctantly picked myself off the recliner at about 1pm and walked back to the bus station. We boarded the bus and left on time. The bus ride was uneventful and when we arrived in Jacksonville at 4pm there was a surprise waiting for me. An unexpected surprise! My family was there waiting for me! I was so happy to see them and I hugged and kissed them for what seemed like hours. It was a total surprise and it made my day, my week, my month! I then checked my bus schedule and realized that I had a two hour layover. I figured that it would be wise to have them drive me the rest of the way to the halfway house. I checked the conditions of the furlough sheet and saw nothing that restricted them from driving me the remainder of the distance provided we stayed on the same direct route to the halfway house. It was the best ride that I had ever.

We got to the Dismas Charities halfway house at about 8pm and I hugged my family and headed inside. The building resembled that of a small commercial plaza that would accommodate three or four stores but the entire space was occupied by the halfway house. I was curious to see what the inside was like. Once inside I was greeted by the lady at the front window. They were very polite and treated me like a human being. It was a pleasant experience to be treated like a real person again. I took a quick breathalyzer, gave a urine sample, gave a fingerprint sample, and then signed of couple of documents and was done. I was then led into the men's dorm and to my dismay this part of the halfway house resembled that of the prison camp that I just came from. It was an open dorm with four rows of double bunks, ten bunks in each row. But I was not complaining in any way. I was so happy to have been reunited with my family so nothing bothered me. There was one plus to the dorm though – it was dark at night and in the morning. There were blinds on the windows! Unlike the prison camp which had no drapes or blinds on the windows, these windows had commercial blinds and that meant no blinding sun to wake up to! This was surely a plus and there was more in store for me to discover.

The next morning I woke up and met a couple of the residents there and chatted with the lady at the front desk. I immediately noticed the less restrictive environment from that of even a minimum security prison camp. We were all allowed to go outside at will, provided we remained within the parking lot area. In the back of the building were picnic tables, a basketball net, and some battered exercise equipment. Battered or not, I was surprised to see it there!

They served lunch at noon and this was also a pleasant surprise. No more long lines and this was real food! The food was excellent and the little cafeteria was clean with a friendly environment. There were two tv rooms and three computers to use. One of the computers had Microsoft Word and some games on it while the other had limited internet access to job finding web sites and some programs that the residents used to request various things such as passes and such. They even had a Wii video game that we could hook up and play when we wanted to.

The payphones were regular payphones without monitors listening to your every word and I could call anyone I wanted without getting an approval first. These little changes were very notable to me and gave the true feeling of being *"halfway home."*

June 11, 2011 – It is Saturday here at the halfway house in Orlando and this place rivals any federal prison institution type setting. I was just sitting here typing up an article on Microsoft Word on one of the computers and was curious about saving my work after I was done. I asked the front desk if I could bring in some computer disks to save my work on. The man said, *"Of course you can. This isn't prison."* I can easily see and feel the less restrictive environment that I am living in now. The people here are all pleasant and the atmosphere is jovial. The best part of all is that I was approved to leave the halfway house on Sunday for two hours to go to a store. And my family is taking me!

It is almost noon here and last night I slept okay. It was amazing waking up to a quiet dark room. It was just unexplainable considering I spent the last seven months waking up to loudspeakers and a bright sun burning my face off. There is still an intercom system but it is not nearly as loud and annoying as the ones in a prison environment. They actually say *"Good morning, breakfast in now being served."*

I am waiting to see if my case manager is going to approve for me to work at my nutrition store. I hope he does as I have to get back to work asap. Other than that I just had lunch, two turkey sandwiches, and brought them back into the tv room to eat while typing on the computer. This type of life is so much more tolerable than the prison camp. I have plenty to do today now that I have access to a computer with some word processing programs on it. Yeah!

June 13, 2011 – Today is Monday and I already have one week down here at the halfway house. I was so excited to have been able to see my family on Sunday. They came down and visited from 12:30 – 2:30. We played Monopoly the entire time and then I was approved to go to the store with them and get some personal items for two hours.

In the last week I have met with a few people here at the halfway house and watched a few videos about the house rules. A probation officer came down and talked to us also. A couple of days ago I also met with my case manager. We discussed the possibility of me working for myself at my nutrition store but it is likely that it will be declined.

Regardless I only have about five weeks left here no matter what the situation is. If I am not allowed to work at my own store then I will try to find a temporary job near my home which is about forty minutes from here.

I have settled in nicely here and have a daily plan together to help pass the time. The first few nights I rested little but then I started resting better once I got used to my new surroundings. I have met many of the other residents, they are no longer referred to as inmates, and it is a pleasant atmosphere here with the exception of a couple of people here who never learned the definition of the word courtesy and respect. For example, one guy likes to talk to his friends loud at night, late at night, while others are trying to rest. Another guy yelled at him last night at about 2am. That was all it took and then it was quiet the remainder of the night. Another point which I forgot to mention is that there is also a women's dorm here. There are only about five females here that I have seen and the population is mostly males. My job assignment is to clean one of the men's bathrooms. It only takes about fifteen minutes per day. Other than that I spend my days reading, writing, working on the computer, watching tv, walking around the building, and working out in the back with the makeshift equipment like a sac of towels attached to a metal bar to curl with. I am hoping to drop another five pounds before I leave here to look good for my family. It is about 3pm as I write this and I am going to go call my family right now. Another point to mention is the fact that the phones are a blessing and no longer monitored and controlled. There is no limits on who you call and how long you talk and it is now trouble free to call my family on the payphone because we have a toll free number for our herb business. I am falling asleep about 1am or so and waking at about 8-9 in the morning. This is definitely halfway home just as the title reiterates.

June 18, 2011 – It is about 11am here in Orlando, Florida. I am ready to start my third week here at the Dismas Halfway House. Last week I filled out a slew of forms to get various things accomplished here. It seems there is a form for everything. First I had to fill out multiple forms to have my vehicle approved for me to drive. This included submitting a copy of my driver's license, vehicle registration, proof of insurance, and driving record. I was approved to drive my vehicle on Friday. This was great news to me! It is so time consuming getting around via bus. Next was a home inspection that had to be conducted by one of the staff here at the halfway house. This inspection is required in addition to the inspection that is conducted by the probation department. Once this was completed my home was approved for me to visit. The best news I got was Friday when my case manager told me that I would be allowed to go home for eight hours on Sunday! I would be allowed to leave from 11am to 7pm and be with my family in my house. I would be also allowed to drive my own vehicle back to the halfway house. So as you can see each little step leads back to normal life. I truly do think the name *"halfway house"* is a valid term for this place.

I have been passing time here by doing everything from exercising, editing my book, reading, writing, watching a little tv, talking to my family, and even playing the Wii video game that they have here. The majority of my time consists of working on my book. It is sunny today so I will spend a little time outside today. Only five weeks left until my life is back! Yeah!

June 21, 2011 – It is almost 10pm here on Tuesday evening. Wow I had one of the best weekends in a long time. I was allowed to go home on Sunday from 11-7 and it was great. My family picked me up at 11am and we went back to our house and talked, played games, and ate some great food. I smiled the entire time and I think I kissed my wife and little girl no less than one thousand times. I have big plans for them both once I am done in a few weeks and Disney World is a knocking. I spoke to my mom and dad also and that was so great too. They were both so excited to talk to me finally on the outside and we talked for a while. I can't wait to bring my family down and see them. I was approved to drive my vehicle therefore my family did not have to drive me all the way back to Orlando on Sunday. When I got back to the halfway house I had to get searched and then take a breathalyzer test. No biggie though. I was so happy to be back in the real world.

Yesterday two U.S. Marshals came down to the halfway house and picked up two of the residents to bring them back to prison. I heard that they both failed their urine drug test. The crazy thing is that another resident got picked up again today. I hear that a lot of people here are smoking herbal marijuana called K2 because it is not detectable in a urine drug test but guess what? They are testing for this K2 herbal weed now and this is getting a lot of people in big trouble. It simply is not worth it! If someone is caught, they not only go back to prison, but probably lose all their good time, RDAP time, and the remainder of their halfway house time! This could lead to extra years on their sentence! No way! Not worth it! Ever!

I was also approved to go job hunting tomorrow from 10-6. I will be driving my truck to Daytona, Port Orange, and Ormond Beach to find employment. Only a few more weeks after this week! Going to sleep soon!

June 28, 2011 – Wow, it has been about a week since I last wrote. I have been busy editing my book about eight hours per day here. I was allowed to leave twice within the last week for eight hours to go job hunting. It was so nice to be allowed to travel up to the Daytona Beach area to look for a job. I met my two best friends for lunch and it was so sweet. The halfway house will not let me work at my nutrition store so I am forced to find some other work for the next few weeks. If I don't find any work then I will be denied any overnight home passes. My job here at the halfway house has been to clean the dining room at 7am and then at 7pm. It is easy, but waking up early to clean up after other people's messes is a drag.

I talk to my family several times per day and it is so nice not having that automated voice talking before each phone call alerting the other person that the phone call is from an inmate at a federal prison. I am not sure if I mentioned it but I was approved to drive my truck and it is now here in the parking lot.

Sunday is my visiting day from 12:30-2:30. My two best friends came down and we played cards and talked the entire time. I taught my little girl and wife how to play Hearts and Oh Hell, two fun card games. It is about 8am here and I am going back to sleep. I just finished cleaning the dining room.

July 5, 2011 – July 4th came and went yesterday. It was very boring and ordinary but on Sunday my family came down and visited me from 12:30-2:30. This is my designated visiting hours each week. It is so sweet seeing my family multiple times per week now! They meet me for lunch while I am at work and then I see them on the weekend at least once. It is about 10pm here at the halfway house and curfew time is almost here. All the residents must go back to the dorm at 10:30pm each night and 11:00pm on the weekends and holidays. I am sitting in the tv room typing this right now.
There are four guys next to me playing dominos and a guy and girl sitting in here also talking and watching tv. I have been able to go to the store and get my haircut while here. It is a matter of requesting passes for these needs and hoping that they get approved. The halfway house has limits on what they can and cannot approve. I got a job last week at a friend's restaurant and I am working there tomorrow from 12-7.
Only a couple more weeks and I am done! It gets noisy in the dorm trying to rest but I am used to it – especially considering where I came from. My new job is to keep the dorm clean. It is mush easier than my last job cleaning the dining room! Everyone crowded around the tv today to watch the Casey Anthony verdict unfold. I am off to the dorm before curfew is called. Bye!

July 12, 2011 – I was just told by my case manager that they are going to send in my paperwork for me to go to home confinement! I am so happy right now I think I could run 100 miles. Other than this great news, my family came down Sunday and we played cards and laughed a whole bunch. I can't believe that I am so close to going home. I am much more comfortable here now that I know a lot of the residents. I even have the second best high score for Wii Golf! Passing time is much easier here than any prison and I am so grateful to be on my last stretch. I am excited to get my book published as soon as I am outta' here!

290 - Reduce My Prison Sentence

July 14, 2011 – You won't believe it! I slept in my bed last night with my beautiful wife in my arms and my little girl in the other room. On Tuesday I was called into the case manger's office and told that they were submitting the paperwork to place me on home confinement for the last couple weeks. I could not believe it! I'm going home to my family two weeks early. Anyway I have been up since 5am working on so many things. I am just truly exhausted right now so I am going to go get a little more sleep – good sleep! I am sporting a very stylish ankle bracelet on my right ankle. It goes anywhere I go and communicates with a little black box that was brought to our house today. I end this note smiling!

13
Prison Directory

Did you know that the modern day prison system began to form shortly after the Revolutionary War? Yes it's true. The 1790's brought with it new ideas for imprisonment. The idea of reforming a prisoner versus the traditional theory of punishing those imprisoned was finally underway. Jails, on the other hand are nothing new in history. Jail cells have been around for hundreds of years. There is documented proof dating back to the year 1166 when King Henry II, the King of England at the time, had ordered jails to be built to house those who had broken his laws.

The U.S. prison system continued to develop into the 1800's when the Quakers, who did not believe in war or violence, constructed the first penitentiary type institution. It was built in the old Walnut Street Jail which was situated behind Independence Hall in Philadelphia, PA. The Quakers also realized that imprisonment should be used to help reform the individual and not solely punish them. Unfortunately, the Quakers used single man cells in which each prisoner was isolated from human contact. The inmates each had their own adjacent exercise yard where they could spend time but they were always alone with no human interaction. This type of solitary confinement slowly caused many of the prisoners to become mentally ill and eventually insane.

Meanwhile, in Auburn, New York, a second prison was built in 1825 using a different approach for prisoners. In the Auburn prison, the inmates were housed together in hopes of solving the emotional problems which developed from solitary confinement. The most serious criminals were still confined alone just as they would have been in Pennsylvania but all other inmates were allowed to work and eat together on a daily basis. The only drawback for the inmates was they were not allowed to talk. The inmates were required to remain silent at all times or face serious consequences such as being placed back in solitary confinement. This new approach in the prison system seemed to be working quite well and the imminent threat of inmates going insane began to diminish in the years that followed.

By 1913 the Pennsylvania method of housing prisoners in solitary confinement was discontinued except for those committing the most severe and heinous types of crimes. By 1876 the first reformatory was established in Elmira, New York. This institution was built to help reform, rather than punish juveniles who have broken the law. These younger prisoners were taught a trade while incarcerated at the informatory. They could serve their time learning and mastering a trade and then have a better chance for a crime free life once released back to the outside community. This type of reform is seen all over in today's world with numerous juvenile detention programs around the nation. With the onset of the twentieth century, also came individualized treatment programs for various offenders. During this time is when inmates suffering from drug and alcohol abuse could seek additional help while incarcerated. Similar programs followed for inmates who were mentally ill and for those who committed sex crimes.

It would be during the 1970's when the prison system began to fall apart. Both the state and federal institutions were flooded with prisoners of all ages, races, and religions. Overcrowding became a huge problem that has since never been corrected. With the crowded prisons came tension. The high tension would frequently result in violence. The violence transformed into racial problems and the racial problems manifested themselves into prison gangs. The most violent prison riot occurred at the Attica Correctional Facility in New York. Hundreds of deaths resulted from this bloody battle.

Today's modern day prisons are still severely overcrowded, filled with corruption, and flooded with gangs. At many prisons the gangs actually run the inner workings of the prison. Without proper funding for new prisons or reformed laws that lessen the length of imprisonment for various crimes, the problem of overcrowding in American prisons will continue to grow with each passing day.

The following is a list of federal prisons operating in the United States. These institutions are classified into five different security levels: High, Medium, Low, Minimum, and

Administrative. Each security level will designate different requirements such as the ratio of guards per inmates required (i.e., higher security means more guards), the types of confinement for the prisoner (i.e., cell type housing or dormitories), the type of perimeter that surrounds the institution (i.e., fences, walls, guard towers, etc.), the presence of security cameras and metal detectors, and the overall restrictions on the compound (i.e., controlled movements, more frequent shakedowns, etc.). Most minimum security institutions will only have one or two guards per each three hundred inmates or so and little, if any perimeter fencing. Minimum security prisons, also known as *"prison camps"* have the least amount of restrictions and are mainly for non-violent offenders serving less than ten years of incarceration. Maximum security institutions, also known as a United States Penitentiaries, will have the highest number of guards per inmate, reinforced perimeter walls, and razor or electric wire fences to contain the inmates. Additionally, all inmates except those housed at a minimum security prison camp are restricted to *"ten minute moves,"* which only allows them to move from one part of the prison to another during the first ten minutes of each hour. Inmates serving time at a minimum security or low security institution usually are housed in cubes while inmates in higher security facilities are assigned to one or two man cells. Regardless of where an inmate is placed, the housing quarters in all institutions are very limited and lacking of any privacy.

Directory of Federal Prisons

AL

FPC Montgomery
Maxwell Air Force Base
Montgomery, AL 36112
Ph: 334-293-2100
Fax: 334-293-2326
Security Levels: Minimum
Camp Population: 860

FCI Talladega
565 E Renfroe Rd.
Talladega, AL 35160
Ph: 256-315-4100
Fax: 256-315-4495
Security Levels: Medium,
High, Minimum Camp
Population: Med/High – 810
Camp - 357

AR

FCC Forrest City
P.O. Box 7000
Forrest City, AR 72336
Medium: 870-494-4200
Med. Fax: 870-494-4496
Low: 870-630-6000
Security Levels: Medium,
Low, Minimum Camp
Population: 3,838

AZ

FCI Phoenix
37900 N 45th Ave.
Phoenix, AZ 85086
Ph: 623-465-9757
Fax: 623-465-5199
Security Levels: Medium,
Minimum Camp/Female
Population: All – 1,248

FCI Safford
P.O. Box 820
Safford, AZ 85548
Ph: 928-428-6600
Fax: 928-348-1331
Security Levels: Low
Population: 848

FCC Tucson
9300 S Wilmot Rd.
Tucson, AZ 85756
USP: 520-663-5000
USP Fax: 520-664-5024
Medium: 520-574-7100
Security Levels: Medium,
High, Administrative,
Minimum Camp
Population: 1,559 (all)

CA

USP Atwater
P.O. Box 019001
#1 Federal Way
Atwater, CA 95340
Ph: 209-386-0257
Fax: 209-386-4635
Security Levels: High,
Minimum Camp/Male
Population: High - 973
Camp - 116

FCI Dublin
5701 8th St., Camp Parks
Dublin, CA 94568
Ph: 925-833-7500
Fax: 925-833-7599
Security Levels: Low/Female,
Administrative/Male
Minimum Camp/Female
Population: FCI - 1248
Camp - 313

FCI Herlong
P.O. Box 900
Herlong, CA 96113
Ph: 530-827-8000
Fax: 530-827-8024
Security Levels: Medium,
Minimum Camp
Population: Med - 949
Camp - 119

MDC Los Angeles
535 N Alameda St.
Los Angeles, CA 90012
Ph: 213-485-0439
Fax: 213-253-9510
Security Levels:
Administrative:
Male & Female
Population: 1,055

MCC San Diego
808 Union St.
San Diego, CA 92101-6078
Ph: 619-232-4311
Fax: 619-595-0390
Security Levels:
Administrative:
Male & Female
Population: 1,116

FCI Terminal Island
1299 Seaside Ave.
Terminal Island, CA 90731
Ph: 310-831-8961
Fax: 310-732-5335
Security Levels: Low
Population: 1,079

FCC Victorville
P.O. Box 5400
Adelanto, CA 92301
USP: 760-530-5000
USP Fax: 760-530-5103
Medium I: 760-246-2400
Medium II: 760-530-5700
Security Levels: Medium,
High, Minimum
Camp/Female
Population: 4,750

CT

FCI Danbury
Route 37
Danbury, CT 06811
Ph: 203-743-6471
Fax: 203-312-5110
Security Levels: Low,
Minimum Camp/Female
Population: FCI - 1,210
Camp - 209

CO

FCI Englewood
9595 W Quincy Ave.
Littleton, CO 80123
Ph: 303-985-1566
Fax: 303-763-2553
Security Levels: Low,
Administrative,
Minimum Camp
Population: FCI - 430
Camp - 165

FCC Florence
5880 State Hwy 67
Florence, CO 81226
ADX: 719-784-9464
ADX Fax: 719-784-5290
USP: 719-784-9454
FCI: 719-784-9100
Population: 3,069
Security Levels: Medium,
High, Administrative,
Minimum; Pop: All – 3,069

FL

FCC Coleman
P.O. Box 1024
Coleman, FL 33521
USPII: 352-689-7000
USPII Fax: 352-689-7012
USPI: 352-689-6000
Medium: 352-689-5000
Low: 352-689-4000
Security Levels: Low, Medium, High, Minimum Camp/Female
Population: 7,491

FCI Marianna
3625 FCI Rd.
Marianna, FL 32446
Ph: 850-526-2313
Fax: 850-718-2014
Security Levels: Medium, Minimum Camp/Female
Population: FCI - 1,251
Camp - 266

FCI Miami
15801 SW 137th Ave.
Miami, FL 33177
Ph: 305-259-2100
Fax: 305-259-2160
Security Levels: Low, Minimum Camp
Population: Low - 1,084
Camp - 398

FDC Miami
33 NE 4th St.
Miami, FL 33132
Ph: 305-982-1277
Fax: 305-536-7368
Security Levels: Administrative Male/Female
Population: 1,656

FPC Pensacola
110 Raby Ave.
Pensacola, FL 32509-5127
Ph: 850-457-1911
Fax: 850-458-7291
Security Levels: Minimum Camp
Population: 691

FCI Tallahassee
501 Capital Cir. NE
Tallahassee, FL 32301-3572
Ph: 850-878-2173
Fax: 850-216-1299
Security Levels: Low/Female, Administrative/Male
Population: 1,275

GA

USP Atlanta
601 McDonough Blvd, SE
Atlanta, GA 30315-0182
Ph: 404-635-5100
Fax: 404-331-2137
Security Levels: Medium, Administrative, Minimum Camp
Population: USP - 1,999
Camp - 441

FCI Jesup
2600 Hwy 301 S
Jesup, GA 31599
Ph: 912-427-0870
Fax: 912-427-1125
Security Levels: Medium, Low, Minimum Camp
Population: FCI -1,170
Low: 593   Camp - 147

HI

FDC Honolulu
P.O. Box 30547
351 Elliott Street
Honolulu, HI 96820
Ph: 808-838-4200
Fax: 808-838-4507
Security Levels:
Administrative
Male & Female
Population: 662

IL

MCC Chicago
71 W Van Buren
Chicago, IL 60605
Ph: 312-322-0567
Fax: 312-347-4012
Security Levels:
Administrative
Male & Female
Population: 711

FCI Greenville
P.O. Box 4000
Greenville, IL 66246
Ph: 618-664-6200
Fax: 618-664-6372
Security Levels: Medium,
Minimum Camp/Female
Population: FCI - 1,212
Camp - 301

USP Marion
4500 Prison Rd.
P.O. Box 2000
Marion, IL 62959
Ph: 618-964-1441
Fax: 618-964-2058
Security Levels: Medium,
Minimum – Pop: All - 1211

FCI Pekin
P.O. Box 7000
Pekin, IL 61555-7000
Ph: 309-346-8588
Fax: 309-477-4685
Security Levels: Medium,
Minimum Camp/Female
Population: FCI - 1,211
Camp - 309

IN

FCC Terre Haute
4700 Bureau Rd. S
Terre Haute, IN 47802
USP: 812-244-4400
USP Fax: 812-244-4791
Medium: 812-238-1531
Security Levels: High,
Medium, Minimum Camp
Population: 3,428 (all)

KS

USP Leavenworth
P.O. Box 1000
Leavenworth, KS 66048
Ph: 913-682-8700
Fax: 913-578-1010
Security Levels: Medium,
Minimum Camp
Population: USP - 1,921
Camp – 415

KY

FCI Ashland
P.O. Box 888
State Route 716
Ashland, KY 41105-0888
Ph: 606-928-6414
Security Levels: Low,
Minimum Camp/Male
Population: FCI - 1,225
Camp - 277

USP Big Sandy
P.O. Box 2067
Inez, KY 41224
Ph: 606-433-2400
Fax: 606-433-2596
Security Levels: High, Minimum Camp
Population: USP - 1,444
Camp - 109

FMC Lexington
3301 Leestown Rd.
Lexington, KY 40511
Ph: 859-255-6812
Fax: 859-253-8821
Security Levels: Administrative, Minimum Camp/Female
Population: FMC - 1,623
Camp - 288

FCI Manchester
P.O. Box 3000
Manchester, KY 40962
Ph: 606-598-1900
Fax: 606-599-4115
Security Levels: Medium, Minimum Camp
Population: FCI – 1,190
Camp - 411

USP McCreary
330 Federal Way
Pine Knot, KY 42635
Ph: 606-354-7000
Fax: 606-654-7190
Security Levels: Medium, Minimum Camp
Population: USP – 1,601
Camp - 126

LA

FCC Oakdale
P.O. Box 5050
Oakdale, LA 71463
FCI: 318-335-4070
Fax: 318-215-2688
FDC: 318-335-4466
Security Levels: High, Low, Administrative, Minimum Camp (Population 2,061)

FCC Pollock
1000 Airbase Rd.
P.O. Box 1000
Pollock, LA 71467
USP: 318-561-5300
USP Fax: 318-561-5391
Medium: 318-765-4400
Security Levels: High, Medium, Minimum Camp
Population: USP - 1,306
Camp - 190

MA

FMC Devens
P.O. Box 880
Ayer, MA 01432
Ph: 978-796-1000
Fax: 978-796-1118
Security Level: Administrative, Minimum Camp
Population: FMC – 1099
Camp - 103

MD

FCI Cumberland
14601 Burbridge Rd., SE
Cumberland, MD 21502
Ph: 301-784-1000
Fax: 301-784-1008
Security Levels: Medium, Minimum Camp
Population: FCI - 1,239
Camp - 298

MI

FCI Milan
E Arkona Rd.
P.O. Box 9999
Milan, MI 48160
Ph: 734-439-1511
Fax: 734-439-5535
Security Levels: Low,
Administrative
Population: 1,467 (all)

MN

FPC Duluth
P.O. Box 1400
Duluth, MN 55814
Ph: 218-722-8634
Fax: 218-733-4701
Security Levels:
Minimum Camp
Population: 852

FMC Rochester
P.O. Box 4600
2110 E. Center St.
Rochester, MN 55903-4600
Ph: 507-287-0674
Fax: 507-424-7600
Security Levels:
Administrative
Population: 904

FCI Sandstone
P.O. Box 999
Sandstone, MN 55072
Ph: 320-245-2262
Fax: 320-245-0385
Security Levels: Low
Population: 1,241

FCI Waseca
1000 University Dr., SW
P.O. Box 1731
Waseca, MN 56093
Ph: 507-835-8972
Fax: 507-837-4547
Security Levels: Low/Female
Population: 964

MO

MCFP Springfield
P.O. Box 4000
1900 W Sunshine
Springfield, MO 65801-4000
Ph: 417-862-7041
Fax: 417-837-1717
Security Levels:
Administrative
Population: 1,113

MS

FCC Yazoo City
P.O. Box 5666
2225 Haley Barbour
Yazoo City, MS 39194
Medium: 662-716-1020
Med. Fax: 662-716-1036
Low: 662-751-4800
FCC Security Levels:
Medium, Low,
Minimum Camp
Population: 3,313

NC

FPC Bryan
P.O. Drawer 2197
Bryan, TX 77805-2197
Ph: 979-823-1879
Fax: 979-775-5681
Security Levels: Minimum
Camp/Female
Population: 920

FCC Butner
Old NC Hwy 75
P.O. Box 1600
Butner, NC 27509
FMC: 919-575-3900
FMC Fax: 919-575-4801
Medium I: 919-575-4541
Medium II: 919-575-8000
Low: 919-575-5000
Security Levels: Medium,
Low, Administrative,
Minimum Camp
Population: 4,452

NJ

FCI Fairton
655 Fairton-Milville Rd.
P.O. Box 280
Fairton, NJ 08320
Ph: 856-453-1177
Fax: 856-453-4186
Security Levels: Medium,
Minimum Camp
Population: FCI - 1,437
Camp - 102

FCI Fort Dix
5756 Hartford Rd.
P.O. Box 38
Fort Dix, NJ 08640
Ph: 609-723-1100
Fax: 609-724-7557
Security Levels: Low,
Minimum Camp
Population: FCI - 3,676
Camp - 419

NY

MDC Brooklyn
P.O. Box 329001
Brooklyn, NY 11232
Ph: 718-840-4200
Fax: 718-840-5005
Security Levels:
Administrative Male &
Female; Pop - 2,510

MCC New York
150 Park Row
New York, NY 10007
Ph: 646-836-6300
Fax: 646-836-7751
Security Levels:
Administrative
Male & Female
Population: 759

FCI Otisville
P.O. Box 600
Otisville, NY 10963
Ph: 845-386-6700
Fax: 845-386-6727
Security Levels: Medium,
Minimum Camp
Population: FCI - 1,106
Camp - 110

FCI Ray Brook
P.O. Box 300
128 Ray Brook Rd.
Ray Brook, NY 12977
Ph: 518-897-4000
Fax: 518-897-4216
Security Levels: Medium
Population: 1,238

OH

FCI Elkton
P.O. Box 129
Lisbon, OH 44432
Ph: 330-420-6200
Fax: 330-420-6436
Security Levels: Low
Population: 2,479

OK

FCI El Reno
4205 Hwy 66 W
P.O. Box 1000
El Reno, OK 73036-1000
Ph: 405-262-4875
Fax: 405-319-7626
Security Levels: Medium,
Minimum Camp
Population: FCI - 1,142
Camp - 251

FTC OK City
P.O. Box 898802
7410 S. MacArthur Blvd.
Oklahoma City, OK 73189
Ph: 405-682-4075
Fax: 405-680-4203
Security Levels:
Administrative
Male & Female
Population: 1,550

OR

FCI Sheridan
27072 Ballston Rd.
P.O. Box 8000
Sheridan, OR 97378-9601
Ph: 503-843-4442
Fax: 503-843-6645
Security Levels: Medium,
Administrative, Minimum
Population: FCI – 1,400
Camp - 481

PA

FCC Allenwood
P.O. Box 3500
White Deer, PA 17887
USP: 570-547-0963
USP Fax: 570-547-9201
Medium: 570-547-7950
Low: 570-547-1990
Security Levels: High,
Medium, Low
Population: 3,870

USP Canaan
P.O. Box 400
Waymart, PA 18472
Ph: 570-488-8000
Fax: 570-488-8130
Security Levels: High,
Minimum Camp
Population: USP - 789
Camp - 131

USP Lewisburg
2400 Robert F. Miller Dr.
Lewisburg, PA 17837
Ph: 570-523-1251
Fax: 570-522-7745
Security Levels: High,
Minimum Camp
Population: USP - 1,552
Camp - 531

FCI Loretto
P.O. Box 1000
Loretto, PA 15940
Ph: 814-472-4140
Fax: 814-471-1660
Security Levels: Low,
Minimum Camp
Population: FCI - 1,269
Camp - 152

FCI McKean
P.O. Box 5000
Bradford, PA 16701
Ph: 814-362-8900
Fax: 814-363-6822
Security Levels: Medium,
Minimum Camp
Population: FCI - 1,304
Camp - 280

FDC Philadelphia
P.O. Box 572
Philadelphia, PA 19106
Ph: 215-521-4000
Fax: 215-521-7220
Security Levels:
Administrative
Male & Female
Population: 1,119

FCI Schuylkill
Route 901 & I-81
P.O. Box 700
Minersville, PA 17954
Ph: 570-544-7100
Fax: 570-544-7224
Security Levels: Medium,
Minimum Camp
Population: FCI - 1,299
Camp - 292

SC

FCI Bennettsville
696 Muckerman Rd.
Bennettsville, SC 29512
Ph: 843-454-8200
Fax: 843-454-8219
Security Levels: Medium,
Minimum Camp
Population: FCI - 1,620
Camp - 124

FCI Edgefield
P.O. Box 723
Edgefield, SC 29824
Ph: 803-637-1500
Fax: 803-637-9840
Security Levels: Medium,
Minimum Camp
Population: FCI - 1,660
Camp - 461

FCI Estill
P.O. Box 699
Estill, SC 29918
Ph: 803-625-4607
Fax: 803-625-5635
Security Levels: Medium,
Minimum Camp
Population: FCI - 1,110
Camp - 279

FCI Williamsburg
P.O. Box 340
Salters, SC 29590
Ph: 843-387-9400
Fax: 843-387-6961
Security Levels: Medium,
Minimum Camp
Population: FCI - 1,614
Camp - 129

SD

FPC Yankton
1016 Douglas Ave.
Yankton, SD 57078
Ph: 605-665-3262
Fax: 605-668-1113
Security Levels:
Minimum Camp
Population: 801

TN

FCI Memphis
1101 John A. Denie Rd.
Memphis, TN 38134
Ph: 901-372-2269
Fax: 901-384-5462
Security Levels: Medium,
Minimum Camp
Population: FCI - 1,218
Camp - 304

TX

FCI Bastrop
P.O. Box 730
1341 Hwy 95 N
Bastrop, TX 78602
Ph: 512-321-3903
Fax: 512-304-0117
Security Levels: Low,
Minimum Camp
Population: FCI - 1,190
Camp - 182

FCC Beaumont
P.O. Box 26035
Beaumont, TX 77720
USP: 409-727-8188
USP Fax: 409-626-3700
Medium: 409-727-0101
Low: 409-727-8172
Security Levels: High,
Medium, Low,
Minimum Camp
Population: 4,461 (all)

FCI Big Spring
1900 Simler Dr.
Big Spring, TX 79720
Ph: 432-466-2300
Fax: 432-466-2576
Security Levels: Low,
Minimum Camp
Population: FCI - 1,331
Camp - 178

FMC Carswell
P.O. Box 27066
J St. - Bldg 000
Fort Worth, TX 76127
Ph: 817-782-4000
Fax: 817-782-4875
Security Levels:
Administrative, Minimum
Camp Female
Population: FMC - 1,520
Camp - 277

FCI Fort Worth
3150 Horton Rd.
Fort Worth, TX 76119-5996
Ph: 817-534-8400
Fax: 817-413-3350
Security Levels: Low
Population: 1,741

FDC Houston
1200 Texas Ave.
P.O. Box 526245
Houston, TX 77002
Ph: 713-221-5400
Fax: 713-229-4200
Security Levels: Low,
Administrative
Male & Female
Population: 835

FCI La Tuna
8500 Doniphan
P.O. Box 1000
Anthony, NM-TX 88021
Ph: 915-791-9000
Fax: 915-791-9128
Security Levels: Low,
Minimum Camp
Population: FCI - 1,341
Camp - 281

FCI Seagoville
2113 N Hwy 175
Seagoville, TX 75159
Ph: 972-287-2911
Fax: 972-287-5466
Security Levels: Low,
Administrative,
Minimum Camp
Population: FCI - 1,904
Camp - 157

FCI Texarkana
P.O. Box 9500
Texarkana, TX 75505
Ph: 903-838-4587
Fax: 903-223-4417
Security Levels: Low,
Minimum Camp
Population: FCI - 1,381
Camp - 338

FCI Three Rivers
P.O. Box 4000
Three Rivers, TX 78071
Ph: 361-786-3576
Fax: 361-786-5051
Security Levels: Medium,
Minimum Camp
Population: FCI - 1,017
Camp - 314

VA

USP Lee
P.O. Box 900
Jonesville, VA 24263
Ph: 276-546-0150
Fax: 276-546-9116
Security Levels: High,
Minimum Camp
Population: USP - 1,488
Camp - 119

FCC Petersburg
P.O. Box 90026
Petersburg, VA 23804
Medium: 804-504-7200
Med. Fax: 804-504-7204
Low: 804-733-7881
Security Levels: Medium,
Low, Minimum Camp
Population: 3,540 (all)

WA

FDC SeaTac
2425 S 200th St.
SeaTac, WA 98198-1091
Ph: 206-870-5700
Fax: 206-870-5717
Security Levels:
Administrative
Male & Female
Population: 902

WI

FCI Oxford
P.O. Box 500
Oxford, WI 53952-0500
Ph: 608-584-5511
Fax: 608-584-6371
Security Levels: Medium,
Minimum Camp
Population: FCI - 1,079
Camp - 200

WV

FPC Alderson
P.O. Box A
Alderson, WV 24910
Ph: 304-445-3300
Fax: 304-445-3312
Security Level: Minimum
Camp/Female Pop: 1,136

FCI Beckley
P.O. Box 1280
1600 Industrial Park Rd.
Beaver, WV 25813
Ph: 304-252-9758
Fax: 304-256-4956
Security Levels: Medium,
Low, Minimum Camp
Population: FCI - 1,811
Camp - 390

FCI Gilmer
P.O. Box 5000
201 FCI Ln.
Glenville, WV 26351-9500
Ph: 304-462-0395
Fax: 304-462-0396
Security Levels: Medium,
Minimum Camp
Population: FCI - 1,212
Camp - 121

USP Hazelton
1640 Sky View Dr.
P.O. Box 450
Bruceton Mills, WV 26525
Ph: 304-379-5000
Fax: 304-379-5039
Security Levels: High,
Low/Female, Minimum
Population: USP - 1,560
Low – 751 Camp - 118

FCI Morgantown
P.O. Box 1000
Morgantown, WV 26507
Ph: 304-296-4416
Fax: 304-284-3600
Security Levels: Minimum
Population: 1,032

Appendix
Inmate's Resources

- The Fair Sentencing Act of 2010 (i.e., The New "Crack Law")

- The Second Chance Act

- June 24, Halfway House Revised Guidance Memo

- Federal Sentencing Table

The Fair Sentencing Act of 2010 S.1789 "Crack Law"

An Act - To restore fairness to Federal cocaine sentencing.

Be it enacted by the Senate and House of Representatives of the United States of America in Congress assembled,

SECTION 1. SHORT TITLE.

This Act may be cited as the 'Fair Sentencing Act of 2010'.

SEC. 2. COCAINE SENTENCING DISPARITY REDUCTION.

(a) CSA- Section 401(b)(1) of the Controlled Substances Act (21 U.S.C. 841(b)(1)) is amended--

(1) in subparagraph (A)(iii), by striking '50 grams' and inserting '280 grams'; and

(2) in subparagraph (B)(iii), by striking '5 grams' and inserting '28 grams'.
(b) Import and Export Act- Section 1010(b) of the Controlled Substances Import and Export Act (21 U.S.C. 960(b)) is amended--

(1) in paragraph (1)(C), by striking '50 grams' and inserting '280 grams'; and
(2) in paragraph (2)(C), by striking '5 grams' and inserting '28 grams'.

SEC. 3. ELIMINATION OF MANDATORY MINIMUM SENTENCE FOR SIMPLE POSSESSION.

Section 404(a) of the Controlled Substances Act (21 U.S.C. 844(a)) is amended by striking the sentence beginning 'Notwithstanding the preceding sentence,'.

SEC. 4. INCREASED PENALTIES FOR MAJOR DRUG TRAFFICKERS.

(a) Increased Penalties for Manufacture, Distribution, Dispensation, or Possession With Intent To Manufacture, Distribute, or Dispense- Section 401(b)(1) of the Controlled Substances Act (21 U.S.C. 841(b)) is amended--

(1) in subparagraph (A), by striking '$4,000,000', '$10,000,000', '$8,000,000', and '$20,000,000' and inserting '$10,000,000', '$50,000,000', '$20,000,000', and '$75,000,000', respectively; and

(2) in subparagraph (B), by striking '$2,000,000', '$5,000,000', '$4,000,000', and '$10,000,000' and inserting '$5,000,000', '$25,000,000', '$8,000,000', and '$50,000,000', respectively.

(b) Increased Penalties for Importation and Exportation- Section 1010(b) of the Controlled Substances Import and Export Act (21 U.S.C. 960(b)) is amended--

308 - Reduce My Prison Sentence

(1) in paragraph (1), by striking '$4,000,000', '$10,000,000', '$8,000,000', and '$20,000,000' and inserting '$10,000,000', '$50,000,000', '$20,000,000', and '$75,000,000', respectively; and

(2) in paragraph (2), by striking '$2,000,000', '$5,000,000', '$4,000,000', and '$10,000,000' and inserting '$5,000,000', '$25,000,000', '$8,000,000', and '$50,000,000', respectively.

SEC. 5. ENHANCEMENTS FOR ACTS OF VIOLENCE DURING THE COURSE OF A DRUG TRAFFICKING OFFENSE.

Pursuant to its authority under section 994 of title 28, United States Code, the United States Sentencing Commission shall review and amend the Federal sentencing guidelines to ensure that the guidelines provide an additional penalty increase of at least 2 offense levels if the defendant used violence, made a credible threat to use violence, or directed the use of violence during a drug trafficking offense.

SEC. 6. INCREASED EMPHASIS ON DEFENDANT'S ROLE AND CERTAIN AGGRAVATING FACTORS.

Pursuant to its authority under section 994 of title 28, United States Code, the United States Sentencing Commission shall review and amend the Federal sentencing guidelines to ensure an additional increase of at least 2 offense levels if--

(1) the defendant bribed, or attempted to bribe, a Federal, State, or local law enforcement official in connection with a drug trafficking offense;

(2) the defendant maintained an establishment for the manufacture or distribution of a controlled substance, as generally described in section 416 of the Controlled Substances Act (21 U.S.C. 856); or

(3)(A) the defendant is an organizer, leader, manager, or supervisor of drug trafficking activity subject to an aggravating role enhancement under the guidelines; and

(B) the offense involved 1 or more of the following super-aggravating factors:
(i) The defendant--
(I) used another person to purchase, sell, transport, or store controlled substances;

(II) used impulse, fear, friendship, affection, or some combination thereof to involve such person in the offense; and
(III) such person had a minimum knowledge of the illegal enterprise and was to receive little or no compensation from the illegal transaction.

(ii) The defendant--
(I) knowingly distributed a controlled substance to a person under the age of 18 years, a person over the age of 64 years, or a pregnant individual;
(II) knowingly involved a person under the age of 18 years, a person over the age of 64 years, or a pregnant individual in drug trafficking;

(III) knowingly distributed a controlled substance to an individual who was unusually vulnerable due to physical or mental condition, or who was particularly susceptible to criminal conduct; or

(IV) knowingly involved an individual who was unusually vulnerable due to physical or mental condition, or who was particularly susceptible to criminal conduct, in the offense.

(iii) The defendant was involved in the importation into the United States of a controlled substance.

(iv) The defendant engaged in witness intimidation, tampered with or destroyed evidence, or otherwise obstructed justice in connection with the investigation or prosecution of the offense.

(v) The defendant committed the drug trafficking offense as part of a pattern of criminal conduct engaged in as a livelihood.

SEC. 7. INCREASED EMPHASIS ON DEFENDANT'S ROLE AND CERTAIN MITIGATING FACTORS.

Pursuant to its authority under section 994 of title 28, United States Code, the United States Sentencing Commission shall review and amend the Federal sentencing guidelines and policy statements to ensure that--

(1) if the defendant is subject to a minimal role adjustment under the guidelines, the base offense level for the defendant based solely on drug quantity shall not exceed level 32; and

(2) there is an additional reduction of 2 offense levels if the defendant--
(A) otherwise qualifies for a minimal role adjustment under the guidelines and had a minimum knowledge of the illegal enterprise;

(B) was to receive no monetary compensation from the illegal transaction; and

(C) was motivated by an intimate or familial relationship or by threats or fear when the defendant was otherwise unlikely to commit such an offense.

SEC. 8. EMERGENCY AUTHORITY FOR UNITED STATES SENTENCING COMMISSION.

The United States Sentencing Commission shall--

(1) promulgate the guidelines, policy statements, or amendments provided for in this Act as soon as practicable, and in any event not later than 90 days after the date of enactment of this Act, in accordance with the procedure set forth in section 21(a) of the Sentencing Act of 1987 (28 U.S.C. 994 note), as though the authority under that Act had not expired; and

(2) pursuant to the emergency authority provided under paragraph (1), make such conforming amendments to the Federal sentencing guidelines as the Commission determines necessary to achieve consistency with other guideline provisions and applicable law.

SEC. 9. REPORT ON EFFECTIVENESS OF DRUG COURTS.

(a) In General- Not later than 1 year after the date of enactment of this Act, the Comptroller General of the United States shall submit to Congress a report analyzing the effectiveness of drug court programs receiving funds under the drug court grant program under part EE of title I of the Omnibus Crime Control and Safe Streets Act of 1968 (42 U.S.C. 3797-u et seq.).

(b) Contents- The report submitted under subsection (a) shall--

(1) assess the efforts of the Department of Justice to collect data on the performance of federally funded drug courts;

(2) address the effect of drug courts on recidivism and substance abuse rates;

(3) address any cost benefits resulting from the use of drug courts as alternatives to incarceration;

(4) assess the response of the Department of Justice to previous recommendations made by the Comptroller General regarding drug court programs; and

(5) make recommendations concerning the performance, impact, and cost-effectiveness of federally funded drug court programs.

SEC. 10. UNITED STATES SENTENCING COMMISSION REPORT ON IMPACT OF CHANGES TO FEDERAL COCAINE SENTENCING LAW.

Not later than 5 years after the date of enactment of this Act, the United States Sentencing Commission, pursuant to the authority under sections 994 and 995 of title 28, United States Code, shall study and submit to Congress a report regarding the impact of the changes in Federal sentencing law under this Act and the amendments made by this Act.

The Second Chance Act of 2007

Title I - Amendments Related To The Omnibus Crime Control And Safe Streets Act of 1968

Subtitle A - Improvements to Existing Programs

Section 101 - Amends the Omnibus Crime Control and Safe Streets Act of 1968 to reauthorize, rewrite, and expand provisions for adult and juvenile offender state and local reentry demonstration projects to provide expanded services to offenders and their families for reentry into society. Sets forth provisions relating to grant applications, requirements for grants, priorities in awarding grants, and reentry plan performance measurements. Requires grant recipients to: (1) develop comprehensive strategic reentry plans containing measurable annual and five-year performance outcomes; and (2) establish or empower reentry task forces to promote lower recidivism. Limits the federal share of a grant to 50% of the project funded under such grant.

Authorizes the Attorney General to provide for the establishment of a National Adult and Juvenile Offender Reentry Resource Center to collect data and assist grantees in carrying out offender reentry programs. Authorizes appropriations for FY2009-FY2010. Limits funding for technical assistance and training to not more than 3% or less than 2% of available funds. Requires the Attorney General to ensure that grants are distributed equitably among the geographical regions and between urban and rural populations, including Indian tribes.

Section 102 - Requires states receiving funds under the Residential Substance Abuse Treatment program to provide aftercare services, including case management services and other support services. Requires the Attorney General to conduct a study on the use and effectiveness of funds used for aftercare services.

Section 103 - Revises the definition of "violent offender" for purposes of the drug court grant program to include an offender who has been convicted of an offense punishable by a prison term of more than one year. Requires grantees to adopt such revised definition within three years after the enactment of this Act. Requires the Secretary of Health and Human Services to revise regulations to incorporate the revised definition.

Section 104 - Authorizes the use of violent offender truth-in-sentencing grant funds under the Violent Crime Control and Law Enforcement Act of 1994 for offender reentry demonstration projects.

Subtitle B - New and Innovative Programs To Improve Offender Reentry Services

Section 111 - Authorizes the Attorney General to award grants up to $500,000 to establish state, local, and tribal reentry courts to monitor offenders and provide them with access to comprehensive reentry services and programs, including programs for drug and alcohol testing and assessment for treatment. Requires grantees to report annually to the Attorney General on the activities of reentry courts.

Section 112 - Authorizes the Attorney General to make grants to state, tribal, and local prosecutors for drug treatment programs that are alternatives to imprisonment.

Section 113 - Authorizes the Attorney General to make grants for family substance abuse treatment alternatives to incarceration for nonviolent parent drug offenders and for prison-based family treatment programs for incarcerated parents of minor children.

Section 114 - Authorizes the Attorney General to carry out a grant program to evaluate methods to improve academic and vocational education for offenders in prison, jails, and juvenile facilities.

Section 115 - Directs the Attorney General to make grants for providing technology career training to prisoners. Authorizes appropriations for FY2009-FY2010.

Title II - Enhanced Drug Treatment And Mentoring Grant Programs
Subtitle A - Drug Treatment

Section 201 - Authorizes the Attorney General to make grants to: (1) improve drug treatment for federal inmates; and (2) reduce the use of alcohol and other drugs by long-term substance abusers while incarcerated or during periods of parole or court supervision. Requires the Attorney General to submit to Congress: (1) an interim report by September 30, 2009, on the best practices for substance abuse treatment in prisons and treatment of long-term substance abusers; and (2) a final report by September 30, 2010, on funded programs. Authorizes appropriations for FY2009-FY2010.

Subtitle B - Mentoring

Section 211 - Requires the Attorney General to make grants to nonprofit organizations for providing mentoring and other transitional services for reintegrating offenders into the community.

Section 212 - Authorizes the Secretary of Labor to make grants to nonprofit organizations to provide mentoring, job training and placement services, and other services to assist certain non-violent offenders in obtaining and retaining employment. Authorizes appropriations for FY2009-FY2010.

Section 213 - Requires the Director of the Bureau of Prisons to: (1) adopt and implement a policy allowing the continuation of mentoring services to offenders after their release from prison; and (2) report to Congress by September 30, 2009, on the implementation of such policy.

Section 214 - Requires the Director to discontinue the Standardized Chapel Library project or any other project that limits prisoner access to reading and other educational material.

Subtitle C - Administration of Justice Reforms
Chapter 1 - Improving Federal Offender Reentry

Section 231 - Requires the Attorney General, in coordination with the Director of the Bureau of Prisons, to establish a federal prisoner reentry initiative to prepare prisoners for release and successful reintegration into the community.
Requires the Director to assist prisoners in obtaining identification documents (e.g., birth certificates and social security cards) prior to release from prison.
Directs the Attorney General to modify the policies and procedures of the Department of Justice (DOJ) for transition of offenders into the community.
Expands the duties of the Director to include reentry planning procedures to provide federal prisoners with information on health and nutrition, employment, literacy and education, and other matters to assist in reentry into the community. Requires the Director to report to the Judiciary Committees of Congress annually on: (1) the progress of the Bureau of Prisons in responding to the reentry needs and deficits of inmates; and (2) recidivism reduction. Requires the adoption of performance measures and goals for reentry and recidivism reduction programs of the Bureau of Prisons.
Requires the Attorney General to: (1) take steps to educate employers on initiatives for hiring former federal, state, or local prisoners; and (2) conduct a pilot program for removing nonviolent elderly offenders (not less than age 65) from prison and placing them on home detention. Requires the Bureau of Prisons to ensure prisoners in community confinement facilities continued access to medical care.

Authorizes the Director of the Administrative Office of the U.S. Courts, in consultation with the Attorney General, to establish the Federal Remote Satellite Tracking and Reentry Training (ReStart) program to promote the effective reentry into the community of high risk individuals (i.e., individuals who violated terms of release or are at a high risk of recidivism). Authorizes appropriations for FY2009-FY2010.

Section 232 - Requires the Attorney General to report to Congress on DOJ practices and policies for the use of physical restraints on pregnant female prisoners.

Chapter 2 - Reentry Research

Section 241 - Authorizes the National Institute of Justice and the Bureau of Justice Standards to conduct research on juvenile and adult offender reentry.

Section 242 - Authorizes the Attorney General to award grants to study parole and post-supervision revocation data and community safety issues.

Section 243 - Authorizes the Attorney General to collect data and develop best practices for coordinating the efforts of state correctional departments and child protection agencies to ensure the safety and support of children of incarcerated parents and the support of relationships between incarcerated parents and their children. Expresses the sense of Congress that states and other entities should use the best practices developed by the Attorney General to protect children of incarcerated parents.

Section 244 - Authorizes the Attorney General to make grants to public and private research entities to evaluate the effectiveness of depot naltrexone for the treatment of heroin addiction.

Section 245 - Authorizes appropriations for FY2009-FY2010.

Chapter 3 - Correctional Reforms to Existing Law

Section 251 - Amends federal criminal code prerelease provisions to expand the authority of the Director of the Bureau of Prisons to place prisoners in a community corrections facility. Requires the Director to report to the Judiciary Committees of Congress on the use of community corrections facilities and issue regulations on placement of offenders in such facilities.

Prohibits courts from entering orders requiring that a sentence of imprisonment be served in a community corrections facility.

Section 252 - Redefines "residential substance abuse treatment" for offenders to allow: (1) an extended treatment period; and (2) the use of pharmocotherapies.

Section 253 - Expands the authority of the Director of the Administrative Office of the U.S. Courts to contract for reentry services for offenders.

Chapter 4 - Miscellaneous Provisions

Section 261 - Amends the Prison Rape Elimination Act of 2003 to extend the date for the report of the National Prison Rape Elimination Commission on the impacts of prison rape, thus extending the Commission's termination date.

New Halfway House Guidance Memorandum June 24, 2010

Most non-violent federal prison inmates will complete their period of federal prison incarceration in some type of Community Corrections Center (CCC) or halfway house, now being called a Residential Re-entry Center, (RRC). Old law and B.O.P. policy, as of December 2002, requires inmates to remain in federal prison until at least 90% or more of their sentence has been completed. Only then did they become eligible for a transfer to a Community Corrections Center. The maximum amount of halfway house time the inmate received was ten (10) percent of his sentence or a maximum of six (6) months, whichever is **less.** Of course the passage of the *Second Chance Act* on April 9, 2008, affected many changes. The *Second Chance Act*, signed by President Bush, provided that, *"the Director of the Bureau of Prisons shall, to the extent practicable, ensure that a prisoner serving a term of imprisonment spends a portion of the final months of that term (not to exceed 12 months), under conditions that will afford that prisoner a reasonable opportunity to adjust to and prepare for reentry of that prisoner into the community. Such conditions may include a community correctional facility."* In addition, the *Second Chance Act* addresses home confinement which is now called *home detention* when it states, *"The* *authority under this subsection may be used to place a prisoner in home confinement for the shorter of 10 percent of the term of imprisonment of that prisoner or 6 months."* Recent B.O.P. policy shifts outlined in the June 24, 2010 **Memorandum** titled, *"Revised Guidance for Residential Reentry Center (RRC) Placements"*, now directs the Unit Team to allow direct placement to home detention rather than placement in a halfway house for some inmates. Of course graduates of the 500-Hour Residential Drug Abuse Program receive up to 180 days (6 months) in RRC's regardless of their term of imprisonment. In other cases some inmates may stay only up to 14 days in a halfway house before being placed in home detention. The inmate's length of stay at a halfway house may be reduced considerably. This results in even less time in prison and less time in a halfway house and more time at home with the inmate's family. Jail Time Consulting explains this process to our clients and assists them to receive the most halfway house time or home detention time possible.

DID YOU KNOW?

Halfway House (RRC) Time- The Second Chance Act allows you to have more and maybe–home detention!

"Knowledge and a strict adherence to the rules and regulations coupled with a complete understanding of the transitional process will prevent the inmate from "violating" and being remanded back to federal prison for the remainder of his sentence."

322 - Reduce My Prison Sentence

SUPREME COURT OF THE UNITED STATES

UNITED STATES v. BOOKER

CERTIORARI TO THE UNITED STATES COURT OF APPEALS FOR THE SEVENTH CIRCUIT

No. 04—104. Argued October 4, 2004–Decided January 12, 2005

Under the Federal Sentencing Guidelines, the sentence authorized by the jury verdict in respondent Booker's drug case was 210-to-262 months in prison. At the sentencing hearing, the judge found additional facts by a preponderance of the evidence. Because these findings mandated a sentence between 360 months and life, the judge gave Booker a 30-year sentence instead of the 21-year, 10-month, sentence he could have imposed based on the facts proved to the jury beyond a reasonable doubt. The Seventh Circuit held that this application of the Guidelines conflicted with the *Apprendi* v. *New Jersey*, 530 U.S. 466, 490, holding that "[o]ther than the fact of a prior conviction, any fact that increases the penalty for a crime beyond the prescribed statutory maximum must be submitted to a jury, and proved beyond a reasonable doubt." Relying on *Blakely* v. *Washington*, 542 U.S. ___, the court held that the sentence violated the Sixth Amendment and instructed the District Court either to sentence Booker within the sentencing range supported by the jury's findings or to hold a separate sentencing hearing before a jury. In respondent Fanfan's case, the maximum sentence authorized by the jury verdict under the Guidelines was 78 months in prison. At the sentencing hearing, the District Judge found by a preponderance of the evidence additional facts authorizing a sentence in the 188-to-235-month range, which would have required him to impose a 15- or 16-year sentence instead of the 5 or 6 years authorized by the jury verdict alone. Relying on *Blakely*'s majority opinion, statements in its dissenting opinions, and the Solicitor General's brief in *Blakely*, the judge concluded that he could not follow the

Guidelines and imposed a sentence based solely upon the guilty verdict in the case. The Government filed a notice of appeal in the First Circuit and a petition for certiorari before judgment in this Court.

Held: The judgment of the Court of Appeals in No. 04—104 is affirmed, and the case is remanded. The judgment of the District Court in No. 04—105 is vacated, and the case is remanded.

No. 04—104, 375 F.3d 508, affirmed and remanded; and No. 04—105, vacated and remanded.

Justice Stevens delivered the opinion of the Court in part, concluding that the Sixth Amendment as construed in *Blakely* applies to the Federal Sentencing Guidelines.

(a) In addressing Washington State's determinate sentencing scheme, the *Blakely* Court found that *Jones* v. *United States,* 526 U.S. 227; *Apprendi* v. *New Jersey,* 530 U.S. 466; and *Ring* v. *Arizona,* 536 U.S. 584, made clear "that the 'statutory maximum' for *Apprendi* purposes is the maximum sentence a judge may impose *solely on the basis of the facts reflected in the jury verdict or admitted by the defendant.*" 542 U.S., at ___. As *Blakely*'s dissenting opinions recognized, there is no constitutionally significant distinction between the Guidelines and the Washington procedure at issue in that case. This conclusion rests on the premise, common to both systems, that the relevant sentencing rules are mandatory and impose binding requirements on all sentencing judges. Were the Guidelines merely advisory–recommending, but not requiring, the selection of particular sentences in response to differing sets of facts–their use would not implicate the Sixth Amendment. However, that is not the case. Title 18 U.S.C. A. §3553(b) directs that a court "*shall* impose a sentence of the kind, and within the range" established by the Guidelines, subject to departures in specific, limited cases. Because they are binding on all on judges, this Court has consistently held that the Guidelines have the force and effect of laws. Further, the availability of a departure where the judge "finds ... an aggravating or mitigating circumstance of a kind, or to a degree, not adequately taken into consideration by the Sentencing Commission in formulating the guidelines that should result in a sentence different from that described," §3553(b)(1), does not avoid the constitutional issue. Departures are unavailable in most cases because the Commission will have adequately taken all relevant factors into account, and no departure will be legally permissible. In those instances, the judge is legally bound to impose a sentence within the Guidelines range. Booker's case illustrates this point. The jury found him guilty of possessing at least 50 grams of crack cocaine, based on evidence that he had 92.5 grams. Under those facts, the Guidelines required a possible 210-to-262-month sentence. To reach Booker's actual sentence–which was almost 10 years longer–the judge found that he possessed an additional 566 grams of crack. Although, the jury never heard any such evidence, the judge found it to be true by a preponderance of the evidence. Thus, as in *Blakely*, "the jury's verdict alone does not authorize the sentence. The judge acquires that authority only upon finding some additional fact." 542 U.S., at ___. Finally, because there were no factors the Sentencing Commission failed to adequately consider, the judge was required to impose a sentence within the higher Guidelines range.

(b) The Government's arguments for its position that *Blakely*'s reasoning should not be applied to the Federal Sentencing Guidelines are unpersuasive. The fact that the Guidelines are promulgated by the Sentencing Commission, rather than Congress, is constitutionally irrelevant. The Court has not previously considered the question, but the same Sixth Amendment principles apply to the Sentencing Guidelines. Further, the Court's pre-*Apprendi* cases considering the Guidelines are inapplicable, as they did not consider the application of *Apprendi* to the Sentencing Guidelines. Finally, separation of powers concerns are not present here, and were rejected in *Mistretta*. In *Mistretta* the Court concluded that even though the Commission performed political rather than adjudicatory functions, Congress did not exceed constitutional limitations in creating the Commission. 488 U.S., at 393, 388. That conclusion remains true regardless of whether the facts relevant to sentencing are labeled "sentencing factors" or "elements" of crimes.

Justice Breyer delivered the opinion of the Court in part, concluding that 18 U.S.C. A. §3553(b)(1), which makes the Federal Sentencing Guidelines mandatory, is incompatible with today's Sixth Amendment "jury trial" holding and therefore must be severed and excised from the Sentencing Reform Act of 1984 (Act). Section 3742(e), which depends upon the Guidelines' mandatory nature, also must be severed and excised. So modified, the Act makes the Guidelines effectively advisory, requiring a sentencing court to consider Guidelines ranges, see §3553(a)(4), but permitting it to tailor the sentence in light of other statutory concerns, see §3553(a).

(a) Answering the remedial question requires a determination of what "Congress would have intended" in light of the Court's constitutional holding. *E.g., Denver Area Ed. Telecommunications Consortium, Inc.* v. *FCC*, 518 U.S. 727, 767. Here, the Court must decide which of two approaches is the more compatible with Congress' intent as embodied in the Act: (1) retaining the Act (and the Guidelines) as written, with today's Sixth Amendment requirement engrafted onto it; or (2) eliminating some of the Act's provisions. Evaluation of the constitutional requirement's consequences in light of the Act's language, history, and basic purposes demonstrates that the requirement is not compatible with the Act as written and that some severance (and excision) is necessary. Congress would likely have preferred the total invalidation of the Act to an Act with the constitutional requirement engrafted onto it, but would likely have preferred the excision of the Act's mandatory language to the invalidation of the entire Act.

(b) Several considerations demonstrate that adding the Court's constitutional requirement onto the Act as currently written would so transform the statutory scheme that Congress likely would not have intended the Act as so modified to stand. First, references to "[t]he court" in §3553(a)(1)–which requires "[t]he court" when sentencing to consider "the nature and circumstances of the offense and the history and characteristics of the defendant"–and references to "the judge" in the Act's history must be read in context to mean "the judge without the jury," not "the judge working together with the jury." That is made clear by §3661, which removes typical "jury trial" limitations on "the information" concerning the offender that the sentencing "court ... may receive." Second, Congress' basic statutory goal of diminishing sentencing disparity depends for its success upon judicial efforts to determine, and to base punishment upon, the *real conduct* underlying the crime of conviction. In looking to real conduct, federal sentencing judges have long relied upon a probation officer's presentence report, which is often unavailable until *after* the trial. To engraft the Court's constitutional requirement onto the Act would destroy the system by preventing a sentencing judge from relying upon a presentence report for relevant factual information uncovered after the trial. Third, the Act, read to include today's constitutional requirement, would create a system far more complex than Congress could have intended, thereby greatly complicating the tasks of the prosecution, defense, judge, and jury. Fourth, plea bargaining would not significantly diminish the consequences of the Court's constitutional holding for the operation of the Guidelines, but would make matters worse, leading to sentences that gave greater weight not to real conduct, but rather to counsel's skill, the prosecutor's policies, the caseload, and other factors that vary from place to place, defendant to defendant, and crime to crime. Fifth, Congress would not have enacted sentencing statutes that make it more difficult to adjust sentences *upward* than to adjust them *downward,* yet that is what the engrafted system would create. For all these reasons, the Act cannot remain valid in its entirety. Severance and excision are necessary.

(c) The entire Act need not be invalidated, since most of it is perfectly valid. In order not to "invalidat[e] more of the statute than is necessary," *Regan* v. *Time, Inc.,* 468 U.S. 641, 652, the Court must retain those portions of the Act that are (1) constitutionally valid, *ibid.*, (2) capable of "functioning independently," *Alaska Airlines, Inc.* v. *Brock,* 480 U.S. 678, 684, and (3) consistent with Congress' basic objectives in enacting the statute, *Regan, supra,* at 653. Application of these criteria demonstrates that only §3553(b)(1), which requires sentencing courts to impose a sentence within the applicable Guidelines range (absent circumstances justifying a departure), and §3742(e), which provides for *de novo* review on appeal of departures, must be severed and excised. With these two sections severed (and statutory cross-references to the two sections consequently invalidated), the rest of the Act satisfies the Court's constitutional requirement and falls outside the scope of *Apprendi* v. *New Jersey,* 530 U.S. 466. The Act still requires judges to take account of the Guidelines together with other sentencing goals, see §3553(a)(4); to consider the Guidelines "sentencing range established for ... the applicable category of offense committed by the applicable category of defendant," pertinent Sentencing Commission policy statements, and the need to avoid unwarranted sentencing disparities and to restitute victims, §§3553(a)(1), (3)—(7); and to impose sentences that reflect the seriousness of the offense, promote respect for the law, provide just punishment, afford adequate deterrence, protect the public, and effectively provide the defendant with needed training and medical care, §3553(a)(2). Moreover, despite §3553(b)(1)'s absence, the Act continues to provide for appeals from sentencing decisions (irrespective of whether the trial judge sentences within or outside the Guidelines range). See §§3742(a) and (b). Excision of §3742(e), which sets forth appellate review standards, does not pose a critical problem. Appropriate review standards may be inferred from related statutory language, the statute's structure, and the "sound administration of justice." *Pierce* v. *Underwood,* 487 U.S. 552, 559—560. Here, these factors and the past two decades of appellate practice in cases involving departures from the Guidelines imply a familiar and practical standard of review: review for "unreasonable[ness]." See, *e.g.,* 18 U.S.C. § 3742(e)(3) (1994 ed.). Finally, the Act without its mandatory provision and related language remains consistent with Congress' intent to avoid "unwarranted sentencing disparities ... [and] maintai[n] sufficient flexibility to permit individualized sentences when warranted," 28 U.S.C. § 991(b)(1)(B), in that the Sentencing Commission remains in place to perform its statutory duties, see §994, the district courts must consult the Guidelines and take them into account when sentencing, see 18 U.S.C. § 3553(a)(4), and the courts of appeals review sentencing decisions for unreasonableness. Thus, it is more consistent with Congress' likely intent (1) to preserve the Act's important pre-existing elements while severing and excising §§3553(b) and 3742(e) than (2) to maintain all of the Act's provisions and engraft today's constitutional requirement onto the statutory scheme.

(d) Other possible remedies–including, *e.g.,* the parties' proposals that the Guidelines remain binding in cases other than those in which the Constitution prohibits judicial fact finding and that the Act's provisions requiring such fact finding at sentencing be excised–are rejected.

(e) On remand in respondent Booker's case, the District Court should impose a sentence in accordance with today's opinions, and, if the sentence comes before the Seventh Circuit for review, that court should apply the review standards set forth in this Court's remedial opinion. In respondent Fanfan's case, the Government (and Fanfan should he so choose) may seek resentencing under the system set forth in today's opinions. As these dispositions indicate, today's Sixth Amendment holding and the Court's remedial interpretation of the Sentencing Act must be applied to all cases on direct review. See, *e.g., Griffith* v. *Kentucky,* 479 U.S. 314, 328. That does not mean that every sentence will give rise to a Sixth Amendment violation or that every appeal will lead to a new sentencing hearing. That is
because reviewing courts are expected to apply ordinary prudential doctrines, determining, *e.g.,* whether the issue was raised below and whether it fails the "plain-error" test. It is also because, in cases not involving a Sixth Amendment violation, whether resentencing is warranted or whether it will instead be sufficient to review a
sentence for reasonableness may depend upon application of the harmless-error doctrine.

Stevens, J., delivered the opinion of the Court in part, in which Scalia, Souter, Thomas, and Ginsburg, JJ., joined.

Breyer, J., delivered the opinion of the Court in part, in which Rehnquist, C. J., and O'Connor, Kennedy, and Ginsburg, JJ., joined. Stevens, J., filed an opinion dissenting in part, in which Souter, J., joined, and in which Scalia, J., joined except for Part III and footnote 17. Scalia, J., and Thomas, J., filed opinions dissenting in part. Breyer, J., filed an opinion dissenting in part, in which Rehnquist, C. J., and O'Connor and Kennedy, JJ., joined.

INDEX

18 U.S.C 3582, 19
18 U.S.C 3582. See Compassionate release
18 U.S.C. 2255. See 2255 motion
18 U.S.C. 3553, 204
18 U.S.C. 3621, 179
18 U.S.C. 3624, 184, See Halfway House
2241 petition, 208
2255 motion, 207
5K1, 123, 136, 204
5K2, 99, 126
A&O, 249
A&O handbook, 173
Aberrant behavior, 104
Abuse in prison, 116
Acceptance of responsibility, 30, 85, 119
Administrative remedy, 182
Admissions & Orientation. See A&O
Appeal, 206
Appeals court, 207
Auburn prison, 291
Bank fraud, 88
Binding plea deal, 43
Booker, 217, 324
BP-10, 185
BP-11, 185
BP-8, 184
BP-9, 185
Case manager, 172, 174
CCC, 170
Cellies, 223
Cellmates, 223
Central Inmate Monitoring, 126
Charitable works, 91
Cheech & Chong, 9
CIM. See Central Inmate Monitoring
Cocaine violation, 126
Coercion and Duress, 110
Commissary, 244
Community correction centers. See CCC
Commutation of Sentence, 168
Compassionate Release, 165
Cop-out, See Inmate to staff request
Count, 226
Criminal complaint, 22
Criminal defense attorney, 12
Criminal history, 36
Criminal history points, 35
Criminal information, 22
Cyril Wecht, 9
DAPC, 158, See Drug Abuse Program Coordinator
Designation and Security Computation Ctr, See DSCC
Designator, 46
Diesel therapy, 45
Diminished capacity. See Reduced mental capacity

332 - Reduce My Prison Sentence

Downward departure, 17
Drug Abuse Program Coordinator, 158, See DAPC
DSCC, 46
DUI, 40, 160
False tax returns, 97
Family ties, 50
Federal defense attorney, 12, 19
Federal Medical Centers, See FMC's
Federal prison camp, 221
Federal Public Defender, 29, 206
FMC's, 68
Fog count, 260
Gambler's Anonymous, 101
GED, 176
Going to prison, 17
Good deeds, 91
Good Time Credit. See GTC
Grow houses, 149
GTC, 210
Guilty verdict, 17
Halfway house, 188, 285
Housing units, 241
Indictment, 21
Inepi ceremony, 269
Inmate Telephone System, 222
Inmate to staff request, 157, 247
Jail cells, 291
Lesser harms argument, 113, 115
Life expectancy argument, 89
Mandatory minimum, 139, 143

Marijuana case, 150, 152
Methamphetamine case, 131, 132
Military and public service, 91
Mitigating factor, 43, 83
Mitigating Role, 121
Naltrexone, 315
National Inmate Appeals Administrator, 186
Not guilty verdict, 17
Notice of Appeal, 206
Omnibus Act, 311
Operation Pipedream, 9
Operation True Test, 9
Pardon Attorney, 168
Penitentiary, 291
Plea bargain, 29, 41
Possession of a firearm, 150
Presentence Investigation Report, 31
Private attorney, 13, 28
Probation officer, 31
PSI, 31
RDAP, 155
RDAP Institutions, 162
Reduced mental capacity, 96
Reentry planning, 314
Rehabilitative efforts, 102
Residential Drug Abuse Program, See RDAP
Residential re-entry centers. See RRC
Revised Halfway House Memo, 180
RRC, 170
Rule 35, 204
Safety valve, 128, 141, 146, 151
Second Chance Act, 311

Security classification form, 46
Self surrender, 45, 238
Sentencing hearing, 44
Sentencing memorandum, 215
Sentencing table, 34
Shot, 229
SHU, 226, 228, 245
Special Housing Unit, See SHU
Statement of reasons, 62, 93
Statute of limitations, 19
Substantial assistance, 123, 126
Team meeting, 175
TRULINCS, 222
Unregistered firearm, 114
Victim misconduct, 94
Victim's conduct, 93
Violent offender, 312
Voluntary manslaughter, 95
Waiver of indictment, 23
Walnut Street Jail, 291
Writ of habeas corpus, 207, 208

 # Quick Order Form

email orders: Orders@ReduceMyPrisonSentence.com
website address: www.ReduceMyPrisonSentence.com

Postal Orders:
Stephen Sharp - Sunbelt Publishing
2134 Springwater Lane (Room B2)
Port Orange, FL 32128

Enclosed is cash, check, money order or credit card payment for _____ books.
Subtotal: _____ books x $24.95 = _____

Sales tax: Please add 6.5% sales tax for products being shipped to Florida addresses.

Priority Shipping
U.S.: $7 for first book and $2 for each additional book.
International: $25 for first book and $5 for each additional book.

Name: _____

Address: _____

City: _____ State: _____ Zip: _____

Telephone: _____

Email address: _____

CC#: _____

Name on card: _____

Exp. Date: _____ (mm/yyyy)

www.ingramcontent.com/pod-product-compliance
Lightning Source LLC
Chambersburg PA
CBHW030909040526
R18240000002B/R182400PG44116CBX00011B/7